CHRISTIAN ETHICS

CHRISTIAN ETHICS

A Case Method Approach

THIRD EDITION

Robert L. Stivers
Christine E. Gudorf
Alice Frazer Evans
Robert A. Evans

ORBIS BOOKS

Maryknoll, New York 10545

Founded in 1970, Orbis Books endeavors to publish works that enlighten the mind, nourish the spirit, and challenge the conscience. The publishing arm of the Maryknoll Fathers and Brothers, Orbis seeks to explore the global dimensions of the Christian faith and mission, to invite dialogue with diverse cultures and religious traditions, and to serve the cause of reconciliation and peace. The books published reflect the views of their authors and do not represent the official position of the Maryknoll Society. To learn more about Maryknoll and Orbis Books, please visit our website at www.maryknoll.org.

This is a substantially revised edition of *Christian Ethics: A Case Method Approach, Second Edition,* edited by Robert L. Stivers, Christine E. Gudorf, Alice Frazer Evans, and Robert A. Evans, Maryknoll, NY: Orbis Books, 1994.

Published by Orbis Books, Maryknoll, New York 10545–0308.
Manufactured in the United States of America.
Manuscript editing and typesetting by Joan Weber Laflamme.

Library of Congress Cataloging-in-Publication Data

Christian ethics : a case method approach / Robert L. Stivers . . . [et al.].— 3rd ed.
    p. cm.
  Includes bibliographical references.
  ISBN–13: 978–1–57075–621–4 (pbk.)
  1. Christian ethics—Case studies. I. Stivers, Robert L., 1940–
  BJ1251.C49 2005
  241—dc22

2005011603

Contents

Introduction

Christian Ethics
and the Case Method

The student pensively approached the case teacher after class and finally mustered some words: "That case really hit home. The characters
were different, but they could just as well have been my family. Not long
ago we went through exactly the same thing." Another student, waiting
for the first to finish, finally edged up and joined in, "And the question that
woman in the front row asked about euthanasia, that's the precise question
I wanted to ask but couldn't find the right words."

These two statements, often encountered in one form or another by case
teachers, reflect something enduring in human behavior: while every individual is unique, ethical problems and questions about what is right or
good are persistent if not universal. These recurrences and the dilemmas
they represent can be recorded and replayed to help others learn to make
better ethical choices. Case studies are one way to capture past occurrences,
and case teaching is a method to enable individuals and groups to make
better choices.

This book is about making ethical choices and forming Christian character. It contains sixteen cases. Accompanying each case study is a commentary by one of the authors that is intended to aid understanding of the case
from a Christian ethical perspective. The purpose of the book is to offer
an approach to contemporary social issues and to underscore the importance of the Christian ethical dimension in the issues and in character
formation. The authors are enthusiastic about the case approach as one
way to prepare individuals and communities to make ethical decisions
and form character. Since the method was first developed at the Harvard
Law and Business Schools, it has moved far beyond these origins, receiving wide acceptance nationally in business and law schools. During the
past three decades it has also been successfully applied to religious studies. This proven track record and personal experience with the case approach

are the bases of the authors' enthusiasm for this teaching and learning approach.

MAKING ETHICAL DECISIONS

Ethical decisions are made on a number of levels. On one level decision-making seems to flow easily. Individuals follow their gut-level intuitions and muddle through situations reactively. This approach may be effective if the individual is caring and the situation is uncomplicated and more or less personal. It is less effective in complex social situations and can be disastrous when the individual is uncaring, ethically immature, or locked into a narrow social world.

On another level making ethical choices is both difficult and complex. Logical and abstract reasoning comes hard to some. In certain situations the decision-maker is bombarded by a bewildering array of conflicting and complex facts. Finding relevant ethical norms or guidelines from Christian traditions to apply to particular situations is difficult at best and can easily be shortcircuited or sidetracked with simplistic appeals to authority.

Once relevant norms are discovered, their application is often tricky. The norms frequently offer conflicting counsel. Indeed, this is the primary reason that ethical decisions are problematic. There is seldom a straight path from a single norm to an easy decision. If there were, no problem would exist. The decision-maker is most often caught between equally attractive or unattractive alternatives. Worse, the path is usually made treacherous by intersecting problems and relationships that complicate situations and suggest exceptions to the rules. Last, and hardly necessary to point out, relationships themselves present complicating factors. The moral decision-maker possesses limited freedom and is quite capable of being arbitrary in its use.

The case method of instruction recounts real ethical dilemmas in order to assist individuals and groups through complexity to good or at least well-reasoned choices. Cases may help sort out the choices and give the person with the dilemma an opportunity to move down the path from the identification of norms through the maze of intersecting facts, relationships, and exceptions to the selection of the best alternatives.

There are many types of case studies. They range from imagined scenarios, to in-depth histories of organizations, to one-page "verbatims" that report a single incident. The cases in this volume are descriptions of actual situations as seen by a writer usually through the eyes of a participant involved in the problem. The situations normally entail a decision to be made that is left sufficiently open to allow students to enter the process of ethical reflection and decision-making.

Such a method is well suited to the study of Christian ethics, for it drives the student to take the insights of tradition and theory, apply them to an actual situation, and then reconsider the adequacy of theory and tradition. Involved in this movement from theory to practice and back to theory are all the elements that go into an ethical decision.

THE ELEMENTS OF AN ETHICAL DECISION

Element I: The Relationship of Faith

A pervasive historical problem for most Christian traditions has been human sin. Sin results from deep-seated anxieties and separation from God, self, others, and nature. It issues forth in specific acts that break relationships. Sin is magnified in groups and hardens in institutions. From another angle, sin is the refusal to accept God's gracious power of love, a refusal that leads to a sense of alienation and judgment

While sin runs deep and is universal, it does not necessarily paralyze the moral life. In his person and work Jesus Christ reveals resources for living with integrity in the midst of sin. Jesus identifies God, the source of these resources, as a power that creates inner wholeness and the possibility of right relationships.

Primary to most Christian traditions is the affirmation of God's power as love. Love redeems humans from sin and reunites them with others without violating human freedom. Love is a free gift, never a possession, and cannot be obtained by an effort of the will alone. The continuing presence of love in all situations is called the work of the Holy Spirit.

The starting point for Christian ethics is *being* in love. This is not something the self can do alone, however. It is something that God does in cooperation with the self, although the self is constantly tempted to think otherwise and take control, so furthering sin and alienation. Being in love is first a matter of receiving love and letting it work in the self to produce inner wholeness and transformation. Action follows being in love. This is more or less the central message of most Christian traditions, although there is considerable variation in particulars. Thus ethics or *doing* has its foundation in being or life in the Spirit. Faith is a matter of relationship, of being in love first with God and then responsively with self, others, and nature.

The word *spirituality* is often used to identify the core relationship to God. God's power is experienced in quite different ways, the common element being the integrated and transformed self that emerges. Most Christians readily recognize the customary religious ways of experiencing God: worship, prayer, singing, participation in the sacraments, and the preached word. God is not limited to these religious ways, but rather, according to most traditions, God is free to be present in a variety of ways consistent with love.

Spirituality, alternatively being in love or being in the Spirit, inspires acts of justice in society and nature and also leads the loving self intuitively to specific acts in particular situations. In coming to decisions, however, other things are needed, because inspiration and intuition by themselves are not always accurate guides for doing what is right or good. This is especially true in complex social situations. The doing of good acts requires thought as well as heart, knowledge as well as inspiration and intuition. The Christian doer, while inspired and empowered, is also sensitive to relationships in specific situations and deeply interested in the facts and theories that give order to situations as well as the traditions that provide ethical norms for human actions.

Sensitivity to relationships involves a strong element of good intentions. It also involves a sense of the Spirit already at work in a situation, of the character of the human actors, and of the needs of plants and animals. Sensitivity to relationships is constantly in tune with feelings and the subtle changes that make certain situations exceptional. It is aware of the self, its state of being, and its tendencies to sin, both in one's own self and in the selves of others.

Interest in the facts and norms that guide decisions are more a matter of knowledge than heart. They require the thoughtful analysis and assessment of a situation, the next two elements in making an ethical decision.

Element II: Analysis

Good ethical decisions and actions depend on good information, and getting good information depends on hard work and a certain amount of savvy. There are several components to consider in analyzing a situation or case study, not all of which apply in any given situation or case.[1] First is to consider how *personal experience* shapes the way the self perceives a situation. One way to do this is for students to ask themselves what they personally have at stake, what personal history—for example, race, class, gender, habits, and attitudes—they bring to the situation.

The second component is *power dynamics*. Who are the key players, and how is powered distributed among them? Whose voices are heard? Whose are ignored?

A third component is *factual information*. Are there historical roots to the problem? What are the key facts? Are there facts in dispute? Are the theories that give coherence to the facts in conflict?

Fourth is the larger *context* of the situation. Most cases are seen through the eyes of a single person and involve personal relationships. The decision-maker must go beyond the close confines of his or her own personal life to see how society and nature affect and in turn are affected by the actions of the people in the case. As the old adage goes: Don't lose the forest for the tree.

Fifth is attention to the *complicating factors* in a situation. Is this an exceptional case? Is crucial information missing? Are there things that are hard to grasp?

Sixth is a careful delineation of *relationships*. Sometimes relational factors produce a situation that is not normal and to which traditional ethical guidelines do not apply. Decision-makers must ask if there are relational or character issues that complicate choices.

Seventh is to identify the primary and secondary *ethical issues* in the situation. Case studies almost always involve multiple issues, and students must select among them in order to focus.

Finally, the eighth component is the identification of *alternative courses of action* to address the issues and the *consequences* of each. What seems to be appropriate action may on second glance reveal consequences that make it inappropriate or even harmful.

Element III: Assessment

The main task in assessment is locating norms or ethical guidelines in the traditions of the church that are relevant to a given situation. In ethics, norms refer to broad directives that provide guidance for moral life. Norms help to determine what usually should be done in a particular situation. They reflect the wisdom and experience of past decision-makers as they faced similar situations and generalized about what is good. Their insights are passed down in traditions and usually offer wise counsel as current decision-makers face the same kinds of situations or even new situations.

Norms

Norms come in many forms. A few illustrations will suffice to demonstrate this variety and to identify the most important norms. Three very important norms are love, justice, and peacemaking. The experience of God's love leads to an intention to love one's neighbor. In Christian ethics justice is a general *principle* and means fairness or equity with a special concern for the poor and those on the margins of society. In the ethic of ecological justice this norm is given further expression in the principles of sustainability, sufficiency, participation, and solidarity (see the case "Klamath Conflicts"). Peacemaking as a norm includes understandings of nonviolence and reconciliation and gives foundation to three normative *perspectives:* pacifism, the justifiable war, and the crusade (see the case "Vietnam and Iraq").

Virtues are norms insofar as they represent patterns of behavior worthy of emulation. The best, but not the only, example in Christian ethics is the person and work of Jesus. The popular but well-worn question "What would Jesus do?" points to how his example is a moral guide for many.

Theological interpretations also guide. Different interpretations of how God is at work in a given situation, for example, are important in cases of life and death. Theological understandings of sin, death, and the work of the Holy Spirit and the church are important to decisions in other cases.

Finally, the most familiar norms are stated as *rules, laws,* and *commands.* The Ten Commandments are the most obvious. In using laws as guides, care must be taken, however, to avoid legalism, the tendency to follow rules slavishly even if the consequences are unloving. In Christianity, all laws and rules are grounded in and tested by love, the most basic guideline of all.

Sources of Norms

Christians look to a number of sources for ethical guidance. The *Bible* has traditionally been the first and most important source. Gleaning ethical guidance from the Bible is not as easy as it might seem, however. The many books of the Bible were written in different periods and reflect quite a variety of contexts and situations. The biblical writers wrote from their own locations in diverse societies and culture. They saw and understood things differently from one another and certainly from persons of the modern age, who live in a thoroughly changed world. Biblical writers sometimes disagreed, and what they thought was ethically acceptable in their own time—for example, slavery—has changed as culture has evolved. Compounding these differences, and complicating matters immensely, present-day decision-makers must interpret what biblical writers meant and then apply these meanings. The Bible does not interpret itself or make decisions. And while biblical scholars have developed a wide range of tools to do the task of interpretation and ethicists offer their best wisdom on interpretation, their disagreements are commonplace. Indeed, ethical conflicts are sometimes matters of interpretation and use of biblical texts.

In spite of these complications, themes do run through the Bible, and these themes can be identified with a degree of accuracy. The biblical writers experienced the same loving God as modern people and faced many of the same problems. The Bible remains a good source of guidance.

Theology is the second source of norms. Understandings of God's power and human sin have already been identified. The nature of God's power as love inspires and leads decision-makers to love their neighbors and to be sensitive to the work of the Spirit in situations. Different understandings of sin lead to conflicting views on matters of sexuality. Seeing sin as deep and universal leads decision-makers to realistic actions that factor in the human tendency to misuse freedom.

The third source of norms is the *historical traditions* of the church. Christians through the centuries have devoted considerable thought to issues of, for example, violence, sexuality, the poor, and nature. The traditions change and sometimes yield a multiplicity of guidelines, but they also show continuity and reflect a certain amount of practical wisdom. Traditions on justice are critical to this volume.

The fourth source of norms is the *church* in its many forms. The three previous sources all grew in church ground. The church ranges from the church catholic or universal, to specific church organizations such as the Roman Catholic Church and specific Protestant denominations, to associations of churches, to the local brick and mortar church, to what in the Bible is referred to as "where two or three are gathered together." Likewise, the ethical guidelines range from traditional historical perspectives, to comprehensive church studies and pronouncements, to rules of church organizations, and to the wisdom and guidance of a good friend.

The final source is the broad category of *secular ethical traditions and other religions.* Christian and secular philosophical traditions in the West have had a close and mutually edifying relationship for centuries. Native American traditions are rich in their sensitivity to nature. Taoism is likewise rich in its search for balance. Buddhism holds to the interrelation of all beings and talks about clinging or desire as the chief problem. Christians are free to appropriate the insights of these other traditions, to enter into dialogue with adherents of these traditions, and to join in common actions.

Using these five sources to establish norms that relate to a given case is complex and requires practice. The situation or case itself offers an obvious starting point. So, for example, if the situation involves violent conflict, norms dealing with violence and nonviolence apply.

Many aids are available to help in locating relevant norms. Concordances help to locate specific words in the Bible and texts containing these words. The critical commentaries that follow each case in this volume identify norms and help with interpretation. Dictionaries of Christian ethics are widely available and provide short summaries for those whose time is limited. Scholars have studied most ethical issues, and their publications usually develop norms. Most major denominations have well-established positions on major ethical issues. Decision-makers are increasingly consulting websites, although the quality of articles found is uneven and caution is advised. If cases are discussed in a classroom setting, teachers may provide background in lectures. Also, decision-makers may turn to the local church, where communities of believers frequently work through ethical issues, often guided by competent leaders.

Conflicting Norms

Once decision-makers have identified the relevant norms and reflected on their meaning for a specific situation, they must jump at least one more hurdle. Ethical problems are frequently encountered because two or more norms conflict. For example, in matters related to the use of violence, nonviolence is an obvious norm. So is justice. The conflict between the two in certain cases has led some Christians to elect the normative perspective of the justifiable war as their guide. So, if a large measure of justice can be won for a small measure of violence, violence may be justifiable if certain conditions are met. Another frequent conflict is between human economic benefit and care for other species and ecosystems.

What should the decision-maker do when conflicting norms make for a close call? There is no one right answer to this question. Prayer helps, but finally choices must be made. Luther's famous dictum, "sin bravely," applies in some cases.

Method

Method is the process of pulling intuitions and norms together and applying them to analysis. No single method of relating norms, facts, theories, contexts, and relationships to one another and to specific situations can be called distinctively Christian. There are a number of methods, each with advantages and disadvantages. The authors have not tried to impose a particular method in their approach either to the cases or to the commentaries that follow them. They are convinced that method is important, however, and that an adequate method seeks to touch base with the elements relevant to making a particular ethical decision.

The case approach is conducive to the teaching of method. A specific case can even be used to focus on method. Over the course of a semester or study series the teacher can use and ask participants to use a single method so that they will acquire skill in employing that particular methodology. Alternatively, the teacher can employ several methods and request that students experiment with and evaluate each. Or finally, consciousness of method may be left to emerge from the process of doing ethical reflection.

The commentaries that follow each case are organized around the elements of making an ethical decision. The commentaries do not spell out how these elements are to be put together to reach a decision. The authors would be remiss, however, if they did not indicate a few typical approaches.

The approach that starts with and stresses norms is called the *deontological* or *normative approach*. The word *deontological* comes from the Greek work *deon*, which means "binding," and refers to the study of duty and moral obligation.

The tendency in this approach is to let norms, rules, principles, standards, and ideals be decisive or binding in making choices. The degree of decisiveness that should be afforded to norms has been a matter of contention in Christian ethics. To call an approach normative means that norms have a fairly high degree of decisiveness. Most of those who take a normative approach, however, are willing to admit some exceptions to norms occasioned by contextual or relational factors and conflicting norms. Used in a flexible way, the normative approach is appropriate. Indeed, the authors are of a common mind that considerable attention should be given to norms in all situations.

The extreme of the normative approach, legalism, presents difficulties, however. Following rules to the exclusion of contextual and relational factors is a problem for Christians because of its rigidity, frequent heartlessness, and the obvious polemic against it in the sayings of Jesus and the epistles of Paul.

The second approach is called *teleological* from the Greek *telos*, which means "end" or "goal." Those who take a teleological approach are interested in achieving an end or maximizing a goal as much as possible. Another way to put this is to say they seek good consequences or results. Hence this approach is also called the *consequentialist approach*. People differ, however, about the goals they seek and the ends they pursue. Some may wish simply to amass wealth and power in life, while others may seek to maximize the welfare of others, including other species. Not all ends or goals are morally desirable, however. For Christians, norms derived from the five sources and especially fundamental norms like love and justice guide evaluation of these ends or goals. Teleologists weigh the costs and benefits of various alternatives as they figure out how to maximize the good they seek to achieve. For teleologists, the ends sometimes justify the means, even morally questionable means in some cases. A weakness here is that teleological thinking can run roughshod over others as it makes ethical concessions in order to maximize the good. So, ends do not justify all means. A strength of this approach is that it takes consequences seriously.

The third approach is called the *areteological approach* or sometimes *virtue ethics* or *the ethics of conscience*. The word comes from the Greek *arete* and refers to excellence of moral character. Those who take this approach think that good ethical decisions will be made by good people. The first task, therefore, is to cultivate excellence of character through education, training, and spiritual formation, that is to say, through the internalization of norms so that they become intuitive. One of the products of this moral formation is the conscience that exists within an individual or community. Those who employ this approach often appeal to their consciences as the basis of their perception of an ethical problem or as a justification for the particular solution they prefer. Ends and means are evaluated in terms of how consistent they are with one's moral character and conscience.

An advantage of this approach is that life is complicated and often requires ethical decisions that have to be made quickly. In situations where norms are not clear or there is insufficient time to calculate costs and benefits, recourse to one's conscience and moral intuition can be a very effective way to exercise ethical judgment. One of the problems, however, is that a sound conscience depends on a well-formed moral character. Many who perpetrate great evils sleep all too well at night. In addition, intuitive appeals to conscience can be very subjective. Ultimately, good ethics requires that reasons be given to justify decisions. Vague appeals to conscience can be a way to dodge this responsibility.

Few teachers have consciously used the case approach to form character. Case discussions are a good resource for character formation, however, and in the process of repeatedly making moral judgments, moral maturity may be expected to increase, or at least that has been the experience of case teachers. Character development may therefore be an unintended positive side effect of the case method. Many teachers may prefer leaving it that way, but there is no reason why character development cannot be made more explicit.

So which of these approaches is the best? All three are good and may be used effectively alone or in combination. The authors suggest a combination, although combinations will not be effective in all cases. Decision-makers should be self-conscious, however, about which approach they are using.

Ethical Assessment

The last step of assessment is actually to do it. Having done the analysis, identified relevant norms, and selected one or more of the methods, decision-makers should evaluate alternative courses of action, strategies, and tactics as well as their viability and consequences. No magic formula or foolproof way exists. The process is dialogical. Norms, methods, and the factors of analysis should be massaged together to find what is appropriate or fitting.

The decision follows. Sometimes difficult to make because alternative courses of action are equally satisfactory or equally unsatisfactory, the relationship of faith calls the decision-maker to decide. Cases do, of course, allow the luxury of "fence sitting," but the ethical dilemmas of life do not. Also, not to decide may be a wise course of action in some cases, but it is a decision nonetheless.

Once a decision has been made and a course of action chosen, these conclusions need to be justified to others. Ethics should normally be a community enterprise. Reasons supporting the decision should be consistent with analysis, appeal to relevant moral norms, use an appropriate method, and carry a sense of proportionality. A well-justified ethical decision will also explain why this is the best choice given the circumstances of the case. In addition, a well-crafted decision will also anticipate and respond to the most significant counter-arguments others may raise.

Element IV: Action

Cases in this volume end with decisions to be made. They are open-ended. Discussions of cases usually end at the point of decision, but in life situations this will not be the case. In this final stage decision-makers are called not only to decide but also to act on their decisions.

Reflection should then follow action so that decision-makers will learn from successes and failures. Finally, there is even a tiny bit of reward. When decision and action are done well, decision-makers may bask in the glow and enjoy the inner peace that follows. And even when things do not turn out all right and mistakes are made, and wrong choices selected, with repentance there are resources of forgiveness. Guilt may be a mark of sin, but it is never the last word in Christian ethics. The Good News is the last word. You are forgiven.

FLEXIBILITY

Cases can be used to form character, to analyze problems, to teach method, to understand human relationships, and to employ a method. The case approach is flexible, and this flexibility makes the goals of the teacher in using the method of great importance. Cases lend themselves to one purpose or a multiplicity of purposes, and teachers need to be clear about what they are trying to accomplish. Purpose should govern the selection of cases, how they are taught, and the outcome. This cannot be emphasized enough. Purpose governs use.

What the authors have not done, and in fact cannot do, is set the purpose for participants and facilitators. We suggest a range of options, for example, introducing students to complex social issues, using cases as an entry into the tradition, the teaching of method, and the development of character, but application must remain with the user. This also means that cases can be misused for the purpose of indoctrination and manipulation. Teachers and students should be aware of this, although misuse of method is not peculiar to the use of cases.

Flexibility has still another dimension. The case method is appropriate to a variety of learning situations from the classroom, to church groups, to the small rump sessions found in coffee shops, dorms, and living rooms. Those who use the method regularly find that it stimulates discussion, breaks up the one-way flow of lectures, and eliminates the silence that often permeates abstract discussions. The method is dialogical and thus meets the needs of instructors and learners who prefer more dialogical approaches. But discussion is only the most frequent way cases are used, and discussion can be more or less structured by teachers depending on their goals.

The method also has internal flexibility. Role plays, small groups, voting, and mini-lectures, a fuller description of which can be found in the Appendix, are only a few of the ways cases can be engaged. Cases are not particularly good for presenting normative material and scientific theories. Experienced case teachers have found that lectures and outside reading are more appropriate for introducing this kind of material. Thus where significant background information is required for intelligent choices, the authors recommend using cases for the purposes of opening discussions of complex problems, of applying theory and the insights of traditions, of bringing closure and decision, and of encouraging the development of a critical consciousness.

ISSUES AND COMMENTARIES

The issues that the cases raise were given careful thought. A characteristic of a good case, however, is that it raises more than one issue. Some cases raise numerous issues, and beyond these are what might be called connecting components. There is no case, for example, that is explicitly about women or men, yet several of the cases address problems associated with the changing relationships of contemporary women and men. Racism is a central issue in at least three cases and a related one in several others. Teachers may want to use these connecting components to structure their courses so themes are addressed consistently.

Each case is followed by a commentary that is provided because past experience shows that interpretive reflections help decision-makers by providing leads into avenues of analysis and assessment. These commentaries are not definitive interpretations. They are the observations of individuals trained in Christian theology, ethics, and the case method. They are not out of the same mold, although they do attempt to use the elements that go into an ethical decision as their starting point. There are stylistic differences and variations in emphasis resulting from their multiple authorship. They are intended as aids not as substitutes for creative thinking, analysis, and decision-making.

As mentioned before, the content of the interpretive reflections is not arbitrary. It is organized around the elements that go into making an ethical decision; however, for the sake of variety and flexibility the authors decided that each commentary did not necessarily have to discuss all of the elements or to do so in the same order. The commentaries are designed to touch base with these elements, although for a given case each element may not be covered with the same thoroughness. Brevity has also governed design. In some of the cases, analysis of one or more of the components does not add significant insight. No doubt in these commentaries there are things omitted that teachers will want to add and points made that facilitators will disagree with and want to comment upon critically.

NOTE

[1] For a variant reading of the following material on making ethical decisions, see James Martin-Schramm and Robert L. Stivers, *Christian Environmental Ethics: A Case Method Approach* (Maryknoll, NY: Orbis Books, 2003), chaps. 2–3.

ADDITIONAL RESOURCES

Crook, Roger H. *An Introduction to Christian Ethics*. 4th ed. Upper Saddle River, NJ: Prentice Hall, 2002.

Holland, Joe, and Peter Henriot. *Social Analysis: Linking Faith and Justice*. Maryknoll, NY: Orbis Books, 1990.

Lovin, Robin W. *Christian Ethics: An Essential Guide*. Nashville, TN: Abingdon Press, 2000.

Martin-Schramm, James A., and Robert L. Stivers. *Christian Environmental Ethics: A Case Method Approach*. Maryknoll, NY: Orbis Books, 2003.

PART I

FAMILY

Case

Rigor
and Responsibility

David Trapp hung up the phone and paused to reflect. He had just spoken with his good friend Al Messer. Al had offered to build the cabin. For several months David and his wife, Nancy, had considered building on the two acres of Clark Lake property left to them the year before by David's uncle. The nagging question returned to David. Now that the means were there, was it right to build?

David lived with his wife and two children on a quiet residential street on the outskirts of Toledo, Ohio. David was a lawyer with a downtown law firm that encouraged him to spend up to 15 percent of his time with clients who could not afford to pay. David always used the full allotment, considering it one way he could respond in faith to a pressing human need. David was also active in community affairs. He was vice-president of a statewide citizens' action lobby for more progressive taxation. Locally, he was on the board of directors of an environmental organization whose goal was the cleanup, restoration, and preservation of Lake Erie, and he led adult education classes at his church. What troubled David the most was relating his sense of outrage at injustice to his enjoyment of good food, travel, and water sports.

Nancy Trapp was a buyer for an office-furniture supplier. Her work involved increasing responsibility, and she found it difficult to leave unfinished business in the office. Recently she had been elected to a two-year term as president of the P.T.A. at the children's school. She had not foreseen the constant interruptions such a position would bring. The telephone never seemed to stop ringing, especially on the weekends when people knew they could find her at home.

Decision-making was more or less a family affair with the Trapps. David and Nancy seldom disagreed on family matters and to David's recollection never on a major one. The children, Darcy and Ben, ages ten and eight, were consulted on major decisions and their voices taken into account.

Nathan Ferguson was the pastor of the local congregation in which the Trapps were active participants. Nathan had recently sold a piece of property he had once intended for recreational purposes. The proceeds from the sale had been donated to a church-sponsored halfway house for drug addicts in downtown Toledo. Shortly after Nathan had sold the property, he had begun to preach and teach in a low-key way on the subjects of possessions, overconsumption, and the materialism of American society. His eventual aim was to have some of his parishioners understand and consider forming a community based on the one in Jerusalem described in the opening chapters of the Book of Acts. He envisioned this community as one that would be environmentally sensitive, hold possessions in common, limit consumption to basic necessities, and give liberally to programs among the poor that were based on a principle of self-reliance.

Clea Parks was David's colleague and an active participant in the church's adult education classes. What amazed David was how she could combine a concern for the poor with a way of living that allowed for occasional extravagances. Like David, Clea made full use of the firm's 15 percent allotment to work with poor clients. She was also on the board of the halfway house for drug addicts. In contrast, she and her husband regularly traveled to Bermuda for tennis and golf and to Sun Valley for skiing. Last year they had flown to the Amazon for an eco-tour. This fall they were headed to the Holy Land for three weeks.

Shortly after the settlement of his uncle's will, which in addition to the two acres included enough cash to construct a modest cabin, David and Nancy had discussed the matter of building. David expressed his ambivalence. He wondered about limits to self-indulgence. His desire for the cabin seemed to be locked in a struggle with his conscience. "How can we build a second place," he asked, "when so many people are living in shelters without roofs or simply do not have a home at all? Can we in good conscience consume as heavily as we do while others are crying out for the very things we take for granted and consume almost at will? And what about the animals? Our consumption contributes to the degradation of their habitat."

He also considered the matter of energy consumption. Again directing his reflections to Nancy, he said: "Think about the energy used in construction and the going to and fro that will follow. Is this good stewardship of resources? Does it reflect our responsibility as Americans to conserve fuel? What sort of legacy are we leaving to our grandchildren, not to mention the lessons we are teaching our own children?"

He then rehearsed once again a pet theme: the excessive materialism of American society. "The Bible is quite explicit about possessions," he insisted. "Possession can easily plug our ears to the hearing of God's word. A person cannot have two masters. The rich young ruler went away empty because he was unwilling to give up his possessions. The tax collector, Zacchaeus, is commended by Jesus for his willingness to give one-half of his possessions to the poor. And Jesus himself lived without possessions, commanding his disciples to do likewise."

He paused to think about this further. "Is it possible," he asked, "to avoid the spirit-numbing nature of possessions short of self-denial? And if I'm not going to opt for self-denial, then I at least have to ask in what way my consumption helps to perpetuate a system that is getting further and further away from the simplicity of Jesus." Again he paused, adding: "I guess it all boils down to the ethics of the Sermon on the Mount that Pastor Ferguson keeps talking about. Does the rigor of the sermon's ethic represent the only valid Christian option? Is it possible to live much in excess of basic needs if this ethic is taken seriously? And if we conclude that the sermon is not a new set of laws, what is its relevance anyway?"

Nancy's response was slow in coming both because she was sensitive to David's imaginative conscience and because she wanted a place to separate herself from work and to teach the children the water sports she and David both enjoyed. "I can understand your commitment," she told him. "It's not a matter of guilt for you. But I just don't feel quite as strongly about those things as you do. The pressure has been getting worse lately, and I feel the need to share with you and the children in a more relaxed setting. The kids are getting older fast, and in a few years they'll be beyond the age where they'll be around to learn water sports.

"The materialism you are so concerned about," she went on to say, "has also made for creative new possibilities. It's not possessions themselves, but how we use them that makes a difference. It's the willingness to give, and we give enough what with the 15 percent of your time and the giving of more than 10 percent of our incomes to church and charity. And think about what giving up our possessions will do. Without programs to transfer our abundance to the poor, giving things up will go for naught or perhaps contribute to the loss of someone's job. That is just the way things are. Think about Al Messer."

David was not quite sure what to make of Nancy's comments. The old nagging questions kept coming back. His conscience would not let him off easily.

Then Nathan Ferguson had begun his sermons and more recently had conducted a series of six sessions in the adult education class that David led. Nathan returned time and again to the teachings of Jesus: to the Sermon on the Mount, to the rich young ruler, to Zacchaeus, to the sharing in early Christian communities, to the call of the prophets to justice and care for the poor, and to Jesus' love for the birds of the air and fish of the sea.

Nathan had not talked in a demanding or accusatory fashion, but neither had he let his parishioners off the hook. To David it seemed that Nathan's every thought had been directed straight at him.

At the office Clea hit him from the other side. At first she had merely commented on Nathan's sermons and classes. She thought Nathan was too much of a perfectionist. She appreciated his concern for the poor and the environment and how possessions can close one's ears to the word of God. She did not, however, see how individual sacrifices produced the social change they all wanted.

She also had a contrasting view of the Sermon on the Mount. "We cannot live the sermon," she explained. "It's impossible, and anyway, it wasn't intended for everyone. Ethical rigor is right for folks like Nathan, but what most of us are called to is responsibility: to the right use of possessions, to a willingness to give, and to advocacy of justice in word and deed. The choice is not between self-indulgence and self-denial. There is a third option: living responsibly with concern for all those issues Nathan talks about and still appreciating the finer things in life."

When David told her about the lake property and Nancy's needs, Clea had begun to push him a bit harder. "Come on, David," she said, half joking, "it's all right with Jesus if you build. Jesus enjoyed life and participated in it fully. The church tradition is quite ambiguous on possessions, wealth, and nature." Another time she put it bluntly, "What right have you to force your values and views on Nancy and the children?" Lately she had been twitting him. Just the other day with a big grin on her face she called him "the monk."

Al Messer's call had jolted David and increased his sense that something had to give. Al had told David that he could build the cabin out of used lumber and had found a place where he could get insulation and double-pane window glass at reduced prices. Al had also indicated he needed the work because business had been a bit slow lately.

Nancy entered the room and guessed what was troubling David. "I know what's bothering you," she said. "If we build, those old questions about the poor, materialism, and limits to consumption will nag at you. You might not even stick to a decision to build. If we don't build, you'll feel you have let the kids and me down and miss your favorite water sports. How should we decide this?"

Commentary

Rigor and Responsibility

Taken at face value this case is about David and Nancy Trapp struggling to decide whether to build a vacation cabin. But at a deeper and more comprehensive level the case is addressed to all non-poor Christians; the issue is how to live as a Christian in a materialistic world where ostentatious luxury, grinding poverty, and environmental degradation exist side by side.

This question of how to live can be given greater specificity by considering the title of the case. Should an affluent family give up what it has and follow the rigorous "holy poverty" of Jesus, or is there an alternative called "responsible consumption" that stresses right use and good stewardship of material resources? Realizing that a continuum of options is possible between the "either" of rigor and the "or" of responsibility, these two options may be contrasted for the purpose of analyzing the decisions the Trapps must make.

Before addressing these two contrasting perspectives, however, there are several related issues that should at least be mentioned. The two most important are poverty and environmental degradation. David and Nancy's decision is not hidden in a vacuum. It stands out in a context where over a billion people are malnourished and live in miserable poverty. It stands out in a global economy in which the gap between rich and poor remains wide. It stands out in an economic system that needs high levels of consumption to stimulate growth and jobs. It stands out in a planetary system where unprecedented numbers of species are going extinct largely due to human actions and where there is serious concern about the sustainability of natural resources and the capacity of ecosystems to absorb pollution. These issues raised by the context of the case are the very issues raised to prominence by this volume.

There are six other issues important for this case but peripheral to the main concerns. The first is family decision-making. How is this family to decide? The second stems from the Trapps' need to "get away." Would the addition of a cabin really solve the more pressing problems of overwork and over-involvement in the community? The third is the matter of educating children. What messages do David and Nancy send Darcy and Ben by overwork and by building a second home? What sort of character are they trying to instill?

The fourth issue is raised by the inheritance. Are David and Nancy really free to give their inheritance to the poor? Although the case does not say, they probably live within the context of a larger family grouping, some of whose members might be a little upset with such unilateral action. The fifth issue is guilt. Should Christians and Americans feel a sense of guilt for their high levels of consumption? And what is the function of guilt in the Christian life? Sixth is the issue of individual action in a world of over six billion people that is dominated by large social organizations. How do people like David and Nancy influence others to do justice and exercise Christianity's call for solidarity? Will individual acts of self-sacrifice make a difference?

Beyond these six issues, there are a number of issues raised by Christian traditions. How should the Bible and theology, for example, guide the Trapps' choice? What in fact do the traditions say about the issues in the case?

THE MAIN QUESTION

So how are Christians to live in a world of continuing poverty and environmental degradation? Most students react to David's dilemma with at least mild astonishment. They seem to assume that consuming goods and services in quantity is the natural thing to do and have difficulty comprehending why building is a dilemma at all. This is not surprising given the daily barrage of commercial advertising whose main purpose is to sell a way of life that encourages heavy consumption. Indeed, heavy consumption has become a way of life to many Americans.

The norm of justice makes the gap between rich and poor and the grinding poverty of so many people that goes side by side with this consumption difficult to justify. The emphasis on material things underlying this consumption is difficult to reconcile with biblical norms on wealth and consumption. The environmental degradation that this level of consumption causes is a serious problem for sustainability of earth's ecological systems. On these grounds David and many Americans have good reason to be troubled by their consciences.

Consider first the norm of *justice*. Justice is rooted in the very being of God. It is an essential part of God's community of love and calls followers of Jesus Christ to make fairness the core of their social response to other persons and the rest of creation. Included in this biblical concern for justice is solidarity with the poor and also with nature.

The biblical basis of justice and solidarity with the poor starts with God's liberation of the oppressed Hebrew slaves in Egypt and the establishment of a covenant with them (Exodus). This theme continues in the prophetic reinterpretation of the covenant. Micah summarized the law:

> to do justice, and to love kindness,
>   and to walk humbly with your God. (Mi 6:8)

Amos was adamant that God's wrath would befall Israel for its injustice and failure to care for the poor (Am 5:21–24). Isaiah and Jeremiah were equally adamant (Is 1:12–17; 3:13–15; 58:6–9; Jer 22:13–17).

In the Christian scriptures the emphasis on justice is somewhat muted in comparison to the prophets, but the concern for the poor may be even stronger. Jesus himself was a poor man from a poor part of Israel. His mission was among the poor, and his message was directed to them. He blessed the poor and spoke God's judgment on the rich. On the cross he made himself one of the dispossessed. In the early Jerusalem community, as recorded in Acts 1—5, the basic economic needs of all members were taken care of as the wealthier shared their possessions so none would be deprived.

Second are biblical and theological understandings of wealth and consumption. Two traditions have dominated, offering two not very compatible understandings of what it means to live sufficiently. One stresses a rigorous response to Jesus teachings, including self-denial, the giving of what one has to the poor, and a radical freedom from possessions. The other accents the right use of possessions and emphasizes responsibility and willingness to share. The first tradition may be called *rigorous discipleship* and the second *responsible consumption*. These are not meant to be polemical titles. Responsible consumption has its element of rigor, and rigorous discipleship is certainly responsible. While the differences between them are significant, it is possible to accept both as valid Christian ways of living.

Parenthetically, these two traditions also give a foundation for solidarity with the poor. Historically, many Christians have identified completely with the poor, even to the point of considerable self-sacrifice. Widely known modern examples, such as Mother Teresa and Dorothy Day, have continued this tradition. At the same time and not so spectacularly, Christians work responsibly in everyday vocations serving Christ with varying degrees of intensity and frugality.

The choice between these traditions is David's dilemma and is worthy of further exploration. The dilemma is the age-old one of the ideal and the real. On the one hand Jesus offers glimpses of the ideal in his teachings on the community of God and in his person. The community of God, he says, is already present with power, and Jesus asks his disciples to live in this power and to drop what they are doing and follow him. On the other hand, paradoxically, the community of God is still to come in its fullness. Reality is a mixture of powers: human power rightly and wrongly used and God's

power of love. God's community of love stands alongside and often in contradiction to human power, and Christians must live in a world where perfect choices are seldom presented.

These two normative traditions both have biblical bases. The Hebrew
scriptures take the responsible consumption side. They praise the rich people
and place a high value on riches gained through honest work (Gn 13:2;
26:13; 30:43; 41:40). Alongside this praise is the obligation to care for weaker
members of society (Am 8:48; Is 5:8–10; 10:1–3). Nowhere do the Hebrew
scriptures praise self-imposed poverty or beggars.

The two sides are found in the teachings of Jesus. His announcement of
the coming community of God carries with it a call for unparalleled freedom from possessions and complete trust in God. The service of God and
service of riches are incompatible (Mt 6:24; Mk 8:36; 9:43–48; 10:17–25; Lk
12:15; 8:14, 18–23; 19:1–10). Jesus tells the rich young ruler who has kept all
the laws to go sell what he has and give it to the poor (Lk 18:18–24). Jesus
himself had no possessions (Mt 8:20; Mk 1:16; 6:8–9; Lk 9:3; 10:4) and prod-
ded his disciples to go out on their missionary journeys taking nothing
with them (Lk 9:3; 10:4).

Nevertheless, Jesus took for granted the owning of property (Lk 6:30;
10:30–37; Mt 25:31–40). He was apparently supported by women of means
(Lk 8:2) and urged that possessions be used to help those in need (Lk 6:30).
Jesus did not ask Zacchaeus to give up all his possessions (Lk 19). He dined
with hated tax collectors and was fond of celebrations, especially meals of
fellowship. The examples echo the Hebrew scriptures' stress on the right
use of wealth and possessions.

This mixed mind continued in the early church. On the one side was the
Jerusalem community where goods were shared in common (Acts 1–5).
This seems to follow Jesus' teachings about radical freedom from possessions. The letter of James offers little solace to the wealthy (Jas 1:11; 2:1–7;
5:1–6). On the other side is Paul, who did not address the problem of wealth,
although he himself seems to have had few possessions and was self-sup-
porting as a tentmaker (Phil 4:11–13). He did, however, stress right use,
made clear his center in Christ, and called on the congregations he served
to support the poor in Jerusalem. The letter to Timothy, while hard on the
wealthy, leaves the door open to right use of possessions (1 Tm 6:6–10, 17–
19).

From these two traditions a dual ethic emerged. For monks and nuns
who surrendered their possessions and elected a life of chastity, holy poverty, and nonviolence, the rigor of Jesus was binding. For the great majority
the rigor of Jesus became "counsels of perfection." It was deemed impossible of fulfillment and therefore binding only on those who would be perfect.

These two ways of living existed side by side with the authority of the
church sanctioning both and holding them together. Implicit in this resolution of the dilemma was a troublesome hierarchy of perfection and the

unbiblical notion of special merits that practicing rigor was claimed to confer. Thus, while the church held things together, it did so at the price of grading perfection and discouraging the rigor of ordinary Christians.

Protestants, following Martin Luther's dictum of the priesthood of all believers, eliminated special merit, but at the price of restoring the dilemma. Monasteries and convents were closed, and all believers were, according to Luther, to serve God in whatever vocation they found themselves. Where there had been two ways of life in one church, now there was one way of life with two tendencies in many churches. Still, rigorous discipleship has continued to the present in the monastic movement within the Roman Catholic Church and in many sects that have flourished in Protestantism.

One statement by Martin Luther during a "table talk" in the winter of 1542–43 catches the mind that is suspicious of wealth:

> Riches are the most insignificant things on earth, the smallest gift that God can give a person. What are they in comparison with the word of God? In fact, what are they in comparison even with physical endowments and beauty? What are they in comparison to the gifts of the mind? And yet we act as if this were not so! The matter, form, effect, and goal of riches are worthless. This is why our Lord God generally gives riches to crude asses to whom nothing else is given.

The biblical witness on consumption follows much the same twofold pattern. The basic issue is frugality versus contentment with a moderate level of consumption.

Theologically the two traditions take their cues from the paradoxical "here, but yet to come" teaching of the early church. This paradox appears in the earliest pages of the Bible. Human beings are created in the image of God (Gn 1) but with Adam and Eve fall away from God into sin (Gn 3). It reappears again and again in the history of Israel as the Israelites wrestle with the responsibilities of the covenant and their own unrighteousness.

Jesus advises his disciples to be sheep among the wolves and to have the wisdom of the serpent and the innocence of the dove (Mt 10:16). For Christians, this paradox is preeminent in the cross and resurrection. The cross is reality at its worst and points to the depth of human sin. Sin is not some minor defect to be overcome by new techniques. Ordering force and occasionally even coercion are needed to keep it in check.

Yet the cross is not the last word in Christianity. It is followed closely by the ever-new word of the resurrection. The resurrection points to God at work overcoming sin and death. It points as well to the possibility of the "new creation" in the lives of individuals and groups and to the creative potential of love and justice. It teaches Christians that while they still live in the age of sin and death, God's love has broken in, there is hope, and their efforts in response to God's love are not in vain. Christians are invited, as a result, to deal with a partly open future in which even small responses can make a difference.

Finally, the paradox is highlighted by Paul's sense that Christians live between the ages. They live in the old age of sin, death, injustice, and limits. Yet they are called to live according to the new age inaugurated by Jesus Christ and made present by the Holy Spirit. Insofar as they live in the old age, Christians give limited support to such things as prison systems, to less than perfect but still functioning economic and political systems, and even to wars of liberation and defense. Living in the old age involves compromises, many of which appear to be "cop-outs" to those who take the rigorous path.

Nevertheless, Christians are not to be serpents or to live according to the old age. They are to live in the resurrection according to the love and justice of the new age. This means pushing beyond what merely is and seeking just and sustainable societies. Living in the new age means witnessing to the ideal and may seem utopian to those who enjoy luxury and even some who follow the path of responsible consumption.

In summary, the rigorous tradition builds on Jesus' call to radical discipleship, his living without possessions frugally and simply, and his freedom from materialism. This tradition calls the disciple to a life of simplicity and sharing. It is a life of commitment to the community of God. And even if all the details are not lived perfectly, at least the disciple should aim in that direction and pray that the grace of God will provide the resources to reconcile aim and action.

As for living between the ages, the path of rigorous discipleship emphasizes the new age almost to the exclusion of the old. This exclusion comes not from failure to see the sin of the old age, but rather from the assumption that Christians are free from the old age through the power of God. Hence radical changes in ways of living come naturally, and followers make these changes with enthusiasm.

The path of rigorous discipleship is attractive. It does not bog down in the inevitable relativities and compromises of the old age. It is simple, direct, and often accompanied by communities that seem full of the Spirit. It is a valid Christian option.

Unlike the path of rigorous discipleship, the path of responsible consumption does not take its main cues from the teachings of Jesus. This does not mean it is less biblical, but that it rests more heavily on the main themes of the Bible, in particular on the theological tension between the old and the new ages. Like those on the path of rigorous discipleship, Christians on this path are concerned for the poor and aware of being tied to possessions. They do not, however, take the frugality and simplicity of Jesus literally or urge the surrender of all possessions.

Reduced to basics, those who follow this tradition wrestle with what it means to live between the ages, taking both ages seriously. In contrast to the heavy stress on the new age, they point to the realities of the old age or to the ambiguity of life between the ages. The problem for them is not rigorous discipleship but how to act responsibly and to begin a process of change that will lead to greater justice and more sustainable communities. Their mood is sober, their programs moderate and reformist in nature. They also have a greater appreciation of material consumption.

This path is attractive to less ascetic Christians and to those who are deeply involved in existing structures. It is a valid Christian tradition and avoids the excesses that sometimes accompany the rigorous tradition. Most important, it accounts for the complexities of living in the world as it is.

While Christianity has been of two minds, it has been clear on one guiding norm, *sufficiency*. Sufficiency for humans is the timely supply of basic material necessities, defined as the minimum amount of food, clothing, shelter, transportation, health care, and education needed to live at some margin above mere subsistence. Sufficiency is, of course, more than a given batch of goods and services. Philosopher Martha Nussbaum has established something she calls the "flourishing life" as the goal of her development scheme. She has advanced two lists of what constitute "the human form of life" and "good human functioning."[1] She insists it is the responsibility of political and economic institutions to ensure that everyone is capable of functioning at a human level. While her lists are exhaustive and beyond the capacity of most governments, they are a good starting place for understanding what sufficiency means.

Sufficiency for other species revolves first around the preservation and restoration of habitat for wild species. Humans do not have the capacity to oversee the survival of many species, but they can cease degrading critical habitats. Habitat loss is a major cause of species extinction. As for domestic animals, more is required. Sufficiency for them means the provision of basic material needs and proper care. This opens up a wide range of options including alternative farming techniques and even vegetarian diets.

Sufficiency must also include future generations. Sufficiency must be sustainable over long periods of time. Another norm influencing the Trapps' decision is therefore *sustainability*. The issue that sustainability raises for the Trapps is whether the forms of consumption they are contemplating degrade the environment. One small cabin on an already developed lake front will hardly do much damage, but if their behavior were to be generalized, it certainly would. The earth can ill afford six billion people who consume as if they were affluent North Americans.

What then are David and Nancy to do? How are they to live? If they will to live responsively to the power of God and to be guided by Christian norms, they will avoid heavy consumption, materialism, and selfish individualism. They will live sufficiently free to pursue rigorous discipleship or responsible consumption as they feel called. They will put trust where trust belongs, that is to say, in God's community, not in material possessions. What this means in practice is something that finally is a matter of conscience. Blueprints and prescriptions are not available.

GUILT

Is David driven by guilt over his own privileged place in the world—white, American, male, intelligent, and wealthy—or is guilt an inappropriate word to describe his struggle with rigor and responsibility? The case does not reveal the answer. Giving David the benefit of doubt, however, it is better to see his struggle as a conscientious effort to deal with an ambiguous tradition and a changing environmental context. Christians like David may be genuinely perplexed as they try to figure out the right course, because valid norms sometimes suggest quite different courses of action.

Even if David did not feel guilty, it is important to recognize that guilt is an all too common human experience and should be taken seriously. Guilt may be a warning sign of serious inner alienation. It may be telling David that he really is living a sinful way of life and needs to change (repent).

More important for those who would categorize David as "guilt ridden" is the possibility that they are projecting their own guilt in order to be free for a life of affluence. To dismiss David's dilemma as guilt is to miss the main point of the case.

Finally, guilt is not something that needs to paralyze action. Guilt may be genuinely experienced and may legitimately point to sin, but it is not the place to rest. Just as the resurrection follows the cross, so do forgiveness and the possibility of new life follow sin and guilt.

INDIVIDUAL ACTION

Does it really make a difference what David and Nancy decide? Does David's struggle over options available to only a select few trivialize the more important problems of world poverty and environmental degradation?

Discussions of individual action are permeated with optimistic and pessimistic extremes. The optimists insist that successful social movements are usually started and led by individuals who are deeply concerned and motivated. They urge their listeners to take the challenge and change the world. The pessimists, in turn, dismiss individual action as not having a chance in a world of large organizations. They urge their listeners to join movements or counsel withdrawal.

Christians are neither optimists nor pessimists. They are hopeful and realistic; hopeful because God is at work in even the darkest times, realistic because of sin. Christians act first in response to the love of God they experience spiritually and only second to achieve results. If good results follow from faithful discipleship, they should be embraced. If they do not, action is still forthcoming because of its spiritual foundation.

This simple truth does away with the debate between optimists and pessimists over individual action. The debate is misplaced. It misses the essential inspiration of Christian ethical action and substitutes reliance on human action alone.

Is David's dilemma trivial? By no means! His struggle with his conscience over appropriate levels of consumption is essential in a poverty-stricken, environmentally degraded world. It is essential for everyone, especially for those who consume heavily or could potentially consume more. Whether it is a cabin, a television set, a new computer, or a trip to the Amazon, personal consumption makes an ethical statement. It says a lot about character. So while David's specific decision will not be recorded in history books, what this generation does to relieve poverty and preserve the environment will.

NOTE

[1] Martha Nussbaum and Jonathan Glover, *Women, Culture, and Development: A Study of Human Capabilities* (Oxford: Clarendon Press, 1995), 76–85. Nussbaum and Glover argue that the "human form of life" consists of (1) mortality; (2) the human body including the needs for food, drink, and shelter, and for sexual desire; (3) the capacity for pleasure and pain; (4) cognitive capability including perceiving, imagining, and thinking; (5) early infant development; (6) practical reason; (7) affiliation with other human beings; (8) relatedness to other species and nature; (9) humor and play; (10) separateness; and (11) space to move around in.

"Basic human functional capabilities" include (1) being able to live to the end of a human life of normal length; (2) being able to have good health; (3) being able to avoid unnecessary and non-beneficial pain; (4) being able to use the senses; (5) being able to have attachments to things and persons outside ourselves; (6) being able to form a conception of the good and to engage in critical reflection about the planning of one's life; (7) being able to live for others; (8) being able to live with concern for and in relations to animals, plants, and the world of nature; (9) being able to laugh, play, and enjoy recreational activities; and (10) being able to live one's own life in one's own surroundings and context.

ADDITIONAL RESOURCES

Batey, Richard. *Jesus and the Poor*. New York: Harper and Row, Publishers, 1972.

Birch, Bruce C., and Larry L. Rasmussen. *The Predicament of the Prosperous*. Philadelphia: The Westminster Press, 1978.

Cobb, John B., Jr. *Sustainability*. Maryknoll, NY: Orbis Books, 1992.

Durning, Alan Thein. *This Place on Earth: Home and the Practice of Permanence*. Seattle: Sasquatch Books, 1997.

Foster, Richard J. *Freedom of Simplicity: Finding Harmony in a Complex World*. New York: Harper Paperback Books, 1998.

Hengel, Martin. *Property and Riches in the Early Church*. Translated by John Bowden. Philadelphia: Fortress Press, 1974.

Luhrs, Janet. *The Simple Living Guide: A Sourcebook for Less Stressful, More Joyful Living*. New York: Broadway Books, 1997.

McDaniel, Jay B. *Living from the Center: Sprirituality in an Age of Consumerism*. St. Louis: Chalice Press, 2000.

Nash, James A. "Toward the Revival and Reform of the Subversive Virtue: Frugality." In *Consumption, Population, and Sustainability: Perspectives from Science and Religion*, edited by Audrey R. Chapman, Rodney L. Petersen, and Barbara Smith-Moran. Washington, DC: Island Press, 2002.

Princen, Thomas, and Michael Maniates, eds. *Confronting Consumption*. Cambridge, MA: MIT Press, 2002.

Rohr, Richard. *Simplicity: The Art of Living*. New York: Crossroad, 1995.

Shi, David. *The Simple Life: Plain Living and High Thinking in American Culture*. Athens, GA: Univ. of Georgia Press, 2001.

Sider, Ronald. *Rich Christians in an Age of Hunger*. Dallas: Word Publishing Company, 2000.

St. James, Ronald J. *The Simplicity Reader*. New York: Smithmark Publishing Company, 1999.

Stivers, Robert L. *Hunger, Technology, and Limits to Growth*. Minneapolis: Augsburg Press, 1984. See Chapter 9.

Yount, David. *Spiritual Simplicity: Simplify Your Life and Enrich Your Soul*. London: Simon and Schuster, 1999.

Case

What God Has Joined

Linda glanced through the large glass window of the restaurant and saw Beth and Jennifer already seated in a corner booth. She hesitated a moment at the door, then moved toward them, hugging and greeting each in turn. They had been good friends in college, but after graduation they had drifted apart. When the fourth member of their college quartet, Joanne, had died of breast cancer eight years after graduation, the remaining three had come together again to support her in her last months and to share the pain of her passing. Over the next two years they had remained close. The lunch today was a kind of a celebration for Jennifer, who had concentrated on her career as an accountant after college rather than marrying and having children like the other three. Now, as the three survivors of the quartet approached thirty-five, Jennifer was engaged to be married to another partner in her accounting firm. Next Saturday there was to be a big party, but this lunch was just for the three of them.

Twenty minutes later, having admired Jen's ring and listened to the couple's wedding plans, Linda was shifting uncomfortably in her seat. She realized both Beth and Jennifer were staring, waiting for her to volunteer information. Finally Jennifer, not the most patient or tactful of the trio, blurted out, "Tell us what's the matter, Lin. We both know that things haven't been great for a while at home, but you seem desperately unhappy. We love you. What's going on?"

It was more than Linda could do to control the gulping sobs that rolled out of her. "I don't know what to do. It's all come back, and I can't go on. David's drinking, and he's hit me. I can't take it anymore."

When Linda had calmed down, Beth pulled the story from her a piece at a time. Beth and Jen knew that Linda's husband, David, had rarely used

This case was prepared by Christine E. Gudorf. Copyright © The Case Study Institute. The names of all persons and institutions have been disguised to protect the privacy of those involved.

alcohol before he lost his job as manager of a bank branch, but both had seen him inebriated at least twice in the last six months. They knew David had not found another job. But both were shocked to hear that he had hit Linda. They immediately asked for details, for neither would have thought David capable of violence. Both remembered the extraordinary gentleness he had displayed in the hospital nursery holding and feeding Megan, the couple's tiny premature firstborn.

Linda began by defending David, citing the pressures of unemployment on him, the stress of seeing their unemployment insurance run out, and the prospect of their savings running out as well. With only the part-time secretarial work that Linda had found with the school board, they would not be able to keep up house payments. "He's drinking, but he's not really drinking that much. He has hit me two or three times but always stops after the one slap. The real problem is me. It's all coming back. I love him, but I can't stand for him to get near me. And he thinks I'm rejecting him, that I don't love him anymore because he doesn't have a job."

Both Beth and Jennifer understood that Linda was referring to her memories of years of sexual abuse by her grandfather. From the time she was eight until his death when Linda was fourteen, her grandfather had used his position as her after-school baby sitter to sexually molest her. Her family had more or less dismissed both attempts she made to tell about the abuse. She later suspected that her mother had been abused before her. When she arrived at college, Linda never dated. When the topic of child incest came up in a sociology class, Linda spoke to the professor, who referred her to individual therapy and to a support group for child victims of incest. After six months of therapy Linda had met David, declared herself cured, and quit the therapy. But both Beth and Jennifer remembered Linda's screaming nightmares and her fear and distrust of men. And they knew that though she kept in touch with her family, she never went back home after college and never left her children with any of her family.

"Are you and David talking, Linda?" Jennifer asked.

"What can I say? He doesn't believe me when I say that he's not the reason I don't want sex. He keeps telling me I was over the abuse years ago, that I have loved sex for all these years, that the only thing that could be turning me off is him. Maybe he's right, and the memories are just an excuse. Maybe I have invented them. That's what mother and Aunt Lucy told me when I was little. That I made them up. I don't really know how I feel, or whether I love him, or what I want to do. But I can't go on. Sometimes I just go and hide in a closet for hours at a time. I can't face anyone. I don't know how I got here—I haven't been outside the house in weeks."

Linda was calmer by the end of the lunch. Both Jennifer and Beth were disturbed by Linda's depression and her expressions of self-doubt and self-blame. They urged her to seek therapeutic help. Beth volunteered to make appointments for both David and Linda separately to see her neighbors, the Spencers, a husband-and-wife therapy team. Beth assured Linda that they worked on a sliding-scale fee schedule.

LONG-TERM RECOVERY ISSUES

Six weeks later, when the friends met after Jen's wedding, Linda reported that some things were better and some things were worse. David had liked Dr. Dan Spencer from the start. By the second session he had stopped drinking, and though there were no more incidents of either verbal or physical violence, David continued to work with Dan Spencer on issues around alcohol and violence. Linda reported that Alice Spencer was pushing her to face the violent episodes, to look at the effect they had had on her and on the marital relationship, and to think about how she might react to violence or the threat of violence from David in the future. David was continuing to look for work in surrounding communities. But he still had trouble accepting that Linda was not rejecting him when she declined sex.

Sitting in Beth's kitchen while Linda's and Beth's children played outside the backyard window, Linda confided, "Sometimes I really do want him to hold me, to give me affection. But the minute it turns sexual, I want to scream. For him, if I don't want sex, I don't love him. He tries sometimes to just be affectionate, but it really hurts him when I panic and push him away from me. Sometimes I can't even stand him being close; other times I want to be held but then push him away later. He complains that he never knows what I want. And I *don't* know what I want. I don't know why it all came back. There was no clue for all those years. We were really happy until he lost his job. But it's been almost a year since we made love, and three months since I was last willing to try."

"What does Alice Spencer think of your situation?" asked Jennifer.

"She says that I need to concentrate not on David or the relationship but on my own feelings. She thinks that's why it all came back—I didn't stay in therapy long enough to heal from the abuse. I'm not good at explaining it, but what the years of abuse did was to teach me to respond to other people's needs and desires and to lose sight of my own. She says now I need to respond to my own feelings, but first I have to learn what they are. And in some areas of my life I don't have a clue as to which feelings are mine and which are David's, or my grandfather's, or even other people's—like yours. So many "shoulds" in my life have come from outside me, without any conscious consideration or adoption on my part. She insists I can heal, that I can find my authentic self. But I don't know. In some things, yes, but I can't imagine ever having sex again and enjoying it without remembering the pain and hatred and ultimate emptiness inside. What does that mean for our marriage? Do I love David? Can I make him wait for what may never happen? Shouldn't I be working on accepting sex so I can stop hurting him?

My rejection is hurting him much worse than his slaps ever hurt me. Can there be a marriage without sex? A real one with love and warmth, the kind we vowed to have?"

Jennifer responded, "That's a tough one. I remember that Christian churches used to forbid totally impotent men to marry, because sex was important to marriage, but I think so long as they had sex once, it didn't matter if they never did again. I don't know. I'm the newly married one here. Can there be a real marriage without sex? Won't that depend on what David wants and needs, too? Do *you* want to be married? Why don't you talk to somebody with some expertise? You like Pastor Link, and we've all known him for years. Why don't you and David talk to him?"

At that very moment David sat in Dan Spencer's office. "All right, all right. I am coming to see that she really is going back through all that past abuse. I don't understand why. I thought she was through it before we got married. She was never tense or nervous about sex, never afraid of being forced or hurt. She knew I would never hurt her. I just don't understand why it came back now, if not in response to me. But I can't do this much longer. I know that when I feel really threatened by her withdrawal that I want to drink too much, and I know that if I drink, the hurt and threat will come out in anger. I don't know how I'd live without myself if I ever forced her to have sex. But not drinking is only a little part of the answer."

David continued thoughtfully, "I know I haven't slept the whole night through in over six months. Some nights I have to get up and get away from her, so I won't start making love to her while she's asleep. I have to go lie down on the couch. I love Linda. When I hold her or hug her or just sit in the car with her driving the kids to Sunday school, I want to make love to her. And I want her to love me. It's not just selfish or lust. I want to give her pleasure, to make her feel better, to show her that she can trust me with her body and her heart. Sometimes I think it would be easier to just stay away from her. But to avoid her, to get separate beds, or even separate rooms when we could afford them, would be like divorce. When will this be over? How long does it take? Will she ever get better? Is divorce the only option?"

When Linda picked up David at Dr. Spencer's, she asked if he were interested in seeing Pastor Link. David agreed and offered to make the appointment. When David called the church, he was told that Pastor Link was out of town for three weeks but that the associate pastor, Reverend Deerick, was available. David made an appointment with Reverend Deerick, explained the general situation to him, and mentioned that he and Linda were in therapy with the Spencers. Reverend Deerick asked for their authorization to speak with the Spencers. When David and Linda appeared the following week for their appointment, Reverend Deerick had briefly discussed the case with the Spencers. Linda and David began by describing their feelings about each other and their marriage, and ended with a flurry of questions about the nature of marriage. Was their marriage over?

Could the wounded child in Linda ever really heal after all these years? If not, would remaining together be merely a hypothetical front, or would it be a heroic fidelity to the vows they had taken? Could there be a real Christian marriage without sharing either genital pleasure or touch and affection? What did the church teach?

When they had finished, Reverend Deerick was still for a few moments and then said: "I'm not sure that anyone can answer all your questions. I have never been married myself. And you probably know that our church, like most Christian churches, is in the midst of rethinking various aspects of our teachings regarding sexuality and marriage. I could tell you what Augustine or Luther would say to you, but I don't think that would do much good. From what you have told me, you didn't marry either to have children or to prevent fornication. You married because you loved each other in a deeply interpersonal way and because you found that the whole of the other person—body and soul—helped put you in touch with ultimate reality, with God. This contemporary understanding of the purpose and goal of marriage is radically different from Augustine's, or Luther's, or any of the other classical Christian thinkers. So their likely advice in this situation—that you purify and consecrate your marriage by giving up sexual intimacy, living as brother and sister as you rear your children—would probably strike you as effectively ending the marriage.

"Our theological tradition simply doesn't give us a lot of useful contemporary guidance about sexuality in marriage. But I do have some suggestions. The first one is personal prayer. I don't mean that you should pray that all this will mysteriously disappear. Prayer is communication with God. Sometimes it is spoken; more often it is silent. Sometimes we write our prayers. Think of prayer as a way of making a friend of God.

"David, I am very moved by your pain and your love for Linda. But you express a great deal of need for her, and that need clearly puts emotional pressure on her. Most men in our society are socialized to fulfill virtually all their intimacy needs in one sexual relationship. Developing an intimate relationship with God could not only take away some of your pain and need, but it could also let you focus on Linda's needs more clearly. Linda, prayer for you could be a source of hope and strength for healing. Some victims of sexual abuse by males have a difficult time with prayer and with God because of the traditional images of God as masculine. You may need to focus on the femininity of God, on God as Mother, to be able to pray. But regardless of what gender you attribute to God, the object is that you let yourself feel God's love for you and God's support for your healing. Feeling God's support for healing could help you feel more legitimate investing so much time and energy in the healing process. A prayerful relationship with God could help you reclaim feelings of trust, self-worth, and responsibility for your own life.

"You both have many questions about marriage and your future that I think only prayer can answer. Prayer can be a process of uncovering, one piece at a time, all our questions about who we are and what we should do. If you like, I would be glad to meet with you periodically to discuss developments in your individual prayer life. Or I have some books or articles you could read, if you prefer."

As David and Linda drove home from the meeting, they wondered how valuable Reverend Deerick's advice had been. In some ways it evoked simplistic notions of passive religion in which prayer is the answer to everything. But Reverend Deerick had supported their therapeutic process with the Spencers as helpful and seemed to want to coordinate this spiritual direction with that process. Perhaps prayer could help David find more patience with Linda's withdrawal and could help Linda feel stronger and more worthwhile. Halfway home Linda asked, "David, do you want to consider divorce as an option? I would understand if you did. I don't think it's right for me to ask you to continue with our marriage if that's not what you want, but for myself I prefer to work on our marriage. I'm just not sure *how* we work on rebuilding it, or what we can legitimately ask of each other. What do you want to do, David?"

Commentary

What God Has Joined

Some of the social and moral issues requiring analysis in this case include alcoholism, domestic violence, and child sexual abuse (child incest). But as David's and Linda's questions indicate, the central question for them is whether they should remain together. This question raises the theological issues undergirding the nature of marriage. Let us begin with the more specific problems.

ALCOHOLISM

Linda and David both seem to treat David's drinking as a minor problem; Beth and Jennifer also seem to accept that judgment. However, Dan Spencer continues to ask about and treat alcohol as a possible ongoing problem, for he is not sure that alcohol is only temporarily a problem due to David's loss of work or Linda's withdrawal. While the use of alcohol has not been regarded as a moral problem within most of Christianity—certainly not within scripture—the abuse of alcohol has been consistently condemned from scriptural times to the present. It is not clear from the case that David's alcohol abuse is part of a larger pattern of alcoholism, but David's misuse of alcohol under the pressure of unemployment and his wife's withdrawal might well signal a pattern of relying on alcohol to cope with pressure.

Research has not determined whether persons who have had trouble with alcohol dependency in response to stress are permanently at risk. Alcoholics Anonymous says yes and insists on lifelong abstinence. There are some people who seem to be able to return to moderate, even abstemious, use of alcohol after an episode of alcohol abuse and to maintain that lower level of use for years. But there are not reliable methods for separating those with such potential from those unable to use alcohol responsibly. If David does not decide to give up alcohol altogether, he needs careful monitoring and oversight of his consumption and response for some time.

DOMESTIC BATTERY

Linda's friends are perceptive to question her facile dismissal of David's violence against her. The Spencers need to elicit from both Linda and David their accounts of violence in the relationship. All too often domestic violence follows a pattern: psychological violence leads to verbal violence, which leads to physical violence (including sexual violence), which may even lead to homicide. It is important to discover whether there has been a pattern of escalation in the violence within the relationship.

Between one in seven and one in four homes in the United States are scenes of domestic violence. Because male abusers often have a series of partners, one in every four US women will be involved at some time during her life in a relationship of domestic violence. Christianity also bears some responsibility for high rates of domestic violence. Violence against women has been tolerated and sometimes actively supported in the churches. In Christianity before mandatory clerical celibacy was imposed at the end of the first millennium, and among Protestants after the Reformation, for example, clergy were encouraged to be especially severe in beating their wives, since their wives were to be examples of wifely submission for other women. Scriptural verses that embody the household code of the Roman Empire, such as Ephesians 5 and Colossians 3, enjoin wives to obey their husbands and husbands to love their wives. These texts were interpreted to require beating as a form of loving discipline, ignoring the fact that the Colossians text reads: "Husbands, love your wives and never treat them harshly" (Col 3:19).

The staggering level of domestic violence in modern society is supported by an attitude of social silence. Neighbors close the windows when they hear slaps, crashes, and shouting next door rather than intervene or call the police. Family members ignore bruises and black eyes in silence or whisper to one another that John and Mary "aren't getting along." Police sometimes treat domestic abuse as if it were another barroom brawl in which both parties are equally at fault and merely need a short separation to "cool down." Too often the churches are totally silent about domestic violence and sexual abuse, assuming that such things do not occur in the homes of church members but only among the unchurched. Such an attitude discourages victims from turning to the church as a resource and fails to call abusers to accountability

Domestic violence is not accidental and is not typically about blowing off steam. Nor is the victim accidentally chosen. Domestic violence maintains control over the spouse. The batterer feels that he is losing control over the spouse and so "accidentally" loses control of himself in violence. Afterward, abusers frequently argue that they should be forgiven because they were not themselves; they were under the influence of alcohol, or temper, or fear, and did not mean the abuse. In fact, batterers' recourse to alcohol is itself usually deliberate, as is the attempt to find issues over which to explode (the quality of dinner, the size of a bill, the behavior of the children, the length of a phone call, and so on). These are pretexts for recourse to violent acts that then terrorize the spouse into capitulating to the control of the abuser. When the violence is done and his control restored, the typical abuser apologizes for the damage, pledges his love, and woos the victim into both remaining in the relationship and forgiving him. Even during this expression of repentance, however, abusers typically refuse to accept responsibility. They insist that the victim was responsible for triggering violence brought on by alcohol, stress, or other factors not under his control.

Given this common pattern in domestic abuse, the Spencers need to ask both Linda and David questions about control in the marriage. Is there any evidence that David's use of violence in response to Linda's sexual withdrawal is part of a pattern of David's controlling Linda through violence or threat of violence? It is important to probe the issue of violent abuse because of Linda's past victimization. Her earlier sexual abuse has obscured her own feelings and interests so that she seems better able to focus on David's suffering and pain than on her own. Does Linda's tendency to brush off the violent episodes mask a low self-esteem that makes her see herself as an appropriate object for violence? Or is her easy dismissal of violence the result of over ten years of knowing David as a gentle, non-controlling partner demonstrating abiding love for her and the children?

Questions need to be asked about violence in either Linda's or David's interaction with their children as well, and about how the children have been affected by David's violence and alcohol abuse and by Linda's emotional condition. We have no indications that either parent has directed violence at the children, and we do not know the ages of these children. The children should be told as much about what is going on with their parents as is appropriate for their ages. Linda and David should explain in simple terms why they are upset, that they are working on their problems, that the children have no responsibility for their parents' problems, and that no matter how they work out their particular problems, the parents will both continue to love the children. Having some idea of what is occurring may help the children feel secure enough to ask for additional reassurance when they need it.

CHILD SEXUAL ABUSE

In the United States one out of every four girls and one out of every nine boys is a victim of child sexual abuse, of which one type is child incest. One of every twenty young girls is the victim of stepfather-daughter incest or father-daughter incest, which is generally considered the most traumatic type of incest, though specific incidents of other types of incest can cause as much or more trauma. In this case we have no mention of Linda's father; her grandfather may or may not have functioned as a father substitute.

The extent of the trauma in child sexual abuse depends upon four factors: the intrusiveness of the abuse; the length of time the abuse continued; the degree of prior trust the victim had invested in the abuser; and the degree of pain, coercion, or threat used to obtain compliance from the victim. We have no information here about the intrusiveness of the abuse or the degree of coercion, pain, or threats in Linda's incestuous abuse as a child. But the abuse continued for several years, and it involved betrayal of trust. In Linda's case the abuser was not only a family member acting in a caretaker role, but the abuse was supported by her primary caretaker's refusal to believe her. Linda's experience is not unusual. Nor is she unusual in experiencing trauma from the incest many years after she thought she had put it behind her. It is often not clear what triggers such memories, but greater social awareness of incestuous abuse of children has supported many unhealed adult victims in getting help rather than remaining trapped in nightmarish fear, distrust, and self-loathing.

The United States is generally considered to have among the highest child sexual abuse rates in the world. But data is not readily available for most parts of the world, and even US data is incomplete. In general, researchers are coming to believe that large numbers of the world's children are at risk for sexual abuse. Both religious and secular cultures here and elsewhere include strong supports for child sexual abuse, including socialization of children to universal respect and unquestioning obedience to parents and other adults; failing to recognize children's rights over their own bodies; and a silence about sex that prevents both information flow and ease of communication around sex, even between intimates. Both church and society, which hold up the family as a protector of children, have been largely blind to familial abuse of children.

Healing from sexual victimization is almost always a long and painful process. When victimization is endured as a child and is unaddressed for decades, the internalization of the abuse, which usually does the most damage, is often unobstructed, even reinforced. In Linda's case, however, it is extremely positive that she did not suppress all memories of the abuse and that she seems to have a history of both sexual satisfaction and intimacy with David. Whatever deficiencies existed within that intimacy (and there are always greater depths of intimacy to achieve), the fact that both partners experienced the relationship as intimate for over a decade testifies to the advantage Linda has over incest victims in general. Many victims find themselves unable to trust others enough for intimacy and unable to feel that they have an authentic self worthy of being disclosed to another. While Linda may always carry some degree of damage from her childhood experience, she may well develop moral strengths from her battle that help her resist and heal from her family's sinful abuse.

It is important for Christians to insist that Linda can heal, both because there is objective evidence of the healing of other victims and because Christians believe in the resurrection, the ground of Christian hope. What Christians mean when they speak of Jesus Christ's resurrection as victory over sin is not that sin ceases to exist. Victims of child sexual abuse are victims of sin. Rather, Christians mean that sin is not final and decisive; because of Jesus Christ's resurrection, others can overcome and recover from the effects of sin. It is through healing from sin that we participate in the resurrection of Jesus. In this case there is a very real possibility that dealing with the present problems in the relationship—the memories that plague Linda, and David's recourse to alcohol and violence—may allow them to reestablish and strengthen their earlier intimacy.

In order for that to happen, David needs to move beyond his present step of acknowledging that Linda is not yet healed from the earlier abuse. He needs to become truly supportive of that healing. Perhaps, as Reverend Deerick suggested, prayerful intimacy with God could alleviate some of David's intimacy needs so that he could become more supportive of Linda's healing. Only support from David himself can remove the sense of demand Linda now feels about David's desire for sexual intimacy. Her feelings of guilt about not being able to give him what he wants echo lessons learned in the abuse and interfere with her ability to concentrate on her own healing process. If David could learn to rely less on sexual intimacy as symbolic of the overall intimacy of the relationship and be more open to emotional intimacy and non-genital physical intimacy with Linda, he could assist Linda's healing and satisfy physically some of his own need to be reassured of Linda's love for him.

At the same time, it would be wrong to demand that David immediately accept a marriage without genital relations or even physical touch. Human beings are integrated persons, and their relationships and growth and development should be integrated. While David seems to be extremely focused on physical and even genital activity for expressing his feelings for Linda and meeting his own intimacy needs, other avenues of interpersonal interactions should be developed in addition to, and not in place of, sexual activity. Genital activity in marriage is an important foundation for other forms of intimacy because of its symbolic power. Both nakedness and the letting go of consciousness and control in orgasm are powerful images of trust and self-giving, of vulnerability. Shared pleasure in sex both rewards lovers for their willingness to offer themselves to the other and bonds lovers together.

Linda should be encouraged to assume that she can heal and that the healing process will include her ability to reclaim her sexual feelings and activity. Healing will mean ending the power of the abuse to dictate her feelings, her actions, and her life. To assume from the beginning that she will never be able to resume a full marital relationship is "victimism," accepting that the effects of victimization are permanent.

SPIRITUAL COUNSELING

Reverend Deerick's offer of support for guiding Linda's and David's prayer life seems to include spiritual counseling around the specifics of their situations. Spiritual counseling when coordinated with psychological counseling frequently complements it and is often the most effective therapy for dealing with lingering feelings of guilt and sinfulness in victims of sexual abuse. Spiritual counseling for Linda might also include encouragement to approach her family as a mature adult who needs to have her suffering and the family's responsibility acknowledged in ways that allow her to get on with her life. We do not know whether she faced her mother (or her aunt) with the fact of her abuse after it ended, whether they feel estranged from her, or, if so, if they know the reason for the estrangement. Even though her grandfather is dead and Linda is not close to her family, she may need, for her own sake, to confront them with her abuse. Spiritual counseling could also help protect Linda from family pressure for premature forgiveness and reconciliation.

MARRIAGE AND DIVORCE

There is little doubt that both David and Linda are experiencing great pain and suffering and asking serious questions about the permanency of marriage. Even though some denominations recognize divorce, Christian understandings of marriage have always taught that marriage should be undertaken as a permanent commitment. Some variety of the "for richer or poorer, in sickness and health, until death do us part" vow has been a part of the Christian wedding service for centuries. The degree of suffering involved is not, in itself, an indication of the appropriateness of divorce. A physician would not help a patient with appendicitis to die merely because the immediate pain is severe. Far more important is the prognosis for restoring health and alleviating the suffering.

For many readers the question of whether David and Linda should remain married is moot, because they are both clear that they love each other. Until the twentieth century there would have been no theological support for the understanding that marriage endures only when love endures, even though it was increasingly common after the sixteenth century to understand that love was a motive for marriage. Because women were not economically franchised, and because of the association of marriage with the bearing and rearing of children, it was assumed that women and children required the presence of the husband/father for their well-being.

Today Christian churches are divided in their understanding of marriage and divorce. The Roman Catholic Church does not recognize divorce and therefore forbids remarriage. However, if Linda were a Catholic, she might be able to obtain an annulment—a declaration that no true marriage ever existed with David—on the grounds that she was not fully free to consent to marriage because of the unresolved trauma of child sexual abuse. Most other Christian churches do not exclude the divorced and remarried, though their preference for permanency is clear. Across denominational lines the criteria that divide marriages in crisis into viable and nonviable categories are disputed among pastors and pastoral counselors. The most common question is whether contractual obligations in marriage endure after feelings of love have been lost. A related question is whether fidelity to the contractual obligations can, over time, rekindle lost feelings of love. Is love more than a feeling? There are no clear answers to these questions, which is one probable reason for Reverend Deerick's focus on personal prayer in response to David's and Linda's questions about the future of their marriage.

A second reason for Reverend Deerick's shift of focus from church teaching on marriage to prayer is that the positive and useful insights on marriage in scripture are embedded within and often distorted by patriarchal depictions of women as men's property. Women achieve virtue through fruitful wombs, sexual fidelity, and homemaking skills. The Mosaic Law and scriptural authors allow little scope for the personhood of women; while a few women are singled out, only an exceptional handful of women are recognized for their own initiatives rather than for their submission or for the fruit of their wombs. For this reason it is difficult to apply any of the scriptural stories or teachings to the crisis in David's and Linda's marriage. From the perspective of many of the communities from which scripture emerged, Linda would have no right to deny David the sexual use of her body, and David would be expected to exercise his rights regardless of her wishes. Linda might not even feel sexual aversion from her childhood memories, for she would have been raised to understand women's bodies as the property of men and might well regard her abuse by her grandfather as a universal hazard of being female. At the same time, the expectations of David and Linda of their marriage would have been significantly different had they lived in scriptural communities. They would have understood the marital bond as characterized much less by interpersonal intimacy and more by contract, especially contract between clans or families.

Theological treatment of marriage as a covenant modeled on the covenant between Yahweh and Israel is a contemporary reversal of the biblical attempt to personalize the covenant relationship. Ancient Israelites came to see their relationship with Yahweh as more personal and intimate than the feudal covenant between lords and vassals that gave the covenant its form and name. The Israelites came to image the covenant as a marriage, the most personal and intimate relationship they knew. In a society in which women were chattel that husbands bought from fathers, the inequalities of power, status, and worth in the divine/human relationship were not barriers to the effectiveness of the analogy. Saint Paul later extended the marital analogy to Christ and the church. But when the contemporary church uses the relationships of Christ/church and Yahweh/Israel relationships to understand and explain marriage, it imports into the marital relationship assumptions about inequalities of power, worth, and initiative between the partners that are alienating, making the analogies less than effective.

Until the modern age, theological treatment of marriage focused almost exclusively on procreation as the purpose and chief blessing of marriage, rather than on the quality of the relationship, which has become the central theological concern over the last few centuries. Few helpful historical resources on the role of sexuality in Christian marriage exist. Between the early medieval era and the Reformation, Christianity taught total impotence as an absolute bar to marriage and sexual consummation of marital vows as necessary to finalize marriage. Before the Reformation, and in Roman Catholicism even afterward, couples were often encouraged to consider Josephite (celibate) marriages, and clergy regularly cautioned couples to abstain from sex on Sundays, holy days, and during Lent, as sex was understood as an obstacle to prayer and contemplation. Procreation was regarded as a sufficient good to justify sexual activity and consequent pleasure. But sexual pleasure was morally suspect and forbidden as a motive for marital sex. The difficulty of resisting sexual pleasure in marriage caused pre-Reformation Christianity and post-Reformation Roman Catholicism to understand celibate religious life as a holier vocation than marriage.

The Reformers raised the status of marriage compared with vowed celibacy and gradually abandoned some of the more negative traditional attitudes toward sex. For the most part, however, the churches of the Reformation continued to understand procreation as the primary purpose of marriage and sex. For limited numbers of Protestant Christians, sexual activity came to be seen as an important way to cherish the spouse and as a source for generating warmth and intimacy that could influence children and the wider community. Among the Puritans and Quakers, for example, new understandings of marriage as primarily a personal bond, within which children were an additional but not the central blessing, gave rise to an appreciation of sex in marriage.

Within American Christianity a positive understanding of sex in marriage has been in tension with a more traditional and more widespread understanding of sex as morally dangerous and sexual desire as something to be resisted by the virtuous. Contemporary Christian theologians are attempting to recover and develop the few examples of positive treatment of body, sexuality, and sex found in Christian theological traditions. Since Christian faith is grounded in the incarnation—the doctrine that the Second Person in the Godhead became fully and humanely embodied in flesh—there should be no room for hatred or suspicion of the human body, its appetite or actions per se.

Some Catholics point out that though the traditions of Catholic moral theology were decidedly anti-sexual, the sacramental tradition regarding marriage incorporated a number of positive elements, including the understanding that sexual intercourse (especially orgasm itself) operates as a primary sacramental sign. Marital sex does not merely represent the spousal love that it signifies but actually contributes to the creation and development of that love. It has even been suggested by a Catholic clergy/lay team commissioned and funded by the US Conference of Catholic Bishops, in its 1986 document *Embodied in Love*, that mutually pleasurable marital sex is perhaps the most accessible human experience of the love that characterizes the Persons of the Trinity.

CONCLUSION

What should David and Linda do about their marriage? Despite all their problems and pain, they both state their concern for each other and act as if they care very much about the other. For that reason they may not want to abandon the marriage now but may prefer to continue work with the Spencers and perhaps to begin seeing Reverend Deerick to work on personal prayer as a means of clarifying what they should do. The teachings of Christian churches on the issues of permanency in marriage and sex in marriage have begun to shift away from fear and suspicion of sex in marriage and from insistence on marital permanence regardless of the costs to those involved. Christian churches have come to see that marital sex can be an integral part of both interpersonal intimacy and communion with the Divine, and that the costs of preserving marriage in some circumstances can include physical and emotional violence and the erosion of self-hood. Ultimately, only Linda and David can decide what level of cost is acceptable to them and to their children in the attempt to rebuild their marriage.

ADDITIONAL RESOURCES

Anjelica, Jade. *A Moral Emergency: Breaking the Cycle of Child Abuse*. Kansas City: Sheed and Ward, 1993.

Black, Claudia. *It Can't Happen to Me: Children of Alcoholics*. Denver: MAC Publications, 1979.

Brown, Joanne C., and Carole R. Bohn. *Christianity, Patriarchy, and Abuse*. New York: Pilgrim Press, 1989.

Ellison, Marvin. *Erotic Justice: A Liberating Ethic of Sexuality*. Louisville, KY: Westminster/John Knox Press, 1996.

Gallagher, Charles A., et al. *Embodied in Love: Sacramental Spirituality and Sexual Intimacy*. New York: Crossroad, 1984.

Gudorf, Christine E. *Body, Sex, and Pleasure: Reconstructing Christian Sexual Ethics*. Cleveland: Pilgrim Press, 1994.

Jung, Patricia, Mary E. Hunt, and Radhika Balakrishnan, eds. *Good Sex: Feminist Perspectives from the World's Religions*. New Brunswick, NJ: Rutgers Univ. Press, 2001.

Ruether, Rosemary Radford. *Christianity and the Making of the Modern Family*. Boston: Beacon Press, 2000.

PART II

VIOLENCE/NONVIOLENCE

Case

A Life for a Life?

There were only two days left in the 2005 Florida legislative session. Manny sighed in relief just thinking about it. He was tired of Tallahassee, tired of commuting home to Sarasota on weekends for the last two months. Florida, unlike many other states, was limited by its constitution to a two-month annual legislative session. The big work—getting agreement on the budget—had just been finished. No one was satisfied with the bill, but that was the nature of compromise, especially at what Manny hoped was the tail end of a recession, when state revenues were low.

As Manny picked up his briefcase and headed out the door of this office he spotted Alice Browner speaking with one of the House members from the Florida Keys. Manny ducked back within his office, shutting the door softly. He liked Alice, but he knew what she wanted and that she might latch onto him if she saw him now. Alice was an unpaid lobbyist for religious groups trying to get the death-penalty statute off the books in Florida. That was not likely to happen any time in the near future; Florida voters tended to be conservative. Polls showed that over 60 percent of them supported the death penalty. Alice's group was full of enthusiasm for full elimination of the death penalty right now, since they had won their struggle to restrict the death penalty to adults, those over eighteen years of age, when the Supreme Court declared capital punishment for minors unconstitutional (March 2, 2005).

The issue of the death penalty for minors had arisen in Florida following a few recent trials that had become media affairs. Three Miami area boys, between twelve and fourteen years of age, had been arrested for murder in the last few years: one for shooting a teacher, another for beating to death a six-year-old girl, and one for slicing the throat of a classmate in

This case was prepared by Christine E. Gudorf. Copyright © The Case Study Institute. The names of all persons and institutions have been disguised to protect the privacy of those involved.

the boys' restroom at a public school. The first two had been tried as adults, and in the first case the prosecutors had asked for the death penalty. But in the end both boys had gotten sentences of life in prison without parole. The case of the one who had killed the six year old while wrestling with her in his home had been a real mess, Manny recalled. The boy's mother had refused to let him take the plea to a lesser charge offered by the prosecutor because she was sure her son would be acquitted. But when he was found guilty of first degree murder, the mandatory sentencing statute kicked in, and he was saddled with life in prison without parole. He had just been released, however, after serving three years, because a court determined that the state should have done competency testing on him before going to trial since there was strong evidence that he was mentally impaired. Now the third of these child-killers was about to be tried, and it looked like he also would be tried as an adult and could face the death penalty. Due to the publicity over the possibility of these very young minors getting death penalties, many Floridians, including Manny, had come to agree with the Supreme Court that the death penalty was inappropriate for minors. His response to the Supreme Court decision had been relief that now he would not have to explain to his strong law-and-order constituents why he was going to support the bill Alice had introduced to exempt minors from the death penalty in Florida.

But now Alice's group and a number of other civic and religious groups were lobbying to end the death penalty in Florida altogether; they had introduced a bill to that effect. With the state budget out of the way, they hoped the legislature would use some of its remaining days to deal with this bill.

Manny had talked to two other House members about the bill just days ago: John Benvenuti from Winter Garden, and Saul Weiss from Jacksonville. Saul had initiated the discussion over dinner one night as they finished revision of an amendment to an insurance bill they wanted passed.

"Do you know how you'll vote if Alice Browner and her group get the death-penalty bill on the agenda?" Saul had asked.

John had responded, "I don't see how I could live with myself if I didn't vote for it, but I don't see how I can get the voters to support such a vote. My district is strong on law-and-order issues, and when it sees death penalty, it thinks 'urban crime,' 'blacks and Hispanics.' My constituents don't see convicted criminals as belonging to the same species as their families and friends."

"Do you really see this as an issue of conscience, John? I didn't know you opposed the death penalty," asked Manny, surprised.

"My church did a program on the death penalty last year, and it really had an impact on me," said John. "You know, since the death penalty was reintroduced in 1973, there have been 119 death-penalty convictions vacated in the United States, and 21 of those have been in Florida—we have had the largest number in the country. Illinois is next with 18, then it drops way down to 8 in Texas and some other states. The program at church brought in the sister of a guy named Smith who had been on death row for fifteen years when another man confessed, and DNA testing—not available when he was tried—proved he had not done the rape/murder for which he was convicted. But it came too late for him; he died of cancer in prison weeks before he would have been released. That's the piece of it that gets me— that some of them really are innocent. That's why the governor of Illinois a few years ago stopped executions and commuted so many sentences. It became hard to have faith in the system's ability to deliver justice. I don't see how I could ever vote for the death penalty. It may cost me my seat. I'm glad we are only part-timers here." He added wryly, "Conscience would be a lot tougher to follow if this were my entire bread and butter." John referred to the fact that he, like almost all House members, had a normal career; they were lawyers, insurance agents, corporate officers, and a variety of other professions, but they earned $29,300 in state compensation for a little more than sixty days of service every year.

Saul shook his head. "I hear you, but that's not where I am. I'm not pandering to my constituents here. I agree with them. There are monsters out there, and they deserve the death penalty. I'm all for improving the justice system—I admit all these people being released from death row doesn't inspire confidence in the system—but I think the answer is to fix the system, not junk it. And don't think for a minute that all these people released from death row are innocent—a lot of the reversals were for police or prosecutor misconduct in the first trials, but by the time those verdicts were reversed evidence had been lost, witnesses had died, so prosecutors simply didn't file for retrials. That doesn't mean those people were innocent. Our job is to write the rules that protect the innocent, and I think the death penalty helps do that."

Manny shook his head. "I just don't know. My district, like John's, thinks killers only come out of urban pits like Miami, that the death penalty is necessary for black and Hispanic criminals and a handful of white 'trailer-trash.' I'm not sure many of them would even care if they knew some of these vacated convictions were clear results of southern racism in the fifties and sixties."

"That's wrong," responded Saul. "But just because there have been racists voting for the death penalty doesn't mean all death-penalty verdicts are racist. I think those prosecutors who decided to try twelve year olds and fourteen year olds as adults were wrong and that they were racially motivated. But they aroused what I think is an overreaction against the death penalty in the Supreme Court and among citizens. I don't have any problem with executing monsters of sixteen or seventeen, maybe even some fifteen year olds. We keep hearing that what we need to do to reform the system is to give judges more discretion in sentencing, instead of tying their hands with mandatory sentences. I say let the judges decide, but give them the option to grant the death penalty if that's what the state asks for and it's appropriate to the circumstances."

"Saul, do you really think that the criminal justice system is ever color-blind?" asked John.

"Are you calling me racist?" asked Saul indignantly.

"No, I'm talking about the racism in our constituents, who so clearly intend the death penalty for minority groups. Or even the system itself—remember that series the *Miami Herald* ran a few years ago that showed the huge differences in how the juvenile justice system treats whites and blacks? When convicted of the same crime and with the same juvenile record, most white youth got probation or community service, and most black youth were sent to reformatories. People who work in the adult system say the same thing happens—whites have more money to hire private lawyers, and so they either get off altogether, or, when they are convicted, get lesser sentences."

"Wait a minute, John," protested Saul. "I do remember that series, and it explained that the reason for the different sentences involved the kids' support networks—family and community. Black kids less often had intact homes with effective parents who could monitor their behavior and also had fewer contacts with community organizations willing to supervise community service. Those sentences were based on the individual situation of the kids, not racism in the system."

"Kind of a vicious circle, isn't it?" asked John. "Because one kid has a father in prison, or who skipped town, and a mother who works three jobs to support her kids, the kid gets into trouble. And the very reasons he got into trouble in the first place are the same reasons he goes to reformatory, while a white kid in the same trouble goes free."

"I can't fix every broken home," responded Saul. "That's not my job. All I'm saying is that not everything that differentiates the races is due to racism. Some differences just occur, and individuals bear some responsibility for what happens to them. Not all kids with absent fathers and overworked mothers get into trouble. These kids had a choice."

As the three of them left the restaurant to return to the session, John and Saul had shifted the talk to procedural moves on the insurance bill, but Manny had been quiet. This was a really tough issue for him.

Manny had grown up thinking that unjust executions only happened in other countries, like Cuba, where one of his mother's brothers had been executed as a young man for opposing Castro. He had always seen the justice system in the United States as a model for the world. But his years in the legislature had taken some of the shine off that model. He saw how large a role politics, personalities, the press of time, and sometimes even corruption had in the creation of laws and state budgets, and it made him wonder if the implementation of laws was necessarily any more careful than the creation of those laws. The best evidence of that, he thought, was the March rape/murder of a nine-year-old girl abducted from her home not too far from Manny's district. It had taken days to discover the body and catch the killer, an ex-con sexual predator who later confessed, because the state database that was supposed to track the registered locations of sexual predators was so out of date that it did not know that the rapist had moved into the girl's neighborhood months before. He tended to agree with his wife, Pina, that these sexual predators seemed to be impossible to reform and that the death penalty was the only way to safeguard society, especially the children.

Now Manny was torn. While he thought he could support capital punishment for sex predators, he knew that there could be cases in which people were wrongly convicted as sexual predators, too. He agreed with Saul that the level of death-row acquittals proved the system was not well run and should be improved, but he wasn't sure it could be fixed well enough to justify capital punishment.

But Manny also knew that Pina would be appalled if he voted for Alice's bill to eliminate the death penalty. The little girl recently killed had been a student at the school where Pina taught kindergarten, and that had made Pina and most other parents see the perpetrator as a threat to all the children there, including Pina's and Manny's two little girls. But it was also true that Manny was a second-term legislator from a pretty safe district, and he and Pina had counted on the income from one more term to finance the master's degree in education she planned to finally begin in the fall. Their oldest son would graduate from a state university in December, and it was supposed to be Pina's turn now, while the younger kids were still in elementary and junior high school. Pina was a kindergarten teacher who had to earn a master's degree soon or lose her job, which she loved. If he lost the November election over this issue, his regular salary would only go up about $6,000 before taxes, because he already took one month of the legislative session as paid vacation from his job and only one month as unpaid leave. From $29,000 to $6,000 in salary for that month was a big drop. Could Pina understand if he not only defended the right to life of sexual predators who preyed on children, but if also, because of his taking that position, they weren't able to fund her return to the university? More than that, how would they manage to send the other kids to college if Pina lost her job?

Manny lifted his head and ended his reverie. Certainly he had waited long enough for Alice to leave. He walked down the hall, hearing nothing. But just as he turned the corner to the elevator, Manny saw Alice. She saw him, waved, and made a beeline toward him. It was crunch time.

Commentary

A Life for a Life?

Christian tradition has not been historically unanimous on the issue of killing. While the first three centuries of Christianity saw a strong pressure for pacifism at all levels, in the fourth century earlier refusals to grant Christian burials to those who had taken life—whether in self-defense, military service, or wantonly—were relaxed, and Christian theologians such as Augustine began to argue that Christians could serve in the army, since the army protected the Roman Empire and, thus, Christianity. From that time on, the dominant Christian position has been that Christians are allowed to kill on behalf of the state in certain situations, and even in some very limited personal situations, notably self-defense.

This teaching has not been by any means unanimous. There have been, especially since the Protestant Reformation, a number of pacifist denominations who oppose killing in all forms. These denominations include the Mennonites, the Amish, the Quakers, the Brethren, and a number of other smaller denominations. Jehovah's Witnesses are often counted with this group, as they oppose all obedience to the state and deny the right of the state to demand military service or any other type of service, including oaths. Many theologians have agreed with the American courts that the Witnesses are not pacifist in the same sense as these other groups, however, since in their theology they insist they will take up arms in the last days to fight in the army of the Lord, punishing sinners.

Christian ethical analysis of this case must examine at least two questions: (1) the justice of capital punishment in general, and (2) whether for Christians there are other values (for example, forgiveness, mercy) that can or should trump justice in capital cases.

CAPITAL PUNISHMENT AND JUST WAR

The dominant Christian position regarding violence has been called the just-war position. Capital punishment has been subsumed under the just-war position, as it, too, argues that at some times the state must take human life in order to defend the common good against serious attacks—war from outside and capital crimes inside. The basic limitation was that the life taken must be guilty. While it could be permitted to kill, it was never permissible to kill innocent life.

The development of the just-war position occurred over many centuries; many theologians and churchmen contributed to it, including Augustine, Bonaventure, and Aquinas. In their arguments defending the possibility of a just war, they often used examples of capital punishment, which was generally accepted. At the same time that Christians generally accepted the need for the state to execute criminals (not always for what we might consider serious crimes), the question of whether Christians should be allowed to be executioners was raised again and again. Many jurisdictions ruled that executioners must be hooded, so that they might avoid some of the moral disapproval that generally accompanied the job.

While there has been a great deal of debate about just war—conditions for just war in particular—within the dominant tradition, there has been little debate about capital punishment until fairly recently. Historically, the self-understanding of the church as an institution parallel to, and similar to, the state, caused the church to assume that the legal system of the state was generally just and efficient. That assumption has been radically called into question in the last century in a new way.

In the past there were occasionally periods in which it was apparent to the church and to the wider society that the law and the legal system itself were being manipulated by the powerful, often by the monarch himself, to produce injustice: innocents wrongfully accused and executed, their property coveted and appropriated. Such things even occurred sometimes within the church itself. But when law and order were restored the interval that had just ended was considered an exception to the normal prevalence of justice.

This world view is still prevalent in many American Christians. The National Assembly of Evangelicals, the Christian Coalition, Christian Reconstructionists, the Southern Baptist churches, the Latter-Day Saints (Mormons), the Missouri Synod Lutherans, and many Pentecostal churches support the death penalty for serious crimes. Important for many of these churches is the biblical evidence that the Hebrew scriptures support capital punishment, even "requiring" the death penalty for over a dozen crimes in addition to murder. Most of these Old Testament "crimes" the churches would no longer see as deserving capital punishment (working on the Sabbath, being disrespectful toward parents, teaching another religion, being an unbeliever and entering the Temple). Furthermore, supporters of the death penalty quote Matthew 5:17–19 to the effect that Jesus intended the Mosaic Law to remain unchanged ("Do not think that I have come to abolish the law or the prophets; I have come not to abolish but to fulfill. For truly I tell you, until heaven and earth pass away, not one letter, not one stroke of a letter will pass from the law until all is accomplished").

But by the twentieth century there were many people who questioned not only the specific workings of one legal system or another, but the very assumption that human systems of legal justice could be more or less just. There were a number of reasons underlying such suspicions. One was the gradual acceptance by the majority of the idea, spread initially by Marxism, that modern societies are class societies in which power tends to be wielded by the wealthy in their own interests. In this conception the legal system functions to support social control by the wealthy elite.

Even many who do not accept that modern capitalist societies *inevitably* have legal systems in which the interests of those with less power and wealth carry less weight recognize that this is often the case. In the United States, for example, analysis of convictions and sentencing throughout the twentieth century have shown that the best predictor of the severity of punishments for murder, rape, and assault is the race of the victim. If the victim is white, conviction rates are higher and sentences are higher than if the victim is black. The second-best predictor is the race of the accused: blacks accused of crimes were convicted more often, and when sentenced for the same crime as whites, got higher sentences than whites when the victims were white, but not necessarily when the victims were black. As in the research reported in the *Miami Herald*, race-based economics undoubtedly plays a part in discrepancies in convictions and sentencing in general, in that higher percentages of blacks are poor and thus forced to utilize overworked and underpaid public defenders, who are not as successful in defending their clients as are the private attorneys more often hired by whites.

The statistics on death-row exonerations, updated March 2, 2005, come from Death Penalty Information Center, whose website includes state by state data on executions and exonerations throughout the twentieth century in the United States. Since Florida first reintroduced the death penalty in 1976, there have been twenty-one exonerations on death row and six instances of clemency. The language used for the reversals of capital convictions is telling. Supporters of capital punishment point out that the vacation of these sentences does not mean that the person is innocent of the crime; sometimes it merely means that there is insufficient evidence to convict, or the process in the trial was faulty. Inevitably, some guilty persons are released, too.

Details on the twenty-one Florida cases in which death-row prisoners were set free illustrate that sometimes the reversals do indicate lack of proof or police or judicial misconduct rather than full innocence. The cases fall into these categories:

- Two were pardoned by the governor after another man confessed;
- Three were set free after another suspect was charged (two) or convicted (one);
- Seven were set free after key witnesses retracted their statements;

- Four were released after new DNA evidence ruled the convict out as the perpetrator;
- One was freed by the appeals court because it said there was no evidence that the death of his wife was a murder;
- One charge was dropped when the prosecutor offered to be a witness for the convict if a new trial were granted; and
- Three were set free when the courts found that the police and the prosecutor had willfully misused evidence; in one case charges were dropped, in two cases the accused were acquitted in a subsequent trial.[1]

The suspicion of unequal justice, supported by many different analytic reports of how the legal system actually works, has influenced American churches, even those with long histories of acceptance of capital punishment. Since 1974 the US Catholic Conference has opposed the death penalty, which was reinstated after a long legal hiatus in 1976, despite over a millennium and a half of ecclesial support for capital punishment. On November 19, 1980, the Catholic bishops of the United States issued a statement in which they declared: "Allowing for the fact that Catholic teaching has accepted the principle that the state has the right to take the life of a person guilty of an extremely serious crime, and that the state may take appropriate measures to protect itself and its citizens from grave harm, the question for judgment today is whether capital punishment is justifiable under present circumstances."[2] Since that time the Vatican itself has become a strong supporter of abolishing the death penalty, frequently appealing in behalf of individual convicts awaiting execution, and the US bishops regularly repeat their opposition to capital punishment.

The Catholic bishops argued that there were significant problems impeding justice within the system of capital punishment, including the possibilities of mistakes, long delays, unfairness in sentencing due to poverty and racism, as well as the extinction of all possibility for reform and rehabilitation in the convict. The bishops pointed to racial and economic inequalities in the system of justice—that the poor and persons of color were disproportionately likely to receive the death penalty when convicted of the same crimes as middle-class or whites convicted.

Regardless of the continued criticism of the death penalty by the Catholic bishops of the United States, a majority of the Catholic population in the United States supports the death penalty. This is also true for many of the denominations that as institutions oppose the death penalty, a group that includes the Eastern Orthodox Christian Churches, the Methodist Church, the Evangelical Lutheran Church of America, the Episcopal Church, the Presbyterian Churches, the United Church of Christ, the Reformed Church in America, and the Unitarian Universalists, and the National Council of the Churches of Christ. Black Christian churches have been especially prominent in their opposition to the death penalty, influenced by the history of lynchings in the United States, in which there was often collusion between officials of the justice system and the lynch mobs, and also by clear evidence of racial bias in the application of the judicial death penalty.

It is also important to understand the premises upon which a majority of Catholics or other American Christians approve the death penalty. When the question is asked in a vacuum (Do you support the death penalty or not?), many respond yes because they understand the alternative to be less than life sentences, which release on parole dangerous people, such as sexual predators who prey on children. When the question asked is whether one favors the death penalty or sentences of life without possibility of parole, there is a significant shift in the numbers, and a slight majority favors eliminating the death penalty. Elimination of the death penalty in the present situation of overcrowded prisons, which exerts pressure on prosecutors, judges, and parole boards to make prison space available by shortening sentences and granting parole, simply has not been acceptable to many.

DNA TESTING DEEPENS OPPOSITION
BY EXPOSING ERRORS IN CONVICTIONS

DNA evidence was introduced into trials in 1989, and by the early 1990s was responsible for freeing hundreds of persons charged with or even convicted of felonies across the nation. Opposition to the death penalty grew beyond the peace churches, black churches, Catholic bishops, and liberals in all the denominations in the mid 1990s, when a number of lawyers and law students began to petition the courts to use the new DNA testing in the cases of death-row convicts. Most of these cases had been tried before DNA testing was available, but the evidence had been preserved through the appeals process and was often still available. The most common DNA evidence involved semen, hair, or skin cells from the perpetrator. By June 2000 eighty-seven people had been released from death row because of DNA evidence, recanted testimony, or other new evidence—one reprieve for every seven executed in the same time period.[3]

As the number of these vacated sentences increased, the Nebraska legislature voted a state moratorium on the death penalty in 1999, which the governor vetoed. The following year the governor of Illinois declared a moratorium on the death penalty in his state, citing statistics that showed that thirteen death-row prisoners had had their convictions overturned since 1977, one more than had been executed during the same period. The numbers continued to rise as police malfeasance in using torture to extract confessions was revealed. Just before the end of his term the governor also commuted a number of death sentences.

The average time spent on death row by the newly exonerated citizens was ten years, but some had spent over twenty. This spate of exonerations led many new groups to question the efficacy of the legal system, for these reversals were not based on difficult-to-understand statistical analysis. They were based on the real-life histories of people with faces who had been unjustly deprived of decades of their lives, and almost of life itself. In the face of these exonerations it was impossible not to conjecture about how many of those who had been executed by the states had in fact been innocent.

To return to the central ethical questions in the case, we must ask to what extent the "errors" in the administration of capital punishment in this nation since 1977 are an inevitable part of a death-penalty system and whether they can be eliminated by reform. About this, people differ. Some point out that the justice system does not only include the original trial and sentencing, but also the very appeal process through which these men were exonerated. ("Men" because only 3 percent of death-penalty sentences are given to females.[4]) They insist that the high number of sentences vacated is proof that the appeals process works.

On the other hand, those who oppose the death sentence point to the fact that two-thirds of the vacated sentences came about through some kind of initiative from outside the justice system itself, usually by volunteer legal organizations, such as the law-school class in Illinois that began the process of appealing for DNA testing in old death-penalty cases there. In the vast majority of capital cases, however, the convict does not have such advocates.

State after state is considering, if they have not already passed, laws that impose new limits on the appeal process at the very time that appeals have been most successful at freeing convicts under capital sentences. In Florida, for example, prisoners, including death-row inmates, who were convicted before DNA evidence was routinely tested, face a state-imposed October 1, 2005, deadline to submit new claims for DNA testing. After that date, evidence may be destroyed and the chance for an exoneration extinguished. Yet the system is seriously backlogged and under-resourced. Anyone who pleaded guilty or no contest, as even innocent people sometimes do, is ineligible.[5] Nor is there any funding to pay lawyers to file DNA petitions. Nearly seven hundred applications are backed up and will likely not be through the system by the deadline. Yet the governor's office lobbied the 2005 Legislature to pass a constitutional amendment that would prevent the Supreme Court from reopening the window of opportunity.[6]

JUSTICE: HIGHEST VALUE FOR CHRISTIANS

Beyond these questions of justice is yet another, often invoked by leaders of Christian churches, about the primary values of the gospel. They ask, When we stand before the throne of God, how do we want to be treated? With justice, or with mercy? What makes God worthy of worship is not power (in the sense of the ability to impose one's will on another), but the power of goodness, of compassion and mercy, even for sinners. This is the center of the incarnation and redemption: God's compassion and mercy for us as sinners. What God asks of us, say many authorities in the Christian tradition, is that we treat others as we are treated by God.

So strong is this argument from within Christian theology that it completely rules out arguments by Christians for retribution in the criminal justice system. Christians may make arguments for sentencing based on the need to protect the innocent in society from future victimization or on the need for action to reform and rehabilitate criminals (in order that they not be a danger to others), but Christians cannot make arguments that invoke the gospel for the necessity of making criminals suffer for their sins. That is not only exclusively God's prerogative, but it is one that God has been shown to forgo in the interests of mercy. Thus the question becomes one of whether or not we live in a situation in which the only way to protect the innocent requires us to give up any hope of rehabilitation in the criminal and end his or her life. Clearly in the past, many societies felt that there was no alternative to capital punishment if society was to be truly protected. But today, the United States is one of only a handful of developed nations that have not abolished the death penalty.

Some have argued that it is opponents of the death penalty who have imposed the heaviest burdens on those sentenced to death, in that they are responsible for the long delays before execution. These delays are not simply years—ten on average, but sometimes twenty or more—spent in prison. Death-row prisoners are kept in isolation. They spend about twenty-three hours a day in their single-person cells, separated from the rest of the prison population, allowed out of the cell only for a shower every other day and a daily half-hour alone in the exercise yard. Two hundred years of prison studies have shown that because human nature is relational, solitary confinement is inhumane treatment that can and often does undermine sanity. Some feel that death-row conditions are so inhumane that it would be better to risk taking the lives of a few innocents by shortening the time between sentencing and execution in order to spare prisoners decades on death row. Opponents of the death penalty, however, insist that the proposals to limit appeals and speed up executions do not simply raise the risk of executing a "few" innocent people. The *average* death-row exoneration occurs slightly more than eight years after receiving the death sentence; cutting appeal time to under eight years means the majority of those now released would be executed. To cut the time till execution to one or two years, as proposed by some, would condemn almost all those who presently are exonerated.

Manny's decision in this case seems to hinge a great deal on his concern for his family. He is worried that his wife may not understand if he votes to end capital punishment, especially if it means that he then loses his seat and she is unable to return to the university. But if Manny's conscience speaks, it should be obeyed, regardless of the political or the personal consequences.

At another level, however, it is possible that his concern that Pina might not accept whatever stance he takes is rooted in a longstanding process of developing shared moral feelings, which is appropriate to marriage. One purpose of marriage is the "perfection of the spouse," as some vows used to say. Spouses often help each other recognize their moral blind spots and address them, and they learn to lean on each other for this. If Manny has been accustomed to take many of his moral signals from Pina, he may be uneasy at taking a differing position on this issue. But conscience is personal. Part of the process of moral development is being able to stand alone, even against our own community and our own family, when God speaks to us in conscience. Manny needs to listen to the voice of conscience and not let his anxieties about whether he will lose his seat, or whether Pina will understand, or how much clout Alice and her organization have, obscure that voice. Perhaps his problem is that conscience is not speaking at all, in which case he needs to continue to gather evidence, listen to both sides, pray, and listen for that voice. If conscience does not speak in a clear voice, then he will need to do the best job he can of weighing the risks and benefits of both options, and choose what seems the better option.

NOTES

[1] Death Penalty Information Center website, "Cases of Innocence: 1973 to the Present," updated March 5, 2005.
[2] US Catholic Conference, "Statement Opposing Capital Punishment," *Focus* 6, no. 10 (December 2, 1980): 2.
[3] Samuel R. Gross et al., "Exonerations in the United States: 1989 Through 2003," Univ. of Michigan Law School (April 19, 2004). Available online.
[4] Victor R. Streib, "Death Penalty for Female Offenders," *University of Cincinnati Law Review* 58 (1990): 845.
[5] R. Ofshe and R. Leo, "The Social Psychology of Police Interrogation: The Theory and Classification of True and False Confessions," *Studies in Law, Politics and Society* 189 (1997): 16.
[6] *St. Petersburg Times*, March 25, 2005.

ADDITIONAL RESOURCES

Costanzo, Mark. *Just Revenge: Costs and Consequences of the Death Penalty.* New York: St. Martin's Books, 1997.
Gross, Samuel R., et al. "Exonerations in the United States: 1989 Through 2003." Univ. of Michigan Law School. April 19, 2004. Available online.
Prejean, Helen. *Dead Man Walking: An Eyewitness Account of the Death Penalty in the U.S.* New York: Random House, 1993.

Ontario Consultants on Religious Tolerance website. "Religious Groups' Policies about the Death Penalty." Posted July 3, 2001.

Steffen, Lloyd. *Executing Justice: The Moral Meaning of the Death Penalty.* Cleveland, OH: Pilgrim Press, 1998.

Westervelt, Saundra D., and John A. Humphrey. *Wrongly Convicted: Perspectives on Failed Justice.* New Brunswick, NJ: Rutgers Univ. Press, 2001.

US Catholic Conference. "Statement Opposing Capital Punishment." *Focus* 6, no. 10 (December 2, 1980): 1–5.

Websites

Death Penalty Information Center
   http://www.deathpenaltyinfo.org
Ontario Consultants on Religious Tolerance
   http://www.religioustolerance.org

Case

Vietnam and Iraq

"What should I say to my grandson about war?" Martin Paxton asked himself. "Should I remain silent, press my ideas on him, or merely point out the options? What Christian perspective makes sense in a world where terrorism and preemptive military strikes have increasingly replaced more peaceful methods of resolving conflicts?" If Congress approves a new draft, how should my grandson respond if he is against the US presence in Iraq?

Then Martin's memory, or perhaps it was his conscience, began to work. The images of his own Vietnam experience came flooding back like an ever-flowing stream. He is "gun boss" on a US Navy destroyer with six five-inch guns. Routine mission: to shell Vietcong positions from two miles off the coast of Vietnam. "General quarters, general quarters, all hands man your battle stations," booms the speaker outside in the passageway. "On station and ready," he reports to the spotter. The radio crackles the coordinates of the target. One round on its way. The spotter over the target in a light plane responds with a "left two hundred, down one hundred yards." Another round, another spot. Then in an electric voice the spotter yells: "You've got 'em on the run. Shoot! Shoot!" A quick correction to fire control, then the command: "thirty rounds, fire for effect!" The noise is deafening. The shock shakes loose twenty years of dust from the overhead. The spotter's voice returns, now even more excited: "You got 'em, you got 'em!" The combat center erupts with cheers. The captain races in from the bridge to congratulate everyone. Back slaps, high fives, and hugs follow. God, it feels good!

Until the wee hours of the morning, that is. Then small voices began to work: "Why did the gunners want to paint coolie hats on the sides of the gun mounts? Why did you hesitate granting their request? Why did you finally say: 'No, I don't think coolie hats would be appropriate?' What are

This case was prepared by Robert L. Stivers. Copyright © The Case Study Institute. The names of all persons and institutions have been disguised to protect the privacy of those involved.

you doing here in Vietnam? Why did you enjoy killing the Vietnamese so much? Who are you anyway, a killer, a Christian, or both? Why didn't anyone prepare you for Vietnam and killing? Why didn't you think these things through before you got here?"

The questions never were answered. Discharge, graduate school, and years running a small business; life has a way of intervening to block introspection just as the decisions of one's children and grandchildren have a way of releasing it. His son Chris had never had to face a situation in which he would be called into the military, although Martin had talked with Chris and his wife, Jan, about his own Vietnam experience. His grandson, Brad, now almost eighteen, when he will have to register with the Selective Service, did not seem to have a clue about military service. When Brad asked his father and mother about the draft and service in the army, Chris and Jan had suggested that he talk to his grandfather. Brad seemed worried by what he was seeing and hearing about Iraq on the television news. Martin felt some of Brad's anxiety, especially since a prolonged US presence in Iraq seemed inevitable. The president had also made preemptive strikes part of his foreign policy, and certain members of Congress were talking seriously about a draft to meet the military's personnel needs.

Martin did not know how much Brad had studied Christian perspectives on war. Brad was a good student and intended to go to college. He attended a Roman Catholic Church on the other side of town with his parents, but Martin had never heard him say much about religion or his own faith. Martin was doubtful that Brad knew very much.

Martin, however, was not without ethical resources for the questions and the new context in which Brad might have to make a decision. Members of the adult education class at his church had recently studied Christian views on violence and nonviolence. The classes had helped him sort out a few things. The early church, he learned, had been pacifist, and a continuing tradition had carried the option of nonviolence to the present in what Ronald Smith, the class instructor and professor of religion at the local college, had called the way of the cross.

A Mennonite from the local area, Jacob Kaufmann, had visited the class on the first Sunday and explained his own pacifism. He spoke about his tradition and his own faith perspective within it. He mentioned the work of prominent pacifists and emphasized how important the church community is to maintaining the nonviolence of the way of the cross. "The church," he said, "takes its cue from the nonviolent but socially active model of Jesus Christ found in the New Testament." He went on to explain that the early church community followed Jesus and his nonviolent ways not so much because Jesus commanded nonviolence but because faith motivates it. "When Christ is truly in you and you in Christ," he said, "nonviolence is your automatic response. Love engenders love. That is the message of Jesus. I can never be a soldier. I must conscientiously object to military service. This does not mean I am passive when it comes to sin. Just as Jesus actively worked for justice in his time, so I am working through the church in mine." Jacob concluded by saying: "This stance may sound naive and idealistic. I am often wrongly accused of both. But let me tell you that I have a deep sense of sin and realize that I may suffer for it."

Martin's friend Jim Everett had pressed Jacob in the question period that followed. "How can I follow the way of the cross in a fallen world?" he asked. "What would you do if your wife and children were attacked?" Obviously Jacob had heard these questions before, because without hesitation he replied: "We are called to follow Jesus, not to make the world turn out right. Ultimately, we are called to suffer, not to inflict suffering. As for an attack on your family, in almost all cases there are nonviolent alternatives."

Jacob's assurance had a certain appeal for Martin. The way of the cross was easy to understand, straightforward, and seemed to fit Jesus' radical call to discipleship and an exclusive reliance on God. He recalled how Martin Luther King, Jr., had used nonviolent tactics to protest unjust segregation laws and the love ethic of Jesus to encourage integration. He also remembered Gandhi, who had made an appeal to Jesus.

Still, Martin was not convinced. "Justice is as important in the way of the cross as nonviolence," he thought. "On rare occasions a large measure of justice can be gained for a small measure of violence. Why prefer the ethical guideline of nonviolence to that of justice in these situations? And who does the dirty work of keeping order in a violent world?"

The next Sunday Ronald Smith presented a position he called Christian realism, out of which comes the just-war doctrine. Historically, Ronald explained, this position emerged after the emperor Constantine converted to Christianity in the early fourth century and the church achieved a favored position in the Roman Empire. Christians took political office and became responsible for the general welfare, including the defense of the empire and the exercise of police functions. The ethical and political task for Christians changed in this situation, Ronald continued. They could not pursue the perfection of Jesus or follow Jesus literally. The best they could do was to use political power to push and pull sinful reality toward the ideal.

"Not best, but better," he insisted, "because best is impossible in a fallen world. The way of the cross may be lived personally, but it is not immediately relevant to politics. We human beings in our freedom can and frequently do ignore the power of God in our midst and alienate our neighbors. God doesn't set things right or organize them for us. We have been given dominion and are responsible for the stewardship of power. To serve one's neighbor, to steward resources well, and to achieve higher levels of justice in a sinful world a Christian must sometimes compromise and occasionally use means that are not consistent with the way of the cross. This is how anarchy is avoided and tyranny prevented. This does not mean the way of the cross is irrelevant or that God does not work in the world. God's love and justice act like magnets pulling us out of sin and moving us to higher ethical levels, and we have a limited capacity to respond. God's power and this capacity are the basis of hope and make 'the better' a constant possibility. Simply put, those of this view are *realists* because of sin and *Christians* because there are resources for making this a better world."

Ronald went on to outline the just-war tradition that is based on Christian realism. "Nonviolence is the norm," he insisted, "but on occasion violence is permissible if its use clearly meets certain criteria." He then set forth the criteria and indicated that they could lead individuals either to enter the military and fight when the criteria were met or selectively to object when they were not. In an aside he observed that our laws make no provision for selective conscientious objection. They require the objector to be opposed to all wars. He concluded by saying that if every nation took the criteria seriously, all war would cease. He paused and added, "But that is a big *if.*"

Martin remembered leaving the class attracted to this position as well, but he was also troubled. How can Christian realism be reconciled with the picture of Jesus in the New Testament? Doesn't the just-war doctrine open the floodgates to abuse? Even Saddam Hussein claimed his cause was just. And Martin remembered what he himself had been told about Vietnam. Each nation is left to judge its own case for the use of violence; most, of course, produce justifications that accord with their own interests. And how about the preemptive strike by the United States on Iraq? Could that be justified especially in hindsight when no chemical, biological, or nuclear weapons have been found and no definitive links to Al Qaeda have been established? Was the removal of Saddam Hussein and the so-called liberation of the Iraqi people sufficient justification to attack, especially when the United States acted without United Nations approval and against the objections of several close allies? Religiously, do the realists take the power of sin too seriously and the power of the Holy Spirit not seriously enough?

The next Sunday Ronald Smith finished up consideration of the just-war tradition by addressing the problem of oppression and the possibility of justifiable revolutions. To present the problems that revolutions create for the just-war tradition, Ronald brought along a colleague who taught Spanish at the college, Maria Gomez. Maria came to the United States in the 1980s from El Salvador, where her life had been threatened because she was suspected of association with known revolutionaries.

Maria led off the discussion by telling her story about the violence and injustice in her native country. She painted a vivid picture of the inequality, injustice, and violence perpetrated by government officials and so-called death squads. Maria ended by noting that some liberationists like her are pacifists. Others justify violent revolutions in certain circumstances. Still others see the overthrow of oppressive regimes as a crusade against evil.

Ronald Smith then asked whether it is justifiable for citizens experiencing severe repression to rise up and violently overthrow those in power. He pointed out that the just-war doctrine requires wars to be initiated by competent authority, which usually means those in charge of the government. Revolutionaries are not competent authorities in most interpretations of the doctrine. "So, how do the citizens of a country protect themselves against oppression?" he asked. "Perhaps we need to modify the doctrine to allow for special cases when, to paraphrase the Declaration of Independence, a long train of abuses tend in the same direction."

Ronald then went on to draw an analogy. "President Bush had a somewhat similar dilemma with Saddam Hussein in Iraq. Almost everyone agreed that Saddam was a violent dictator who deserved removal. But at what point do you act to remove him by force, and who is the competent authority to decide?"

The discussion ended, and Ronald turned to the third of the primary Christian traditions, the crusade. He had not been able to find anyone to represent this tradition. "This does not mean the crusade is dead," he suggested, "only that few are willing to state it in its classic form. It is still alive, however, in the enthusiasm that surrounds going to war and in the tendency to demonize opponents and to see ourselves as highly virtuous. Among Christian conservatives today it receives support from those associated with 'dominion theology' and the Left Behind series of books. These movements depict both a radical dualism between good and evil forces at war with each other and an all-powerful and sometimes violent God. Dominion theology sees a perfected society in which execution would be the punishment for a number of crimes. The Left Behind series of books and movies envisions seven years of violent tribulation before Jesus returns."

"In the Christian tradition," he went on, "crusaders base their violent actions on the holy-war texts in Deuteronomy, Joshua, and Judges. They see the call to stamp out evil and the designation of themselves as God's agents as God's clear commands. Serving in the army of the righteous is a Christian responsibility."

Ronald dismissed this position by claiming it improperly literalized the biblical texts and then misapplied them. "Faith in God is the real significance of the texts." Then he added: "The portrayal of God in these texts as a general who commands and leads the holy army of the righteous in violent combat is incompatible with the picture of Jesus in the New Testament and the biblical witness taken as a whole. Even the picture of the holy army is inadequate. While holy warriors can usually identify the sin of their enemies, they seldom see their own sin." He concluded by observing that crusades are usually the bloodiest kinds of war and are especially dangerous today, given the destructiveness of modern warfare and the potential for terrorists with modest means to create massive destruction and death.

Martin agreed but reflected on the depth of the good-and-evil dualism in each of us. "Wouldn't we all like to stamp out evil if we could?" he mused. "And how like us it is to represent our own cause by our best ideals and our opponents by their worst deeds." Martin also reflected on the comments of one of his employees who had been deeply troubled by the events of 9/11. She had passionately linked Osama bin Laden to evil and even used the word *crusade* to support the need to eliminate him.

The final Sunday Ronald opened the class up to a discussion of the US presence in Iraq. He reviewed the events leading up to the strike, the justifications for it, the actual invasion, and the troubled aftermath that many observers likened to Vietnam, some even calling it a quagmire. "On the one hand, in attempts to justify the war, I heard echoes of the just-war tradition. Saddam Hussein was also linked to terrorists, and some argued that our soldiers in Iraq are protecting Americans from having to fight on our own soil. On the other hand, preemptive strikes are questionable under a strict interpretation of the just-war doctrine. Further, placing Saddam Hussein on an 'axis of evil,' demonizing him, and picturing ourselves as saviors, as some did, suggest a crusading mentality. As for the pacifist perspective, it was largely ignored and occasionally ridiculed," he concluded.

"So how are we as Christians to think about war in general and this war in particular?" Ronald asked the class. "Which of the Christian perspectives is the most appropriate, and how are we to advise young people who face the prospect of service in Iraq, draft or no draft?" The class went at it with intensity, and Martin listened carefully, not quite sure where he stood and how his own experience in Vietnam applied. The discussion stayed with him into the evening. The need to talk to his grandson took on greater importance. "I might be able to quiet my own conscience about Vietnam, but what do I say to Brad? Should I advocate the way of the cross and conscientious objection to serving? Should I suggest the realist's option that allows for just wars in oppressive situations and counsels selective conscientious objection in others? Or should I tell him to still his doubts, do his duty, and serve his country? After all, that's what I did." But more important than my advice is the question of what Brad should do. He faces a range of options. What is best for him?

Commentary

Vietnam and Iraq

Two generations of the Paxton family have matured since the Vietnam War. They know little about My Lai, the Tet offensive, Khe Sanh, or the final capitulation. The troubled waters stirred up by injustice, massive demonstrations, rhetorical flourishes, and challenges to traditional authority have stilled. But beneath the surface currents of conscience and unresolved identity created by the Vietnam War still run deep in the memories of veterans, although they seldom recount them anymore. Few of their children and grandchildren know the face of war or think to ask. Now, on the occasion of a phone call from his grandson Brad, Vietnam veteran Martin Paxton has a chance to pass on some of his memories and possibly some of his wisdom about the face of war, the morality of the preemptive strike in Iraq, and the Selective Service System.

Participation in killing presented a real challenge to Martin's conscience. Brad now faces a challenge to his conscience as he wrestles with the reasons given for invading Iraq, the ongoing presence of US troops in the country, and the increasing possibility that Congress will reinstate the draft. His challenge is both old and new. It is old because conscientious struggling with the use of violence is as old as violence itself. It is new because Brad is young and has never addressed violence as a matter of conscience. It is new also because there is no draft, Iraq is not Vietnam, globalized terrorism is now a considerable threat, and the United States is more powerful militarily than any of its potential enemies.

The relationship between Vietnam and Brad's decision about conscientious objection is important. They are related on the personal level through the exchange of thoughts and feelings. They are also related through the three Christian perspectives on violence presented in Martin's adult education class. Finally, they are related through the education Brad has received in the Paxton family. Martin's ambivalent conscience, which includes his lament about not being prepared for killing, has no doubt been communicated to Brad.

CONSCIENTIOUS OBJECTION

Brad's remarks about the war in Iraq and his inquiry about conscientious objection do not clarify whether Brad objects to all wars or merely to what he might consider unjustifiable wars. This ambiguity may come from a lack of information in the case. More likely, Brad does not know the difference between conscientious objection and selective conscientious objection, and how the law treats each.

From 1948 through 1972 the US government used a combination of draft and voluntary recruitment to fill the ranks of its armed forces. By 1973 Congress had put the draft on standby status because a majority felt it was no longer needed and because it had become a platform for protesting the Vietnam War. Voluntary recruitment became the sole source of new soldiers. Draft registration continued until 1975, when it was suspended. In 1980 registration was reinstated, but the draft remained on standby status.

That is the status of the law today. All males ages eighteen to twenty-six are required to register by filling out a form available at the post office. Failure to register can result in a fine, imprisonment, or both. After registration, the name of the registrant is entered into an electronic database for possible future use.

To make use of these names to induct draftees into the Armed Forces requires an act of Congress with the signature of the president. In an emergency a law to classify and induct could be passed on very short notice and be accompanied by all the emotions of nationalism that often cloud clear thinking. The Selective Service Administration is mandated by law to produce untrained men for induction into the Armed Forces within 193 days of the reinstatement of the draft. Students may be deferred to the end of their current semester but no longer. Seniors in college may be deferred to the end of the school year.

Were such legislation enacted, local draft boards would quickly form, classify all those who are registered, and begin calling individuals for induction, first from the twenty-year-old age group according to a rank order of birthdays determined by a lottery. Eighteen year olds and nineteen year olds will probably not be called until they are twenty. If Brad were classified 1A and his name came up, he would receive an induction notice and have ten days to report. It is within this ten-day period that he would have to set in motion the machinery for deferment or exemption on grounds of conscientious objection. While the law makes room for conscientious objection to all wars, there is no provision for selective conscientious objection, that is, objection to particular wars. Such a provision would open up a host of problems for the military and the government.

Once Brad made an application for conscientious objection, the draft board would postpone induction and set a date for a hearing when he could present his case. His application would be judged on the basis of three criteria: (1) that he is opposed to participation in war in any form; (2) that his opposition is by reason of strongly held moral beliefs; and (3) that he demonstrates sincerity.

If his application were successful, Brad would be reclassified in one of two conscientious objector categories. He might be asked to perform alternative duty or be drafted for noncombatant duty. If not successful, the local board would have to declare in writing the reasons for its rejection, which Brad could appeal to a Selective Service District Appeal Board and from there to a National Appeal Board.

If all appeals fail, Brad has several options. He may volunteer for one of the Armed Forces or be drafted. He could leave the country or go "underground" and try to avoid being caught. Finally, if caught, he may be prosecuted. During the Vietnam War many young men evaded the draft. Some were caught and sent to prison, the sentence usually being two years. Under a reinstated draft it is unclear how much effort the government would expend hunting down evaders and prosecuting them.

The vast majority of conscientious objectors are registering for the draft, but a number of alternatives exist, including refusal to register and the indication of conscientious objector status in the margins of the form in the process of registration. The task for Brad is to think through the ethical implications, decide if he is a conscientious objector, and make his decision about registration. If he elects to be a conscientious objector, he should seek the advice of a draft counselor and begin preparing his supporting material.

With the continuing violence in Iraq and troop commitments there and in other parts of the world, the army is hard pressed to meet its needs. As a result, there are rumblings in Congress about reinstating the draft. The Selective Service System is also reactivating and restaffing long dormant draft boards. Pressures to reinstate the draft are not only a matter of the army's needs but are also fueled by the inequities of the all-volunteer army, which attracts a disproportionate number of lower-income men and women and members of minority racial-ethnic groups. Very few sons and daughters of the wealthy, well born, and well educated are serving in Iraq.

THE VIETNAM WAR

The Vietnam War is not over. The hand-to-hand combat has long since ceased, but the meaning of the experience has not been settled. The Vietnam upheaval has never been adequately worked through, and, as time passes, it looks more and more as if it never will be. Americans either cannot or will not come to terms with this costly war, its justifications, and a divided nation. Now with war in Iraq it looks less likely they ever will.

Martin appears bothered by two things. The first is the destruction of a social myth about the United States, and the second is the destruction of a personal myth about himself. For Martin and many other Vietnam veterans, the destruction of their social and personal myths and the lack of adequate replacements have resulted in lost identity and the inability to comprehend what they went through.

The 1950s saw the United States with newfound power. Victorious in World War II and economically unrivaled, Americans had reason to be content with themselves in spite of serious unresolved social problems. They also had a vision with roots. American social mythology depicted a new city set on a hill free from the cynical entanglements and imperial ambitions of old and decaying Europe. Stories of the American frontier told of rough but moral and hardworking pioneers pushing back the frontier and bringing civilization in behind. Those who resisted were pictured either as uncivilized and in need of American technology and virtue or evil and in need of a crusade.

The frontier closed in the nineteenth century, but its mythology remained open-ended in spite of changing conditions and rude shocks such as the Great Depression. The mythology was skillfully manipulated by politicians such as John F. Kennedy with his New Frontier. It was exploited by those who saw the spread of communism in Asia as the latest evil in need of a crusade and the Vietnamese as candidates for American liberties, technology, and virtue.

In the end this pervasive social mythology was not able to carry the day for an entire nation. The harsh realities of racial violence and the injustice and inconclusiveness of the Vietnam War combined to explode the myth, at least for a vocal minority. For men and women such as Martin Paxton, the bell is now cracked and no new bells have yet been cast.

Martin could not have avoided participation in this mythology. He would have been brought up on westerns, war movies, and patriotic instruction. The path of least resistance would have led him to the conclusion that for the first time in history, here was a moral nation. Because he was brought up in a middle-class America that almost without question saw itself as morally right, he probably saw himself and his nation as inheritors and purveyors of that morality. Abundance would have shielded him from the violence of poverty and class conflict. Entering the Navy was probably as natural as eating his mother's apple pie.

That beneath the mythology of the American dream and his own place in it lay a different reality would have only been dimly perceived. It apparently was not the injustice of Vietnam or the oppression of racism that revealed this reality to him, at least not initially. Rather, it seems to have been his participation in and apparent enjoyment of killing and the acids of uncomfortable dreams stimulated by a vigorous conscience. The eruption of the combat center with the "happy" news of death killed Martin's false consciousness and left him with a good dose of guilt.

In a like manner, Vietnam blew the top off the dormant volcano of the American dream. Martin's crisis was the nation's crisis. The problem for both Martin and other Americans is how to build new mythic mountains to give order and justice to their landscapes. Martin may be building one in his Christian journey, but the nation still seems adrift, unsure about the American dream.

In Christian terms the problem is repentance and new life. Repentance must be the beginning of Martin's journey. The first step is to realize that he is one of those individuals who is capable of killing and enjoying it. Such an admission is hard for most individuals. It forces the sacrifice of the proud self and produces vulnerability. Citizens of modern nations have much more difficulty because pride is so strong and so central to national identity. For the United States with its glowing self-image and righteousness to admit that the Vietnam War was unjust may be too much to expect.

The guilt Martin feels is a sign of God's judgment and his first step toward repentance. But the recognition of judgment is not the end of the story. God forgives, and this forgiveness opens the door to new life. As soon as Martin goes through the door of repentance, the process of coming to terms with his role in Vietnam will begin. There are indications this process has already started.

The prospects for America in its continuing mental struggle are not as good. Nations have far fewer resources for coming to terms with their own injustices. Continuing infatuation with military supremacy does not improve the prospects. The church will have an important role to play in whatever rethinking takes place, for it has resources for announcing judgment, for coming to terms with guilt, and for moving beyond it.

Any rethinking that goes on must address Martin's question and lament: "Why didn't anyone prepare me for Vietnam or killing?" That question points up a shortcoming in the education of children in the United States. Experiences differ, of course, but a child of Martin's generation would normally have been exposed only superficially to peace education. History texts of his generation emphasized kings and great victories. The pacifist side of the Christian tradition was a well-kept secret, even in Sunday school. The media glorified violence and past wars as much as they do today.

It is no wonder that Martin found himself on the firing line before he even had thought things through. His option was "sign up, do your duty, and serve your country." Is it not a problem that the state sees its internal cohesion as so important that it tries to make certain that doing your duty is the only option that can receive a hearing? Does this mean the church failed to present the full range of normative perspectives out of its own traditions? Or is the failure to question, to explore, and to reflect Martin's own? The answer is yes to all three, and from an ethical perspective the point is that those who grapple with life-and-death decisions ought to be exposed to moral perspectives on violence. The state's need for compliance with its will and certainly the church's role in supporting the state do not warrant the exclusion of such perspectives. Young men and women should have access to different options regarding the use of violence.

THE WAR IN IRAQ

The fall of communism in 1989 and the dissolution of the Soviet Union left the United States without major military rivals. During the 1990s leaders struggled with how to use this power effectively. The Gulf War in the early 1990s and involvement in Somalia and the Balkans seemed to push these leaders in the direction of selective military intervention with a few troops for a short period of time. Different administrations sought the support of international bodies such as the United Nations for these interventions. They seemed to have a sense of the limits of military power.

With the election of George W. Bush in the fall of 2000 and the events of 9/11, a new direction was taken that has yet to play itself out. Bush called it the war on terrorism. This new war was militant in attitude, often unilateral in direction, and justified preemptive strikes and regime change, all in the name of protecting US security.

Not long after the events of 9/11, a small group centered in the Pentagon began to lobby for the removal of Iraqi leader Saddam Hussein by force. They claimed he possessed weapons of mass destruction (WMDs), including chemical and biological weapons, and the capability to use them on his neighbors in the Middle East and even the United States Many were persuaded by Saddam Hussein's record of using chemical weapons in his war with Iran in the 1980s and on his own people. They further claimed he was actively pursuing the development of nuclear weapons—indeed, that he would soon accomplish this aim. They also linked him to Al Qaeda, the terrorist organization led by Osama bin Laden responsible for the events of 9/11. In making these claims they apparently relied on intelligence gathered from dissident Iraqis bent on deposing Saddam Hussein.

They portrayed Saddam Hussein as a tyrant, the incarnation of evil, pointing to his invasion of Kuwait and the treatment of Shiites in his own country following the Gulf War. George W. Bush placed Iraq with Iran and North Korea on an "axis of evil." Those lobbying to remove Saddam Hussein pictured themselves as liberators bringing democracy and economic well-being to the entire Middle East. They steadfastly denied that Iraq's large reserves of oil had anything to do with their plans. In October 2002 Congress approved a declaration that gave President Bush wide latitude to initiate a preemptive strike.

Members of this group also seemed to have made some critical assumptions. They thought the invasion would be over swiftly; indeed, President Bush declared it over in May 2003. They assumed the war could be won with relatively few troops and casualties and that the Iraqis would welcome the troops with open arms. Finally, they predicted that any occupation would be brief and quickly followed by a friendly democratic regime in which democracy and capitalism would flourish and become a model for the Middle East. These assumptions seem to have been more idealistic than realistic. This is ironic because they spoke as if they were the hardheaded, no-nonsense, balance-of-power Republicans of the past.

The invasion of Iraq began in March 2003. It was led by the United States but joined by Great Britain, Spain, Italy, and a few other countries. The

United Nations Security Council refused to give its approval. Some in the Bush administration dismissed the United Nations as irrelevant. France and Germany, much to the disdain of the Bush administration, refused to support the United States

Things have not turned out as well as expected, despite official statements to the contrary. Instead of quickly deposing Saddam Hussein and making a quick exit, it now appears that US troops will remain in Iraq for an indefinite period with the possibility of a civil war between rival Muslim groups after departure. US troops have found no WMDs. The claim for nuclear potential was based on manufactured intelligence. The bipartisan commission that investigated the 9/11 terrorist attacks concluded that there did not appear to have been "a collaborative relationship" between Al Qaeda and Saddam Hussein, although contacts that did not amount to anything were made by the two parties at a meeting in the Sudan. That leaves the tyranny of Saddam Hussein as the main justification for a preemptive strike, a justification that has apparently satisfied many Americans who support the war.

The invasion was swift. Saddam Hussein fell from power in three weeks and was later captured. Some Iraqis welcomed US troops, although most were initially noncommittal. Looting soon became commonplace. The Bush administration dismissed the Iraqi army and most police, leaving US troops with the job of maintaining order as new Iraqi forces were trained. Increasing numbers of insurgents targeted US troops, Iraqi collaborators, and the country's infrastructure. US casualties mounted, and Iraqi deaths, while uncounted, were estimated in the tens of thousands. To quell the insurgents, the US Army allowed them to keep their weapons and stay in place as long as they remained invisible. Iraqi acceptance of the occupation declined with the deteriorating situation and revelations of prisoner abuse by US troops.

Was the deposing of Saddam Hussein worth a preemptive strike? Are bleak prospects only the pessimistic projections of the president's determined critics? Is this war justifiable? These are the questions that each American, not just Martin and Brad, needs to ask.

IRAQ AND VIETNAM

Although in many ways Vietnam and Iraq are similar, the differences are considerable.

1. They are very different in terms of climate and topography. Vietnam is mountainous and tropical; Iraq is flat and arid.
2. They have very different cultures. Vietnam is Buddhist with a small Christian minority; Iraq is Muslim with a small Christian minority.

3. The sectarian divisions in Iraq (Sunni and Shiite) are more pronounced than they were in Vietnam.
4. Oil was not an issue in Vietnam.
5. The Vietcong (Vietnamese insurgents in South Vietnam) did not possess WMDs. Saddam Hussein had used chemical weapons in his war with Iran in the 1980s.
6. The Cold War struggle against communism was the United States justification for the Vietnam War; communism is not an issue in Iraq.
7. Terrorists were not a factor in Vietnam, although the Vietcong used guerilla tactics.
8. The Vietcong had outside help from the North Vietnamese, China, and the Soviet Union. Iraq had relatively little outside help, indeed, economic sanctions had inflicted considerable suffering.
9. The US troop commitment was far greater in Vietnam, as were US casualties.
10. US troops in the Vietnam War volunteered and were conscripted; no draft has been in effect for the war in Iraq.

The similarities are striking, however.

1. US leadership perceived both Vietnam and Iraq as tests of US resolve.
2. Both wars led to situations where there seemed to be no way out.
3. Neither war was officially declared.
4. Both wars involved insurgents who were difficult to distinguish from the general population and who effectively used guerilla tactics to counter overwhelming US military might.
5. The United States set up nondemocratic regimes in both countries that were given mixed receptions.
6. Both wars initially received mixed receptions at home and abroad.
7. Both wars might have been avoided with policies of containment rather than military action.
8. Critics accused US leaders in both wars of deception, the manipulation of intelligence (the Gulf of Tonkin incident and the supposed WMDs), and the use of national symbols such as the flag for propaganda purposes.
9. US forces abused prisoners in both wars.
10. Both wars caused considerable collateral damage.
11. The justifications for both wars included elements of the crusading tradition. Vietnam was viewed as a crusade against communism, Iraq as a crusade against the "axis of evil." Crusaders saw the United States as the army of the righteous.
12. The United States tried to win the hearts and minds of the Vietnamese and the Iraqis with mixed success.
13. Both Iraq and Vietnam had been occupied by colonial powers in the twentieth century.

CHRISTIAN OPTIONS

Available to Christian thinking on conscientious objection and the Vietnam War is a normative tradition of great variety and richness. Three distinct historical options are presented within the case itself. The Mennonite Jacob Kaufmann offers the pacifist option. Professor Roger Smith discusses two options: the crusade and Christian realism, which includes the just-war tradition. Maria Gomez, who raises the question of justifiable violence in a revolutionary situation, assists Smith in discussing the just-war tradition.

Pacifism

Pacifism appears first in the case. Christian pacifism is linked with what is called the way of the cross. Jacob Kaufmann presents a modern version of this very traditional perspective, a version often associated with theologian John Howard Yoder.

The way of the cross starts with and stresses what it believes to be the New Testament view of Jesus Christ. According to this perspective Jesus unambiguously models and calls Brad and Martin to only one option, which is normative for life in society. No other options are valid; no other path but discipleship is authentically Christian.

This option takes its cue from Luke 1:46ff. and Luke 4:5–8. In these texts Jesus is announced as an agent of radical social change who scatters the proud, puts down the mighty, exalts those of low degree, and sends the rich away empty. These texts portray Jesus in a new light. Jesus introduces a nonviolent but politically active way of life for Brad and Martin to live in the midst of the world. This way is best seen in the cross, where Jesus stands up to Pilate but does not resort to mob violence or coercive political power to achieve his ends.

The way of the cross is not a new law. It cannot be forced on Brad or Martin, for its essence is freedom. It must be chosen by the disciple with recognition of its true costs, the ultimate being readiness to suffer. While all are called, few will follow because of the high costs. The few who follow will gravitate to small, sharing communities, for the church is the essence of the way.

The way of the cross almost always runs counter to conventional wisdom because of its single-minded commitment to Jesus Christ and nonviolent methods and its unwillingness to compromise. A distinct counter-cultural way of living emerges. As disciples, Brad and Martin would be called to live simply, bear hostility, serve others, and be filled with God's self-giving love. The way is emphatically nonviolent. Violence is antithetical to God's love, even when some other good seems to justify it.

The use of nonviolent methods is not the same as being passive, although some pacifists embrace a passive mode. Jesus did not condone sin and was aware of the pervasive reality of violence in a fallen world. He resisted it at every turn. Nor did he give in to the power of Rome. Likewise, Christians are called to resist up to the point of using violence. At that point resistance takes the form of suffering. Gandhi, King, and the tactics of nonviolent resistance offer models for those who choose this option.

Finally, the way involves a radical break with calculations of consequences, power balances, and prudence. As followers of the way, Brad and Martin would not be responsible for getting results, making things come out right, or moving society to some higher level of moral endeavor. If good results come, fine. If not, then they simply persevere. They are called first, last, and always to the way of active but nonviolent resistance to evil and injustice.

Pacifism was historically the first of the three Christian traditions on violence and nonviolence. The early church was pacifist and continued in this way until the early fourth century. Pacifism continues to be the perspective of the so-called peace churches and monastic orders. It involves a spectrum of options from nonresistance to nuclear pacifism. Pacifists are opposed to the war in Iraq as they are opposed to all wars. For Brad, the way of the cross points unambiguously to conscientious objection. For Martin, it calls for repentance and active resistance to all forms of violence in the future.

Christian Realism

Roger Smith presents the second option, Christian realism, which is presumably his own. In our time the best-known exponent of this position was American theologian Reinhold Niebuhr.

Christian realism has its roots both in Luther's two-realms doctrine and Calvin's call to transform society. The nomenclature reveals the essence of the perspective: the holding together of idealism and realism.

Idealism is a disposition to be loyal to norms or to some understanding of goodness or right. Christian idealists usually look to the Bible and the tradition for their normative understanding and stress adherence to the rules and principles that they find in these sources.

Realism is the disposition to take full account of sin and other elements that frustrate the realization of the ideal. It starts with the way things are and stresses the brokenness of history, limitations, and the pride of individuals and groups. Instead of pushing single-mindedly toward the ideal, the realist asks: Where do we go from here?

In Christian realism Brad and Martin must keep the ideal or normative pole of the tradition together with the realistic pole of the way things are.

Realism without idealism degenerates into cynicism; idealism without a sense of sin becomes illusion.

Brad and Martin are called in this view to live in freedom on the knife edge between idealism and realism and to act politically to move the present situation toward the ideal without the illusion that they can or must achieve the ideal. The political task for them is not the rigorous following of the ideal, however important the ideal may be, but the use of political and sometimes even military power to establish the most tolerable form of peace and justice under the circumstances.

The idealism in this perspective comes from an understanding of God's work in Jesus Christ. Jesus Christ reveals the wisdom and power of God to be self-giving love untainted by self-interest or group-interest. This ideal is not achievable because of sin. Nevertheless, approximations of the ideal are possible because God's power of love is constantly at work in human affairs and human lives.

God's love judges and convicts Brad and Martin. It breaks their pride and prevents illusion. It brings humility and repentance. As a result, Brad and Martin can undertake political tasks motivated by God's love but with a healthy sense of their own sin as well as the sin of others.

The cross and the resurrection free Brad and Martin to work in the midst of suffering and contradiction and to serve without the need for reward. God's love is also a power at work in the world. It creates the possibility of justice and peace and sustains Brad and Martin against the power of sin.

The realism in this perspective comes from an analysis of human sin. Sin is the inevitable alienation that results from self-centered or group-centered attempts to gain security from the anxieties of the human condition, for example, using guns or waging war in response to political frustrations. This tendency to seek security in and through the self or the collective is strong in individuals, stronger still in groups. While individuals have a limited capacity for repentance, for shifting themselves to God, and for relationships with other people, this potential is greatly reduced in groups. It is impossible, for example, for groups to love each other.

Such realism does not lead to pessimism and withdrawal. Rather, it leads to a new awareness about groups. Different norms apply. If groups cannot love, then the appropriate norm is justice under law. Groups can achieve some semblance of mutual regard and justice by balancing power against power. This view of groups as having a different set of norms from individuals is called the two-realms doctrine. In it, the earthly realm is governed by justice, law, rules, and the sword; the divine realm is ruled by love, the gospel, and sensitivity. Brad and Martin, provided they find their center in the divine realm, are freed by the cross and resurrection of Jesus Christ to live and work in the earthly realm and to get their hands dirty as soldiers.

Indeed, the task for Brad and Martin is to serve in the earthly realm within reason, doing what is needed to make it a better place to live. They are called to exercise power and, insofar as they are able, to move the inevitable power balances that are prematurely called justice to higher levels of freedom and equality.

The call to exercise power in as ethical a manner as possible leads to the principles of the just war. In the best of times Brad and Martin should work for justice and peace using nonviolent means. In the worst of times, when neither justice nor peace is possible, violence is sometimes the least of evils.

In such situations Christian realism considers violence, if not good in itself, at least acceptable as long as certain conditions are met. There are seven conditions or criteria for a just war:

1. Last resort: All other means to achieve a just and peaceful solution must have been exhausted.
2. Just cause: The reason for fighting must be the preservation or restoration of peace with justice against a clearly unjust adversary.
3. Right intention: The intention of the violence must be the establishment or restoration of peace with justice.
4. Declared by legitimate authorities: Only legitimate authorities may declare war; private, self-appointed defenders of justice are disallowed.
5. Reasonable hope of success: While success does not have to be guaranteed, the useless sacrifice of soldiers, no matter how just the cause, is ruled out.
6. Noncombatant immunity: Civilians without direct connection with the opponent's war effort must not be intentionally attacked.
7. Proportionality: The force used should be proportional to the objective sought; the good sought should exceed the horrible evil of the violence.

The problem with these criteria is that each group that uses them is judge in its own case. The result is that unjustified and inflated claims are often made to satisfy the criteria. Critics wonder if this tradition is not honored more in the breach to sanction unjustifiable wars than to prevent them. Hitler persuaded enough Germans that his cause was just. He used justice as "window dressing" for the naked exercise of power.

The fourth criterion is also a problem because it seems to rule out justifiable resistance to oppressive regimes. Some would amend it to permit the use of violence in situations of oppression.

Finally, another criterion has emerged in recent years but has yet to find its way on to many lists. Increasingly, broad international support is required before a nation engages in a justifiable war. The United States sought such support at the start of the war in Iraq, but the United Nations Security Council refused to give it.

This perspective puts pressure on Brad and offers several alternatives on Vietnam for Martin. Christian realists do not reject military service out of hand but are prepared to resist fighting in an unjust cause. Unfortunately, current law does not allow selective conscientious objection, that is to say, objection to a particular war. To be considered for conscientious objector status, one must object to all wars. Realists must therefore serve or take the legal consequences in the event that they conscientiously choose resistance. If convicted, they will probably serve time in prison.

Martin, should he accept this perspective, must decide on the justifiability of his own involvement in Vietnam and what to advise Brad. If he sees his involvement as unjustified, which seems to be the case already, he should seek forgiveness and new life in Jesus Christ. He should also relate to Brad the lessons he has learned over the years as his conscience has reacted to his experience in Vietnam.

Finally, this tradition calls all Christians to judge whether the wars in Vietnam and Iraq were justifiable. US leaders claimed that both wars were justifiable. In both cases they met with bitter dissent. Brad and Martin, and all Christians, are left with the task of making this judgment.

Crusade

The final option presented in Martin's class is the crusade, which historically has been an option but does not appear to be so in this case. One reason the crusade has been popular is its simplicity. It divides reality into good and evil. The crusader is always on the side of the good; the enemy is always the incarnation of evil. God wills the eradication of evil, hence the crusader is justified, even commanded, to kill. Another source of its popularity is its compatibility with tribalism, that seemingly natural human inclination to favor one's own group and accept without question its rituals, perspectives, and aggressions.

The crusade has had its moments in Christian history. It was at work in the conquest of the Promised Land by the Hebrews. The so-called holy-war texts, for example Deuteronomy 7:1–2, 13:15–16, and 32:41–42, depict God as commanding and even leading the conquest. In 13:15–16 God is portrayed as commanding what amounts to genocide. Pope Urban II used this text successfully in the Middle Ages to rescue the Holy Land temporarily from the forces of Islam. During the Vietnam War it was used in some Christian circles to call for opposition to "atheistic communism." In the Iraq War, Saddam Hussein was placed on the "axis of evil" and put near the top of everyone's all-tyrant list. The United States, in turn, was pictured as the agent of redemption.

In the case study the crusade is seen as foreign to the teachings of Jesus. Its dualism of good and evil is simplistic in the extreme, especially in its naivete about the sin of the crusader. Its embrace of violence is so alien to the central Christian experience of faith as to make a mockery of it. For these and other reasons Ronald Smith, the teacher, was correct in dismissing it as an option. It is out of the normative bounds of Christianity and offers no guidance to Brad or Martin. Its ethical importance today is that of a historical artifact and an example of what to avoid.

Still, the crusade is alive and well, not only in the claims of US leaders, but also to some degree in the emotional response to the war in Iraq and in the outpouring of war patriotism in support of the war. It is also alive and well on the Christian Right and Islamic extremist groups, such as Al Qaeda, who stretch the meaning of *jihad* to justify their use of violence.

CONCLUSION

The two primary issues in this case are what Brad and other young men his age should think about war in general, and what they should do when their nation is involved in a specific war. Responding to an induction notice might become a part of these questions.

Today, no one is being drafted, but the United States is deeply involved in an increasingly difficult military action in Iraq. The military is hard pressed and stretched thin. Volunteers are coming disproportionately from lower-income groups; most college students are safe in their residences letting others do the fighting.

Women are not subject to the draft, although many are volunteering, and some have been killed in Iraq. Increasingly, the secondary issue of drafting women is being discussed, and women are investigating where they stand.

Martin himself faces two secondary issues. How should he resolve his own conflict of conscience about Vietnam, and what and how should he advise his grandson about military service.

Finally, the case raises the issue of US involvement in Vietnam and Iraq. Were these military actions justifiable in terms of Christian norms?

ADDITIONAL RESOURCES

Bainton, Roland H. *Christian Attitudes Toward War and Peace.* Nashville, TN: Abingdon, 1960.

Bell, Linda A. *Rethinking Ethics in the Midst of Violence: A Feminist Approach to Freedom.* Lanham, MD: Rowman and Littlefield, 1993.

Clarke, Richard H. *Against All Enemies: Inside America's War on Terrorism.* Boston: Free Press, 2004

Gray, J. Glenn. *The Warriors.* Rev. ed. New York: Harper and Row, 1967.

Lahaye, Tim, and Jerry B. Jenkins. *Left Behind: A Novel of the Earth's Last Days.* Wheaton, IL: Tyndale House, 1996.

Long, Edward L., Jr. *Fighting Terrorism: Responding as Christians.* Louisville, KY: Westminster/John Knox Press, 2004.

Míguez Bonino, José. *Doing Theology in a Revolutionary Situation.* Philadelphia: Fortress Press, 1975.

Niebuhr, Reinhold. *The Children of Light and the Children of Darkness.* New York: Charles Scribner's Sons, 1944.

Odum, Mel. *Apocalypse Burning.* Wheaton, IL: Tyndale House, 2004.

Rushdoony, R. J. *The Institues of Biblical Law.* Nutley, NJ: Craig Press, 1973.

Sider, Ronald J., and Richard K. Taylor. *Nuclear Holocaust and Christian Hope.* Downers Grove, IL: InterVarsity Press, 1982.

Stone, Ronald H. *Reinhold Niebuhr: Prophet to Politician.* Nashville, TN: Abingdon Press, 1972.

Woodward, Bob. *Bush at War.* New York: Simon and Schuster, 2002.

Yoder, John Howard. *The Politics of Jesus.* Grand Rapids, MI: Eerdmans, 1972.

- Just War Theory
- Virtue Ethics
- Teleo - gral
- Deont. = Kydism

PART III

JUSTICE

Case

The Cost of Security

The monthly meeting of university deans was turning ugly. It was March, and the immediate issue was graduate assistantships for the following fall semester, especially assistantships for out of state, mostly international, students.

"There must be something the university can do," insisted Mary Ann Suarez, dean of Arts and Sciences, the largest faculty in the university. "We already had severe imbalances before the new SEVIS system was in place, but now it is intolerable. The graduate program directors in Arts and Sciences are very upset. Each new story of visa screwups brings a handful of people to my office demanding action by the university."

The problem under discussion was visa problems for mostly male graduate students from majority Muslim nations. Peter Waters, dean of the graduate school, agreed. "It is beginning to affect admissions, too. We're finding that a graduate assistantship offered to a student from the Middle East, Pakistan, Indonesia, or Malaysia has only a 30 percent chance of resulting in a warm body showing up in September, because he can't get a visa to come to the United States. Departments that have experienced no-shows are more likely to offer that graduate assistantship and its funding to a Chinese or an Indian student, because non-Muslims move more quickly through the visa process. In some schools and departments there is a shift toward women for the same reason—they don't get as much scrutiny."

Mary Ann retorted, "That's a real generalization, Peter. We have non-Muslims and women who are hung up in this process, too. The whole visa process has gotten much more complicated. Many US embassies do not have the staff to do the rigorous kind of background investigations now demanded, so everyone is delayed."

Ankur Singh, dean of the School of Engineering, responded that he saw no reason for the university to get involved with the Office of Homeland Security over visas, as that was a political issue: "Yes, there are some problems with visas and with SEVIS, the new process of Homeland Security for tracking international students through automatic university computer monitoring. But scrutiny is necessary since 9/11, and the kinks will get worked out in few more years. And after all, we have many more applications from international students for graduate assistantships than we could ever fill. So for a few years they go disproportionately to Chinese and Indians. So what? This is a form of foreign aid, and who says US foreign aid has to be the same for all nations?"

"Well, that may work all right for your school," Mary Ann retorted, "because virtually all your top foreign applicants are from China and India. But in the humanities, that's not where the stars are!" The background to Mary Ann's angry, pointed remarks was ongoing resentment over the suspiciously high GRE scores of numerous Chinese students. Many universities had applications from hundreds, even thousands of Chinese students who posted combined verbal and math scores of 1500+ out of a possible 1600. This put them in the upper reaches of the top 1 percent of all those taking the test, English speakers included. On the basis of these scores, Chinese applicants, most but not all of whom were applying in the fields of science and technology, had been displacing all other ethnic groups in the competition for graduate assistantships in this university and many others. Upon arriving on campus, however, many of the Chinese students demonstrated a much lower than expected level of English reading, writing, and speaking ability. The GRE had issued global notices about the "anomaly" of the Chinese scores but as yet had no evidence as to how the tests were being "cooked" in China. This testing issue was merely exacerbating a situation in which Asians had already come to predominate as both science and technology faculty and student bodies in American graduate schools.

Peter Waters replied, "No, Mary Ann, it doesn't affect the science and tech fields as much, but they have their own issues. I do agree, though, that on some of these points the Ohio university system does need to intervene with Homeland Security. This visa problem doesn't just affect new international students applying for admission. Ultimately it affects our budgets from the state when students in whom we have invested years of financial aid are prevented from completing the Ph.D. because they can't get a visa to come back and defend the dissertation. We have another case in environmental studies. Unlike the last one, a Pakistani who could not get a visa to return after he completed his fieldwork research for the dissertation in Papua, this one was an Indonesian who already had a dissertation defense scheduled when his mother died. He went home for a brief visit and was not allowed back in. He has been petitioning for eight months to get a new visa. We can't find out what the delay is. Neither can the US Embassy in

Jakarta, which had him checked out; he came up clean. He had been here for six years, a star student, no political involvement at all. He even married an American. She is beside herself at the possibility that, without a degree, he may not have much of a career in Indonesia and may not be able to live anywhere else."

Winston Duff, the new dean in the School of Hospitality Management, inquired: "That is a tragedy, of course, but how does it affect university funding?" The other deans all turned toward him upon hearing his question, which had forcefully reminded them of his newness in the system. Peter replied, "Because at the graduate level, our principal method of funding from the state is based on graduations. To keep up the number of graduations, we give aid in the form of graduate assistantships to well over half our graduate students and virtually all our international students. When they accept aid they must carry a full-time load of credits, which, if we mentor them through the dissertation in a timely fashion, results in a Ph.D. graduation within five or six years. When they don't graduate, our aid package shrinks. Unfunded American students work to put themselves through and so are only part-time students. They take two or three times longer to complete the degree, if they ever do."

"The risk to funding—that's the reason we shouldn't put on white hats and beat our heads against the Homeland Security wall," said Ankur flatly. "The country is panicked and sees all Muslims as terrorists. Until that changes, we are going to have problems with these students. So let's simply choose to admit and fund US citizens and those internationals who can get in easily, and not risk our aid packages."

Fred Roberts, dean of the School of Education, who normally said little at these meetings, demurred: "Aside from the fact that not all of our schools have the luxury of doing as you suggest without seriously lowering standards, it sounds like accepting racial profiling to me. I'm sure glad that the faculty who looked at my graduate application years ago didn't say: 'Gee, look at this, a black guy with good grades and scores, but he's from an undistinguished school and is already married with two kids. He is going to have a really hard time getting through, and will probably take longer because he's going to have to work. We'd better take that middle-class white kid who is more likely to graduate on time instead.'"

"Amen!" shouted Sherilee Jenkins, dean of the School of Health Sciences. "After the 2000 election, how can anyone make this kind of argument? Many of my family and old neighbors back in Florida tried to vote and got turned away from the polls because they had the same names as some of the 167,000 Florida ex-cons who have no civil rights for the rest of their lives. Florida commissioned a company to compile a list of names of the ex-cons but was too cheap to have the names linked to Social Security numbers. Even though the company told the state that the names alone were not sufficient to identify those who should be barred from voting, the list was given to the precincts and used to purge the voter rolls. You know how many George

Jacksons there are in the state of Florida? Hundreds, literally hundreds. This hit blacks worst because the range of last names is so much smaller among blacks. Well, this is one of the same issues these international students have. One of our Muslim students went home for the summer to India, and because he has the same name as some accused terrorist who is over twenty years older than he is and no relative whatsoever, he cannot get cleared for a visa. His name is on the wanted list; because hundreds of innocent people have that same name, none of them can get visas, either. Yes, people are concerned about terrorism and people are concerned about crime. But justice is justice—it shouldn't depend upon whose ox is being gored."

Fred Roberts sat up a little straighter and added, "Most developing countries don't have things like Social Security numbers, and many of my students tell me that their cultures don't use patronymics. Indonesians, for example, usually have one, two, or even three first names but no family name. So the system that we are using to identify terrorists—lists of marked names—cannot identify them."

Tony Schwartz, dean of the Law School, fidgeted. "We have been talking about this for an hour, but only in very general terms. Let's focus on what steps we should take. Can we change the calendar for giving notice about teaching assistantships to give more time for these affected students to get visas? It won't help the ones with terrorists' names, but it might help those whose visas just take months longer due to the extra scrutiny. And shouldn't we all have longer backup lists, in case our first choices don't get visas?"

Ankur and Mary Ann both began speaking at once: "No, we can't . . . " "That won't work because . . . " Ankur deferred to Mary Ann. "Tony, we can't back the process up any more. Because the provost doesn't get the budget from the state any earlier, he can't tell us how many graduate assistants we are each going to get. We can't know how many to make offers to until we know how much money we will have."

"Furthermore," Ankur added," it takes a few months to get US visas in almost every country. If we say that June 1, or even July 1 or August 1, is the date by which foreign students must have a visa or lose their awards, we will compound the problem by denying awards to hundreds of students whose visas are now granted at the end of August. Most student visas aren't granted until the last few weeks before the term begins."

"What worries me most," said Peter, "are the statistics I am hearing from admissions officers all over the country. International applications are down as much as 40 percent this year. Many of the best international students decided not to take on the extra hurdles of US admission. They are going to Britain, Germany, France, Australia, or even southern and eastern European countries rather than the United States. Who knows how serious the future effect of this shift will be on the quality of medical care or technology development in this country? Being able to skim the cream off the annual crop of the brightest students in the world has raised standards throughout

American universities for years, not to mention the benefits from many of those graduates who remained in the United States. What will be the effect on the quality of education and future technology if we cannot recapture this market?"

Amador Martinez, dean of the School of Business, had become impatient and insisted, "It's not our place to debate such questions. I have tried to sit back and listen because I know this issue affects most of you much more than it does my school, although it has some impact on us, too, especially regarding Latin American students. As an American, I think we are not dealing with the central issue here. We are at war, and the enemy is one who does not come out in the open but hides. How many of the 9/11 terrorists came into this country on student visas? Most of them! So what if there are a few glitches in the SEVIS system in the beginning? We need stricter scrutiny of foreign students applying to come to this country. War calls for unity and necessitates some sacrifice. The loss of international students and possibly some state funding are the sacrifices that our universities are called to make. It is not nearly as much as our soldiers and their families are giving, and we should not complain about it."

Mary Ann and Peter burst into speech simultaneously: "No!" Peter nodded to Mary Ann, who continued: "I doubt anyone here disagrees that we are at war, or that war imposes a variety of costs. The issue here is whether or not this particular cost is necessary. I had hoped to stay out of politics, but it seems to me that our government is ignoring the huge benefits that our nation derives from international students and tourists. If the US government is going to impose much stricter scrutiny of visas, it should enlarge the embassy staffs who do the background checks. Furthermore, there is no reason why the system cannot become more sophisticated, so that it can differentiate a twenty-five year old from a fifty-five year old with the same name. All of us here are dealing with the shift to the new PeopleSoft technology." Mary Ann paused for an audible groan. "As required by law, this system will no longer identify students or staff or faculty by Social Security number but by a variety of indicators. We know that it is possible to identify a person by a combination of name, birthplace, age, and a number of other characteristics. Our question must be: Why hasn't this been done for visa applications? We don't question the need for greater scrutiny of international students; we question the efficiency of the process designed to provide that scrutiny. There seems to be more 'costs' than are necessary."

Amador responded, "I understand, but it seems to me that we could bend some, too. For example, what reason in the world is there that a doctoral student cannot defend his dissertation in a video conference? The university could be more innovative." Amador's College of Business was heavily involved in courses taught over the Internet and had many students throughout Latin America.

"Of course we could," Peter replied. "Amador is right that in some cases we do have remedies at hand if we modify our own policies. This will not solve the overall problems but could help individual students, especially those who have already begun their graduate work with us and got caught in the changes."

Ankur asked impatiently, "So is this just a gripe session about SEVIS, or do you have a specific proposal for us to consider?"

Peter responded slowly and deliberately: "I think that both American self-interest and our own responsibilities to the developing world and its individual students require us to press President Hollings [the university president] to push the Ohio Board of Regents to lobby our Senators and Congressmen for changes to the SEVIS system. The graduate students we send back to Africa, Asia, and Latin America are wonderful ambassadors for the United States in a time when we could use supporters in other nations. And many of them are the best hope that their nations have for improvements in the economy, technology, public health, and other areas of development. Beyond that, our own society has become dependent upon foreign graduate students becoming our own scientists, doctors, engineers, and nurses."

Amador sat up straight and slammed the palm of his hand on the table: "Do you know how dangerous it is for the university to become politically involved? And I don't just mean with the federal government! If we are seen to criticize the present administration, which is how this proposed activity would be seen, we would be taking on its state party, too, which happens to control the legislature and our funding! This is a crazy suggestion, and I can't believe President Hollings will support it."

Mary Ann responded: "Of course it's dangerous. But isn't it also dangerous to do nothing and lose these bright minds from all over the world? Do we have no responsibility to the international students who have already enrolled with us, who turned down opportunities to study in other nations to come here? We have to weigh the risks against our responsibilities and the best interests of all groups involved. And so will President Hollings."

Peter suggested: "I see the coffee is here. Let's take a ten-minute break, come back, take a vote, and see if we can move on to the budget shortfall." Everyone stood and moved toward the hall where the coffee service was set up.

Commentary

The Cost of Security

Questions

Who is my neighbor? Since 9/11 this question haunts the United States in issue after issue. How much should we be willing to trust a stranger? Are we obliged to go out of our way for strangers in general? For our international students? For individuals of another nation and/or another religion? One of the ongoing disagreements in Christian ethics is whether we have greater obligations to those to whom we have personal ties (families, friends) or contractual agreements (students, patients, clients) than to people we do not know. Some argue that our priority should always be for those with the greatest need. Jesus' parable of the Good Samaritan only partially answers this question; it says we need to act as a neighbor to those who are in need. But we do not know what other obligations, if any, the Good Samaritan set aside to help the wounded man. It is also unclear how inclusively the "need" of the stranger ought to be construed. Is the need of a robbed and beaten man left in a ditch by the road equivalent to the "need" of a student from a developing nation for an American Ph.D.?

Henri Nouwen, renowned writer on Christian spirituality, has described one of the major spiritual developments in a Christian's life as moving from hostility to hospitality.[1] Hostility, or defensiveness, he says, stems from insecurity, from feelings of vulnerability, feelings of not being worthwhile. Hostility is rooted in a failure to understand God's gratuitous love for us, a love that makes us worthwhile. Hospitality, on the other hand, is rooted in an understanding that we are loved with an unconditional, limitless love, and can trust in that love to care for us. The understanding that we are loved thus frees us to care for others, even to risk ourselves in caring for others. We are called, in short, to offer to others the care that God offers to us, and to do this not only for those who are closely connected to us but also for strangers. We are commanded to love our neighbors, so such love is an obligation, but ideally the love of neighbor is experienced not as an external obligation, but as a unconscious response to being loved, as an overflow of love from God to us and from us to others.

In this case there seems to be general agreement that both the self-interest of the university and the optimal moral response would be to retain its customary nondiscriminatory hospitality toward international students. The disagreement is over whether, under the present circumstances of the US war against terrorism, efforts to preserve this hospitality are worth the potential risks that would accompany these efforts.

For those who see the situation primarily in terms of institutional self-interest, the risks of activism in behalf of international students may well outweigh the benefits to be gained. A goal of preserving and strengthening the university is not at all inappropriate in Christian ethics, in that universities are generally understood as promoting the common good. Thus we can entertain the argument that any policy that threatens the general mission of the university—providing higher education for diverse groups from the state and the larger world—should be avoided. But for Christians, love of neighbor requires that the welfare of others must also be considered—*all* the others affected by this decision. As the case shows, even within the institution not every group is equally affected by the decision to be made here: some schools and faculties are much more involved than others. Undoubtedly, those *most* affected are the international students who face the most intense visa scrutiny—those from Muslim-majority nations, especially in the Middle East. If every person is potentially our neighbor, then the interests of all stakeholders must be considered. Sometimes the good of maintaining a generally beneficial institution is not sufficient to justify a protective policy that has disproportionately negative effects on one particular group, especially if that protective policy demands a stance that seems incompatible with gospel directives on being hospitable.

HOSPITALITY IN THE OLD TESTAMENT

From a Christian perspective, hospitality to strangers has always been a central moral value. Many theological arguments about hospitality are based in the Old Testament, in which it was clear that various peoples of the Near East recognized a universal obligation to offer hospitality to strangers. This was essential if there was to be any possibility of safe travel or trade. Hospitality was indeed the best test of the virtue of a person, precisely because it involved one's treatment of a stranger, one to whom was not related and whom one might never see again. Hospitality was one of the tests God made for Abraham. After Abraham and Sarah welcomed and cared for the strangers sent by God, they were blessed with their long-awaited child (Gn 18). Abraham's nephew Lot also welcomed the strangers sent from God and protected them from the citizens of Sodom, thus sparing his family the destruction that followed (Gn 19). It was the violation of the law of hospitality that brought on the destruction not only of Sodom and Gomorrah, but later also the city of Gibeah and most of one of the tribes of Israel, that of Benjamin (Judg 19—20).

HOSPITALITY IN THE NEW TESTAMENT

Nor did hospitality disappear as a virtue in the shift from the Old to the New Testament. In fact, one of the central characteristics of the ministry of Jesus, inclusive table fellowship, is based upon the virtue of hospitality. Jesus was well known and often criticized for inviting to his table in Capernaum a very mixed lot: sinners as well as religious leaders (Mt 9:10– 13; 11:19; Mk 2:15–17; Lk 5:30–32; 7:34–40; 15:1–2). His preaching was full of exhortations not to discriminate when calling guests to dine in one's home: "But when you give a banquet, invite the poor, the crippled, the lame, and the blind" (Lk 14:13). Jesus' parables more than once illustrated the ideal householder—God—inviting not only the highborn but also people off the street to his banquet. In his parable of the Sheep and the Goats (Mt 25:31–46), Jesus suggests that it is foolish for humans to divide others into neighbors and strangers, since only God knows who is estranged from God. As Hebrews 13:2 reminds Christians: "Do not neglect to show hospitality to strangers, for by doing that some have entertained angels without knowing it."

In fact, it was based on both Jesus' teaching and his own example that the early church developed the practice of inclusive table fellowship—of inviting to the eucharistic celebration the rich and the poor, the powerful and the weak, Jews and Greeks, slave and free, men and women, all those who followed Jesus' path. All mixed together, and all were equal in the Lord, as the baptismal formula in Galatians 3:28 stated.

Hospitality became one of the qualities looked for in ministers of the gospel in the early church: "A bishop must be above reproach, married only once, temperate, sensible, respectable, *hospitable,* an apt teacher, not a drunkard, not violent but gentle, not quarrelsome, and not a lover of money" (1 Tm 3:2); "a bishop . . . must be *hospitable,* a lover of goodness, prudent, upright, devout, and self-controlled" (Ti 1:7–8).

DIFFICULTIES IN MAKING HOSPITALITY UNIVERSAL

While it would be difficult indeed to argue convincingly against hospitality as an important Christian virtue, it is not so difficult to question how this virtue might apply to this case. Many would argue that it is not the same thing to invite all believers into the fellowship of salvation and to invite all foreign youth to earn graduate degrees in the United States. While hospitality supports a very strong argument for bringing international students from poor nations to centers of higher education in the United States, it might not necessarily dictate the distribution of those students. Justice would insist on institutional efforts to assist already admitted international students to complete their degrees in the United States, but justice, too, offers only a limited argument for admitting one group of students from the developing world over another group, especially in the face of what may be severe political risks to the institution and its future ability to educate both US and international students. Applicants that are not accepted—whether Muslim or Chinese or Hindu—may well be denied higher education in the developed world, and thus may have more limited career opportunities than they would have had if they had been admitted. But as far as material damages to the individual international student go, there is no patently greater damage to the Muslim student in not being accepted than there would be for a poor person from another developing nation. But there may be nonmaterial damages.

Some would make the pragmatic argument that for this university to shift its graduate aid from students in Muslim or Arab nations at the same time that other US universities are for the same reasons shifting their graduate aid from students in Muslim or Arab nations will create a perception of American enmity toward Muslims. That could exacerbate anti-US sentiment already present in those populations and even increase the possibility of terrorist activities against the United States. Thus it might well not be prudent for the university community to acquiesce to this shift in aid.

An analogous argument from pragmatism in the contemporary United States might be that racial profiling, for example, in traffic stops, should not be done because it may arouse anger in the targeted (African American) population that could overflow onto police and even bystanders. This may be true, but it is not the central moral argument. The moral argument would be that there is no general basis for preferring—or handicapping—one group over another. It is one thing to admit more Indians to an engineering program because more Indians apply and more Indians have high test scores on the entrance exams; it would be another thing entirely to admit more Indians (or any other group) because their admission involves the least paperwork and delays than admitting Pakistanis or southern Thais. The criteria for discriminating must be relevant to the end of the selection process. To select students on the basis of convenience for the university is to treat them like things, choosing the ones most easily acquired. But if persons are ends, then choices among them will be based on criteria that are (a) internal to them as individuals, and (b) relevant to what they are being selected for.

The proposed policy shift based in pragmatic acquiescence with national security policy of the moment *is* discriminatory, even if the motivation for the shift is neither personal nor based on race, ethnicity, or religion, but only on convenience. As Americans learned in the civil rights movement, unjustified discrimination leaves scars regardless of the motivation behind it. Nat Turner of slave rebellion fame revealed a "truth of the heart" to those who asked him why his insurrection had killed not only brutal slaveowners but also some liberal whites who treated their slaves well. He responded that from the perspective of the slaves, the liberal whites were far worse, and more hated, than those whites who supported slavery whole-heartedly, because they knew better but still refused to risk anything at all to correct the abomination before them. They just went along with the majority, choosing the easiest path.

OTHER OPTIONS

At the same time, there are other options than confronting the Office of Homeland Security. While the departments of the university may not know exactly how many graduate students they will be able to fund in any one year, they do have a historical sense of how many they had this year, last year, and the year before. Therefore they could send out early acceptances to at least part of their list. Even if they hesitate to make definite offers, they could inform students of where they stand in the process: "In the past five years the Department of History has had seventeen, nineteen, eighteen, twenty, and twenty-two doctoral fellowships, and we anticipate a similar number next year. While we cannot award fellowships until we receive final notice of our budget for next year, you are number twelve on our list of students to be funded. We suggest that you make an appointment for a visa interview with an Embassy official immediately as the wait is often long. Secure your vaccinations soon. We will be sending out the necessary I-20 request form for the visa within the next few weeks." As a corollary of such a policy, the department should work with the international students' office so that some portion of the slots available over the last few years be released early, so that some I-20 forms could be sent even before the final budget amounts are known. In schools with relatively stable financial histories, that portion available for early release might be very high—75–80 percent—while in universities with more erratic funding levels 50 percent might even be a little too high for comfort. To adjust procedure in this way would not only give international students from countries with more US security scrutiny extra time to obtain a visa, but it might gain the university a higher proportion of those students it wants to attract by issuing its invitations before other schools.

No matter which way universities decide to deal with this problem, the administrators who develop the process should be able to honestly explain, without embarrassment, to a student who was not admitted why that decision was made. That does not mean that explaining should be easy; many truths are hard to deliver. But even hard truths can be delivered honestly when the process is fair. Not many of us would be comfortable telling a student: "We didn't accept you because we didn't want to bother finding a way to adjust our admission processes to accommodate the new security situation prevailing in the United States. It was easier to take students from other parts of the world." There is nothing of the gospel in such a message. There is nothing of love of neighbor, or hospitality, or inclusive fellowship.

CONCLUSION

Christians often have difficulty moving from the realm of personal responsibility to that of collective, particularly institutional, responsibility, because we tend to understand the moral stance of Christianity—love your neighbor—in terms of emotional feelings and attitudes towards others. It is difficult to ask institutions to feel love and then act on it, and many Christians consider institutions—states, universities, companies, and others— as not bound by moral imperatives beyond those that bind the persons within them. That may be. But if the corporate entities are not bound by moral imperatives, the individuals within them, who determine the policies of the institution, *are* bound by moral imperatives. Institutions do not make decisions or implement them—individuals within them do. Individuals do not have immunity from moral imperatives for the decisions they make within institutions, whether those decisions create institutional policy or merely implement some piece of that policy.

In a recent news story a Kansas City schoolteacher gave a group of high-school students an F on an assignment for cheating. Parents complained so strongly to the school board that an F was an overreaction to a level of cheating that was common that the school board ordered the teacher to raise the grades of the cheating students. The teacher resigned. In moral terms, the school board demanded that the teacher cooperate in evil. The teacher refused—and paid the price of conscience. The fact that there is often a price to be paid for exercising moral conscience does not excuse Christians from that exercise. This is the place in Christian life that the cross erupts. According to the gospels, Jesus probably could have escaped the cross if he had kept his mouth shut about the plight of the poor and sick, the distortion and extortion in the Temple cult, the pride and hypocrisy of the Pharisees, and the greed and irresponsibility of the Jewish ruling class. The cost of seeing his mission through to the end was the cross.

The cross can be accepted, but it should not be cultivated or pursued. Perhaps in this case the university should not seek a battle with Homeland Security. It should definitely pursue whatever in-house changes in procedure could support earlier award notification of international students. Externally, the university might see if there are other universities concerned and evaluate the possibility of acting, as Peter suggested, through the Ohio Board of Regents to press Ohio Senators and Representatives, or acting nationally, in cooperation with many other universities, to influence Congress.

NOTE

[1] Henri Nouwen, *Reaching Out: The Three Movements in the Spiritual Life* (New York: Doubleday, 1975).

ADDITIONAL RESOURCES

Deck, Sylvia Cirone. *Ministry of Hospitality*. Kansas City: Sheed and Ward, 1996.

Freedman, Samuel G. "Grad School's International Glow Is Dimmed by Security Concerns." *The New York Times*. October 27, 2004. B10, 4.

Hoover, Eric, Brock Read, Burton Bollaq, Richard Monastersky, and David L. Wheeler. "Closing the Gates." *The Chronicle of Higher Education* 49, no. 31 (April 11, 2003), A12–21.

Koenig, John. *New Testament Hospitality: Partnership with Strangers as Promise and Mission*. Philadelphia: Fortress Press, 1985.

Palmer, Parker J. *The Company of Strangers: Christians and the Renewal of America's Public Life*. New York: Crossroad, 1997.

Case

The Agenda:
Preference for the Poorest?

"The first item on the agenda is Don Brown's report from the fund-rais-ing committee on the capital campaign," declared Will Jennings, a black Episcopal priest who, as chairperson of the board of trustees of the Com-munity Land Trust, chaired its monthly meeting.

"Well, you'll all be pleased to hear that the capital campaign raised $420,000 on the condition that we buy land and houses in the West End south of Grant Street and build or rehab for $35,000 or less," said Don proudly. "We had a large number of contributors, and eleven large corpo-rate gifts. All six committee members worked very hard. As you can see in the written reports I am handing out, the fund-raising committee suggests that it become a standing committee of the board, with its members board members."

At that, Kitty Bailey, a middle-aged black woman who had been execu-tive director of the Community Land Trust for seven years, snapped to attention. She had had several run-ins with Don since he had assumed con-trol of the fund-raising committee. Don had come to the trust as a volun-teer through a social-action project in his church. He had recently retired as a vice-president of a large multinational corporation. When Kitty asked Don to take on the much-needed capital campaign, he recruited friends to fill the other five positions on the fund-raising committee. In Kitty's opin-ion, the other members of the committee were like Don—white, well-to-do suburbanites. She was convinced, however, that they were neither familiar with black urban poverty nor comfortable with the trust's poor black resi-dents, who, under the bylaws, made up the majority of the board. Kitty admitted that, having herself spent twenty years escaping from the poverty of the projects of the West End, she was perhaps overly sensitive to slights to the poor black residents. But she suspected Don's proposal was a move toward a bylaws revision lowering the level of resident participation on the board.

Before the applause died down for the extraordinarily high sum raised—more than twice the goal of the campaign—Frank Hart, the attorney on the board, asked a question. Most of the other board members had thought Kitty's recruiting of Frank when she first accepted the directorship was very impressive; he was a partner in the largest, most prestigious law firm in the city. Few knew that Kitty and her husband and Frank and his wife were good friends, or that Kitty and her husband were godparents to the black child adopted into Frank and Tina's white family ten years before.

"Don, that's a fantastic amount you have raised," praised Frank. "But why the restrictions? Why only south of Grant Street, when you know that we have options on at least four properties north of Grant? And why the $35,000 limit on building and rehab costs? That's less than the last Audley Street house. Who set these restrictions?"

"The donors. No restrictions, no money," said Don.

"Don," said Frank, "I've looked through the report, and I don't see a donor list. How much money is restricted, by what donors, and why do those particular donors want us to work only south of Grant Street?"

Don replied, "The committee made a decision to accept the restriction in order to qualify for large corporate donations. There is at least twenty years of work for the trust in rehabbing and building low-income housing south of Grant, so the restriction is no handicap."

Morita Adams, the most outspoken of the resident members, declared, "Well, it don't take no brains to figure out where that restricted money comes from. Who wants to keep the trust from buying parcels north of Grant? The developers, the big real-estate companies, and their banks. I bet Koul Brothers Construction, Park Place Developers, and State Bank want to expand their Liberty Street project south."

Sarah Hawkins, a white Methodist minister and a new board member, looked bewildered. "I don't understand. Those groups have lots more money than the trust does and can outbid us for any piece of property they want. Why should they worry about us? Property values all over the West End are so low that even outbidding us they can get anything they want for a song."

Will Jennings explained, "Developers need large tracts of land downtown, Sarah, because they build for the upper-middle class. They have learned that the white middle class will not buy into a neighborhood near poor black neighbors. For whites to move downtown, developers need large enclaves of exclusively middle-class housing. The trust was set up in 1978 to stop gentrification in the West End so that what remained of black low-income housing would not disappear, leaving blacks dispersed and homeless.

When the trust buys the land, it legally separates the land from the house and sells the house, retaining a repurchase option on any future sale. We lease the land to the house buyer for $1 per year. Our low-income residents have decent housing, the security of home ownership, and the ability to leave those homes to their children and grandchildren. However, once the trust gets a piece of property in the center of a neighborhood, the developers have to look elsewhere, because they won't ever get the whole area."

Don strenuously objected to Will's explanation. "Look, the developers aren't villains here. The city needs to develop the downtown ring in order to expand the tax base so it has the money to fund social-service projects in places like the West End. The condos and townhouses and the new shopping areas are good for the downtown and good for the black residents too. You make it sound like a good thing to have miles of rotting and abandoned housing that only the desperately poor would consider. If blocks of rotting, empty buildings north of Grant Street are torn down and replaced by new housing and commercial developments, then all the West End will be safer, more attractive, and more prosperous."

Kitty impatiently interjected, "But Don, how can it be a good thing for the poor black population to have their housing bought and torn down to build upscale communities where they can't live and where they aren't even welcome to walk because they are regarded as potential criminals? Last year, when the Liberty Street development opened, I went up on my lunch hour to look it over. Two uniformed guards demanded ID, then followed me—only me, not any of the whites walking around—up and down the street. And I was a middle-aged black woman in a business suit. Imagine how they'd respond at night to young black men who wandered in for ice cream at the deli!"

Frank repeated his question about the amount of the total that was restricted. After hearing that $200,000 of the $420,000 was pledged on condition that the trust abandon the West End north of Grant Street, Frank introduced a motion that the board decline the $200,000 restricted donation and use the remaining $220,000 to implement existing board policy and goals. To Don's obvious dismay, the motion passed nine to six.

SAFETY AND DEVELOPMENT: FOR WHOM?

Will Jennings nodded to Jim Meadows, the trust's construction supervisor, as he addressed the board. "The next item on the agenda is the building inspection campaign announced by City Council last week. Jim will tell us how it affects us."

"Well, as far as I can tell," said Jim, "if the city inspectors aren't on the up and up, we have some serious problems, especially the six vacant properties we recently bought and the fourteen on which we have options. Frank tells me city law allows the city to do just about anything it wants with buildings that are unsafe to live in. Being unsafe to live in can mean anything from not complying with the latest building code to being structurally dangerous. The worst case is that they condemn all our properties and institute immediate demolition. Almost as bad would be to give us thirty to sixty days to complete repairs or face demolition. We could rehab from two to four houses in sixty days, but never all of them. If the city gives us a year, though, we could rehab them all and continue much as we have, with only a little more attention to the time between purchase and rehabbing."

Chairperson Will Jennings asked, "What do you mean, if the city is on the up and up? Is there something fishy here?"

Kitty intervened: "There are strong rumors and suspicions in all the low-income housing organizations downtown that the City Council is working with the developers on this one. Other low-income housing groups have also been buying dilapidated and condemned buildings from both private owners and from the city with the idea of keeping upscale developers out of the West End. Due to a shortage of rehab money, three or four buildings sit empty for every one that gets rehabbed and rented out to low-income people. A lot of people think the city means to use inspectors to mandate demolition of those buildings in the name of safety and obtaining a facelift for the city. The real object would be to increase the tax revenues by making the advocates for the poor give up properties that prevent upscale development of poor neighborhoods."

Father Phil Cahill, a white pastor from St. Joseph's, the Catholic parish in the West End, suggested: "Let's not get paranoid. We should follow the law and assume that we will be safe."

Kitty responded: "The problem is, Father, we don't have time to follow all the building codes in the law. Most of the buildings in the city aren't up to code because for decades only new buildings have been inspected. Even now they are only going to inspect empty housing and housing owned by nonprofit organizations. Does St. Joe's or the rectory have a sprinkler system as required for buildings in which public meetings are held? An electrical system with breakers, not fuses? Nothing we own now is up to code; if it were, we would have sold it to a resident. In the year we need to meet code, this campaign could demolish all the West End's low-income housing before we can buy and rehab it. The irony is that despite the City Council's rhetoric about making downtown housing safer for the poor, few of the real firetraps where the kids have lead poisoning, the furnaces don't work, and the stairwells are rotted through will even be inspected because they are occupied and/or privately owned."

Will addressed the group, saying, "Can we agree that until we have further information, Kitty should employ as many paid and volunteer crews as she can locate to rehab our buildings?" All nodded immediately, and Kitty began a list of contacts to call.

Morita raised her hand and asked: "I need to put my kids to bed in thirty minutes. What's this last item on the agenda about target population?"

THE POOR, THE POORER, AND THE POOREST

Will responded: "Thanks, Morita, for calling us back to the time. Father Phil and Sarah wanted to address the board concerning their unease at the change in the trust's target population over the last few years. Father Phil, Sarah?"

Father Phil recalled: "There have been a lot of changes in the trust in the last few years. And I know that some of them were necessary. We weren't very organized before Kitty assumed the directorship. Seven years ago we had ten houses and three apartment buildings. Most of them were in terrible shape, and we didn't have the money to fix any of them. We were slum landlords, though we didn't make any money. We veterans on the board reluctantly went along with selling the apartment buildings in order to concentrate on single-family home ownership. There are other organizations that concentrate on housing the elderly poor, alcoholics, addicts, and the mentally incompetent who can never be candidates for home ownership. *This* organization should stick with its stated purpose of providing home ownership to the poor. But in the last three years our average cost for houses at purchase rose from $8,500 to $20,000, and our average rehabbing cost rose from $20,000 to nearly $42,000. The trust was begun as a form of Christian outreach to the poorest. But the poorest cannot afford monthly payments of over $400 for mortgage, taxes, and insurance, which is what we have to charge on these houses on twenty-year mortgages at 3 percent. Our ministry must be to the poorest of the poor."

Sarah added: "I know of two families in the West End who want to buy homes in the trust but have been priced out by the increases. Some of our people just cannot afford more than $75–100 per month; their gross family income is $900 per month or less. Many of them make only minimum wage. Most can't get forty hours of work a week. Those who *do* get forty hours still barely bring home $175 per week. These people are the real poor, not people who make $1,200–1,500 per month or more and can pay $400 per month. We want to propose that the Community Land Trust go back to the pricing levels of five years ago and set a limit of $20,000 per house."

Morita waved her hand to speak, but before Will could nod, another resident, Carla Hancock, who rarely spoke, burst into speech: "My brother bought one of those first houses for $16,000. Mine cost me $32,000, twice as much. But mine is a house to be proud of; it ain't falling apart like his. All his got was new windows and doors, the roof patched, and a new sink and toilet. Now his plumbing and electric fell apart, his roof leaks something awful, all the floors sag, and they are afraid to use the toilet for fear of falling into the basement. Lots of poor people can't afford houses like mine. But those first houses was a rip-off, 'cause poor people can't afford to both buy 'em and fix 'em decent. My brother Cass figures he got took again. He's still living in a slum, not a decent house. And he owe forever."

Frank Hart added, "Father, I agree that the price of the houses is an important issue and that we can't let prices get too high. But if we are ever going to help the West End become a strong, stable neighborhood with decent housing, we need to offer housing that continues to be both decent and affordable over the long run. Carla is right. Most of those early owners couldn't afford both the mortgage and the major repairs necessary. If we do the major rehab and reroof, rewire, replumb, brace the floors, replaster where needed, and put in a new furnace and replacement windows, the new owners will have ten to twenty years before they face major repairs. By then their income will have increased, if only by inflation, and the fixed amount of the mortgage will be a smaller part of their income. With really good housing available, those families who are making it are more likely to stay in the neighborhood, to fight to keep it free of drugs and crime, and to care about the schools and the parks. We have to find ways of making communities work, not just hand out leaky lifeboats to drowning people. That way we never get ahead, and they're never saved."

Kitty interjected: "The only way to sell houses that are safe and in decent repair and still keep the price under $20,000 is to increase the amount of subsidy in each house by $10,000–15,000. To do that means either to rehab and sell 40–50 percent fewer houses a year or to raise more money for subsidies."

At that, Reverend Hawkins suggested that the board might want to rethink turning down the restricted funds that Don Brown had raised. "What good does it do to keep the area north of Grant Street free of gentrification if we can only afford to rehab and house a handful of families a year? We could work for seven to ten years just in the area south of Grant."

Kitty responded, "But if developers take over north of Grant, there are thousands of poor people who will be displaced. Where will they go? The city and county have virtually no low-income housing anymore. There are twice as many families with Section 8 vouchers as there are landlords willing to accept them, and the places that do accept them are often dangerous, decrepit, and stuck out in some out-of-the-way suburb with no public transportation. We need to preserve as much of the West End as we can, and not just look to what we can rehab and sell in the next seven years."

Just then the clock struck nine. As the board prepared to adjourn, Sarah suggested that perhaps the trust should commit itself to helping as many of the "least among us" as possible and trust God to make it work. Will announced that the proposal of Sarah and Father Phil would be the first agenda item next month. Each board member should think and pray to prepare for a decision.

Frank, who took turns with Kitty driving to the board meetings, dropped off Morita and Carla at their homes near the trust office and then headed north toward Kitty's home. Once on the highway, he asked how she felt about the discussion on serving the poorest. "It's a real dilemma for me," she replied. "I really do believe there are individual and social obligations to serve those who are in greatest need. But I can't see overlooking the many who could take care of themselves if they just had a little help in the beginning. I could spend all our yearly budget on food and shelter and medical and psychiatric help for Dan, Morita's ex-husband, who is certainly among the poorest. But he's been so damaged by crack that he'll always be dependent. I'm not arguing that he should be ignored. It's just that I can't believe God wants us to ignore the Moritas who are left to raise the kids in order to serve the Dans of the world."

Frank responded: "I agree—if two people have fallen into a hole and I only have enough strength to pull one out, I should pull out the one who is most likely to help me pull the other one out, not the one who is the weakest. We could probably all agree that it would be wrong to focus on the hopelessly damaged, like Dan, and ignore the Moritas and their kids. But remember last year when you pointed out that our selection process for home ownership preferred welfare families over the working poor, because they often had as much or slightly more income but also had Medicaid and income security that the working poor don't? Your concerns then weren't all that different from those raised tonight. And I had to agree with you." Troubled, he added: "Perhaps Sarah is right, and I don't have enough faith in God. If I did, maybe I wouldn't worry about what we do with the poor down the road when south of Grant is full and developers have taken over the northern part of the West End. Or maybe the real issue for me is that I'm not sure I could sustain hope if I worked only with the poor who seem the most hopeless."

Kitty nodded, "I know what you mean. I'm glad we have a month to think about it."

Commentary

The Agenda:
Preference for the Poorest?

The participants in this case would probably disagree as to the specific issues in the case. Perhaps most could agree that racism is one issue here, but the explanations of how the racism is illustrated might be very different. For example, Kitty might point to the proposal to dilute the black resident majority on the board with white members of the fund-raising committee as racist because it would prevent the residents from controlling their own community. Don might see resistance to such a proposal as racist in that persons who would contribute more to the organization were rejected in favor of those who would do less on the basis of race. Many people might see no evidence of racism in this because no person or group seems motivated by hatred based on race.

Some social analysts have insisted that the very character of racism has changed in US society. They argue that racial injustice is no longer best understood in terms of racist intent but of consequences and that the inequality of persons of color in US society is maintained no longer by segregation laws but by impersonal economic structures and practices that have been responsible for the formation of an underclass of persons of color. Structural aspects of postmodern capitalism, especially a permanent surplus of labor and low rates of economic growth, they argue further, obstruct efforts to eradicate or escape from that poverty-stricken underclass. Thus an implicit question is whether any of the proposed actions in this case are racist, or whether the black poverty in the case merely reflects the effects of past racism in US society. This question forms one aspect of the central question that has already been framed by the board in terms of Christian spirituality and ethics: Who are the poor?

LOVING GOD WHO LOVES THE POOR

The basic obligation of Christians, according to Jesus, is to love God "with all your heart, and with all your soul, and with all your mind," and to "love your neighbor as yourself" (Mt 22:37–39). To love God is to commit ourselves to the fulfillment of God's intentions for creation, in which love of neighbor is central. It was Yahweh's action of rescuing the Hebrews from slavery in Egypt that revealed the nature of Yahweh's love. In the same way Jesus later taught that love of neighbor is demonstrated through meeting the needs of our neighbor, which thus gives a priority to the needy neighbor. To come to the aid of the needy takes precedence over formal worship. Jesus declared the good neighbor to be the Samaritan who stopped to aid the robbery victim. The priest and the Levite had passed by without helping because they were unwilling to risk the ritual uncleanness that would temporarily bar them from Temple worship.

Many scripture scholars note that Jesus' warning that it is easier for a camel to pass through the eye of a needle than for the rich to enter the realm of God may not have referred to the eye of a sewing needle but to the pedestrian gate of a city, which was also called the eye of a needle. The implication is clear. It would be difficult for a camel to enter the pedestrian gate. It might have to kneel, and it could not be done at all if the camel were carrying a full load on its sides. But it was certainly possible. The issue is not the size of the camel but the attitude of the camel and how much unnecessary burden the camel carries. The implication, then, is that a radical conversion to a humble, unencumbered condition is necessary if the rich are to enter the realm of God. Part of that conversion involves aiding the needy. Members of the Community Land Trust board agree that they, and all Christians, are called to a preferential option for the poor. That preference for the poor does not exclude love of other persons who are not poor, but it does give priority to the needs of the poor precisely because of their need.

The board is called to reflect on what a preferential option for the poor means in terms of both the goals and the strategies to be pursued. Following their goal of "as many families as possible in home ownership," Don and the fund-raising committee were willing to make compromises to restrict housing development to a limited section of the downtown West End. Their goal is worthy, but it assumes an understanding of poverty solely in material terms. Such thinking fails to understand that these people lack not only decent housing but the ability to exercise responsibility for their community. They need better homes, and they need to build and direct their own community. Living in poverty over time robs individuals and communities of the ability to make choices, to control their own lives and communities. Unless poverty is actively resisted by communities, it makes people powerless and dependent. Inevitably, powerlessness and dependence wear away feelings of dignity and self-worth as well as the ability to feel beloved by God and other persons. Without these, communal bonds weaken and break. Involuntary poverty is sinful and affronts God our Creator/Parent because it kills and maims bodies and souls, individuals and communities.

The requirement that the black residents form the majority of the board was undoubtedly chosen as part of a larger attempt to restore to individual poor black residents their ability to make decisions and control their lives and community. At the board meeting the residents seem for the most part passive. Though they constitute a majority of the board, only two speak. No resident is identified as chair of a committee. On the one hand, if this level of contribution to meetings is typical of the residents on the board, it is not surprising that Don and his committee may think they have more to offer the Community Land Trust board. On the other hand, if the ravages of poverty are to be overcome, there must be a process in which the residents learn to discern and articulate the interests and aspirations of their community and then go on to achieve them. That process has the potential for providing the needed individual dignity and communal autonomy to reassert control over their lives and community.

JUSTICE AND CHARITY

Although the fund-raising committee probably does not see itself this way, its goal seems to be more akin to traditional notions of charity than to social justice as understood by many Christian churches today. One of the most obvious differences between justice and charity is how power is distributed. Justice distributes power so that the weak become stronger and better able to care for themselves. Charity meets people's immediate needs in ways that keep them dependent. Members of the fund-raising committee are well-intentioned, and they are attempting to alleviate the poverty of their black neighbors by providing opportunities for home ownership. They undoubtedly see their own relationship to the black residents who benefit from the Community Land Trust as based in love. But real love is effective. In this case, effectiveness includes empowerment of the residents. The fund-raising committee could have accompanied its bid for board membership with a proposal to expand the number of residents on the board to preserve the black majority, or with some alternative aimed at preserving residents' responsibility. The effects of the proposed deal—$200,000 for a Community Land Trust retreat from north of Grant Street—work against empowerment by dividing the existing West End community, benefiting the trust through the sacrifice of that part of the community north of Grant Street.

HONESTY IN POLITICS

The City Council decision to inspect residential property in the greater downtown area, if it is followed up and thus forces owners to fix unsafe buildings or forfeit them, is an ambitious undertaking with the potential to improve the living standards of many poor residents. But a policy is only as good as its procedures. The procedures guiding implementation of this new policy are not clear. As Jim Meadows says, the new policy could force the trust to speed up the process between purchase and rehab. This would mean the trust and other low-income organizations would have fewer empty, rotting buildings to become eyesores or havens for drug dealers and gang violence, an effect of the inspection policy that would greatly benefit the West End. Alternatively, the new policy could also be implemented in ways that demolish whole neighborhoods and encourage rebuilding of upscale rather than low-income housing. Whatever procedures are implemented must, in order to be just, be imposed upon all groups equally. If Kitty is right that the inspection will only include vacant buildings and those owned by nonprofit organizations, the inspection would be discriminatory and would undermine its declared intent to protect the poor.

The interest of the City Council in expanding the tax rolls by bringing more middle-class people downtown is understandable. Since the late 1960s the shift of the middle class to the suburbs, the move of many industrial plants to developing nations, and the relocation of many corporate headquarters to smaller cities or to suburbs of large cities have severely shrunk the tax base of many cities. The decaying infrastructure of many large US cities—their bridges, sewers, subways, streets, and harbors—also begin to demand increasingly large infusions of capital.

Persistent unemployment, gentrification trends, and federal cuts in welfare and food stamps have increased the need for low-income housing at precisely the same time that cities are hard pressed to continue basic services such as fire, police, street repair, and schools. The rise in crime in the 1980s and 1990s and the consequent rise in the expenses of the criminal justice system, added to the expanded medical costs of both the AIDS epidemic and illegal drug use, had brought many large cities to the breaking point years before 9/11 ratcheted up the costs of providing security. During the 1990s the cost of new housing began to rise precipitously, as did land across the United States, thus pricing market-rate housing out of the reach of much of the working poor. This trend has accelerated in many cities since 2000.

The federal government has also contributed directly to the housing crisis faced by the poor. Under the Reagan administration the low-income housing projects in the federal Department of Housing and Urban Development's planning and implementation pipeline dropped from just under five hundred in 1980 to fewer than seventy-five in 1988. Those few projects that were implemented under the Bush administration were disproportionately restricted to the elderly and the disabled.

Few cities are able to take on the increased burden of funding sufficient low-income housing to accommodate those in need. Many cities see luring the middle class back into the city as the only path to a tax base sufficient to allow the city to continue to provide hospitals, police and fire services, street repair, and garbage service. Housing for the poor cannot be dealt with in isolation from these other issues. Protecting the integral existence of poor communities so that empowerment can take place within those communities entails an ongoing tension with the push for gentrification. The City Council may be legitimately torn between the two; nevertheless, inspection procedures should be just and not unduly favor one group.

The trust might do well to reject the paranoia Father Phil warned against and join with other concerned organizations in publicly negotiating with the City Council for reasonable renovation schedules for inspected buildings below code. Kitty and members of the board might use their media contacts to encourage TV and newspapers to investigate dangerous privately owned housing in order to generate support for expanding the inspection program. A local TV news report filming broken stairways and furnaces, peeling lead-based paint, and grill-less windows in buildings exempted from inspection could be very powerful. Such actions should be understood not just as savvy politics but as part of an effective strategy for implementing a preferential option for the poor.

One of the issues in the inspection that does arise in the board discussion is the effect of the inspection on homelessness. Organizations such as the Community Land Trust face a dual problem—the overall lack of new low-income housing, which was the major cause of the rise of homelessness in the 1980s and 1990s, and the destruction of low-income, often minority communities in old center cities. Inner-city poor have been dispersed for decades to government housing spread around large metropolitan areas. While many of the intentions behind this dispersal were benign, its effects were not. The dispersion has produced the disintegration of communities and neighborhoods, followed by the failure of many new recipient communities to welcome or include the new residents from the clearly demarcated "projects." The poor in the projects become excluded from political decision-making. Their former leaders, who no longer represent a coherent community, are silenced.

A vigorous inspection program would improve the quality of available low-income housing, especially if it includes occupied, privately owned units. But the more effective an inspection program is in raising the quality of housing, the more likely it is to lower the number of available units of low-income housing. Some owners will be either financially unable or unwilling to invest in the necessary repairs and will abandon the buildings. Other owners, forced to invest in their property, will evict low-income tenants before the rehab process and upon completion will rent to middle-class tenants from whom they can recover their investment. Not all of the nonprofit organizations will be able to renovate all their units in a timely manner, and some units will be demolished. Without new low-income units, homelessness will increase. Here, too, it is necessary to decide which poor to aid: those whose safety and comfort will increase due to an inspection policy, or those who will be forced into homelessness by an inspection policy.

WHICH NEIGHBOR?

Housing is a complex avenue into the contemporary phenomenon of poverty, in part because low-income housing is dependent upon issues such as employment and wage levels. Under full employment and what Catholic social teaching has called a just wage (a wage that supports a worker, a spouse, and children and allows for saving toward property ownership), homelessness would cease to be a major social problem. But modern society has not enjoyed, and does not soon expect to again enjoy, full employment. And many workers do not earn a just wage.

Low-income housing presents some interesting situations for examining the consequences of various interpretations of the preferential option for the poor. Father Phil and Sarah interpret the preferential option to mean that the poor are favored over the rich, and the most poor over the least poor.

Since the gospels do not pass down to us any discourse by Jesus regarding this question, we must look to the activities of Jesus himself. On the one hand, Jesus did seek out the poorest, though these were not always the most materially poor. If we ask what groups Jesus championed in his ministry, it would be accurate to answer that he championed the cause of the most excluded, the most afflicted, the most discriminated against. The poor, the crippled, the sick, the dying, women and children, and even the despised prostitutes and tax collectors all received special treatment from Jesus.

On the other hand, it would also be accurate to say that it was not Jesus who sought out these poorest of Israel, but they who sought him, and he who responded to them. The geography of Jesus' wandering ministry and his directions to the disciples he sent out in his name make clear that he directed his ministry at the settlements of the Jewish inhabitants, farmers and fishermen, not at the wealthy trading communities of the Gentiles (Mt 10:5–6). The gospels tell us again and again that within the Jewish communities the sick and the children were "brought to him" and that tax collectors, prostitutes, and those begging favors sought him out.

Perhaps the speech of Jesus that most directly speaks to this issue of preference for the poorest is the story of judgment in Matthew 25. Jesus concludes that the Lord will say to the righteous, "Come, you that are blessed by my Father, inherit the kingdom prepared for you from the foundation of the world; for I was hungry and you gave me food, I was thirsty and you gave me something to drink, I was a stranger and you welcomed me, I was naked and you gave me clothing, I was sick and you took care of me, I was in prison and you visited me" (Mt 25:34–36). And when they asked when they did these things, the Lord will say, "Just as you did it to one of the least of these who are members of my family, you did it to me" (Mt 25:40). All these different needy make up the group of the "least" of the Lord's family; there is no attempt to rank caring for the sick compared to giving a drink to the thirsty, and no attempt to rank the different degrees of sickness. In Jesus' own ministry he exorcised demons, cured the sick, defended children; in short, he responded to a variety of needs.

The members of the Community Land Trust have concentrated their energies on providing housing, and, in fact, providing home ownership. In doing that they have already determined that they will not be working with the most needy individuals within the community of the poor, for the most needy are not ready for the level of responsibility that home owner-ship demands.

The most needy are those who are the furthest away from Jesus' model of fully human persons able to accept the costs demanded of disciples to extend themselves in unconditional love of neighbor. The most needy are those who no longer have hope for salvation, who have accepted the world's judgment that they are not worthy of the love of God. Support for the most needy must be offered in small doses, demanding smaller efforts, lest the poorest become discouraged at their failures and their despair is reinforced.

This is not to say that Father Phil and Sarah do not have a point in call-ing attention to the rising costs of Community Land Trust homes. If home-ownership programs are not appropriate for many of the most poor, per-haps the trust should more carefully attempt to aid the poorest among those capable of home ownership. On the one hand, it would be a mistake to use the resources of the trust to aid those who would be able to effect the same step into home ownership by themselves, though on less favorable terms. On the other hand, the finances of the poor are very fragile. Luck has much to do with the ability of poor families to keep up mortgage payments in programs like the Community Land Trust: sickness and accident, burglary or vandalism, car breakdown, fire, and many other misfortunes can send poor families into bankruptcy. They usually do not have insurance to pro-tect them from the financial effects of misfortune. For this reason it may not always be helpful to stress differences of $300 a month between families. Factors such as the size of the family, the health of the family, and even the strength of the family's support network can all make the "richer" family the truly poorer one. Perhaps a compromise could be worked out, in which the trust would continue to reach out to its present family pool but incor-porate some families who look like good prospects for home ownership despite their lesser incomes. The cost of homes for such families could be partially subsidized by the trust on a sliding scale.

Using Community Land Trust funds to subsidize some of the rehab costs for some of the poorer families is better than the trust's earlier policy of doing less than total renovation. The already precarious financial situation of the poor, their lack of savings, and their lack of insurance make the risk of buying a house that may soon need major repairs too high. What is the effect on a new home owner of discovering that his or her house needs a new furnace or a new roof? What if replacing the windows is necessary in order to afford to heat the house? One effect is material: because the down payment used every penny of savings, the repair cannot be done. Meanwhile, a faulty furnace endangers the lives of the family, as well as the value of the house. Another effect is more spiritual. Persons whose lives are spent in poverty in minority communities that are deteriorating and spilling over with crime and pain have a difficult time sustaining hope. A common defense in the lives of the poor after a certain amount of suffering is to refuse to hope lest repeated disappointment completely undermine their ability to cope. To raise the hopes of the poor only to dash them due to inadequate renovation is cruel. It is to place stumbling blocks in front of the poor.

"If any of you put a stumbling block before one of these little ones who believe in me, it would be better for you if a great millstone were fastened about your neck and you were drowned in the depth of the sea. Woe to the world because of stumbling blocks! Occasions for stumbling are bound to come, but woe to the one by whom the stumbling block comes!" (Mt 18:6–7)

The most likely objection to a compromise that uses Trust funds to subsidize costs for lower-income families is that it would lower the number of families who could be helped into decent, affordable home ownership. Because Kitty as executive director is involved in the lives of residents and their communities, she could undoubtedly tell horror stories about the lives of persons on her waiting list for homes: mothers bringing new babies home from the hospital in winter to buildings with no heat, children whose levels of blood lead are dangerously high from eating flaking lead-based paint from the walls, and handicapped elderly people negotiating rotted stairs without handrails. How does the benefit of including some lower-income poor in the home-ownership pool weigh against the disadvantage of delaying the move to safe, affordable homes for families like these?

CONCLUSION

Perhaps the tension on the board could best be dealt with through a communal retreat experience. The board might invite the members of various committees that report to the board, as well. The fact that the board members seem to have a self-consciously Christian identification and share a theological tradition, even though there may be differences of interpretation, gives them a decided advantage over many other groups that must engage in translating values and norms from one religious or moral system into another. Since Will Jennings, Don Brown, Phil Cahill, and Sarah

Hawkins are connected with churches, the board should have many resources for finding an outsider trained in leading groups in reflection on the implications of Christian faith for specific pastoral praxis.

A retreat could not only help ground greater understanding of, and respect for, the perspectives of others, but it could also remind the board members that love and justice and the identity of the poor in the gospel must always be interpreted. Their meanings will be different in different social locations in different historical periods, and they will appear different to different individuals. We have no way of knowing whether the true interpretation (God's) corresponds to one particular human interpretation, to no human interpretation, or somehow incorporates and/or transcends all of them. There are no easy choices in this case, no clean answers. Prayer and reflection by Christians in this case should help create a spirit of humility and openness that facilitates action on behalf of justice. Recognition that each of our perspectives is limited should make it easier for the nonresidents on the board to support a process that aims at the residents not only chairing the board and making up the majority of its members, but also taking full responsibility for the future of their larger community. As Christians who lead by serving, the role of the nonresidents should be a self-consciously temporary one, aimed at making themselves superfluous as quickly as possible.

ADDITIONAL RESOURCES

Cone, James H. *Martin and Malcolm and America: A Dream or a Nightmare?* Maryknoll, NY: Orbis Books 1991.

Fallis, George, and Alex Murray, eds. *Housing the Homeless and the Poor: New Partnerships among the Private, Public, and Third Sectors.* Toronto: Univ. of Toronto Press, 1990.

Goetz, Edward Glenn. *Clearing the Way: Deconcentrating the Poor in America.* Washington, DC: Urban Institute Press, 2003.

Gudorf, Christine E. *Victimization: Examining Christian Complicity.* Philadelphia: Trinity Press International, 1992.

Mar, Peter-Raoul, Linda Rennie Forcey, and Robert F. Hunter, eds. *Yearning to Breathe Free: Liberation Theologies in the U.S.* Maryknoll, NY: Orbis Books, 1990.

Retsinas, Nicholas P., and Eric S. Belsky, eds. *Low Income Homeownership: Examining the Unexamined Goal.* Cambridge, MA: Joint Center for Housing Studies; Washington, D.C.: Brookings Institution Press, 2002.

Williams, Rhonda Y. *The Politics of Public Housing: Black Women's Struggles against Urban Inequality.* New York: Oxford Univ. Press, 2004.

PART IV

THE ENVIRONMENT

Case

Oil and the Caribou People

Ron Blanchard had eagerly accepted the invitation from Bill Sanders. As head of social ministries at church headquarters, Bill had invited Ron to represent the church and society committee of their denomination at the clan gathering of the Gwich'in people during mid-June in northeastern Alaska. Ron had never been above the Arctic Circle in mid-summer. The prospect of visiting such a remote place and learning more about Native American culture seemed like high adventure and something good for his social-studies teaching at Western High School in Seattle.

Now that the trip was over, he had to produce a report on the gathering for the church and society committee. Bill Sanders had also asked for Ron's recommendation on proposed oil drilling in the Arctic National Wildlife Refuge (ANWR) on the north slope of Alaska's Brooks Range adjacent to the Gwich'in reservation. Bill indicated that sixteen other religious organizations and thirty-two Native American groups had already endorsed Gwich'in opposition to the drilling. The Gwich'in, it seemed were interested in gathering further support and so had invited Bill to send a representative.

The Gwich'in are Athabascan people with a population in the range of five to seven thousand. They live primarily in northeastern Alaska and northwestern Canada. Legend and archeological evidence support a long human presence on the lands now inhabited by the Gwich'in. Traditionally, the Gwich'in roamed the boreal forests of the region as hunter-gatherers in bands of six to eight families. They lived a harsh life in an unforgiving land with cool summers and long, frigid winters when starvation was an ever-present danger.

Over the last century, this rigorous way of life has radically changed by a regrouping in larger social units in small villages. The arrival of the

This case was prepared by Robert L. Stivers. Copyright © The Case Study Institute. The names of all persons and institutions have been disguised to protect the privacy of those involved.

Episcopalian missionaries, the building of schools, and the acceptance of modern technology, in particular the rifle and snowmobile, hastened these changes. Ron learned that Gwich'in opposition to oil exploration stems from the threat they perceive to their main source of subsistence, the Porcupine Caribou Herd, and to the culture and spirituality they have developed in relation to the herd. The Porcupine Herd, with approximately 130,000 animals, is one of the largest herds of caribou in the world. It winters south of the Brooks Range on Gwich'in lands. In spring a great migration takes place. First the females and then the males trek through the passes of the range onto the north slope, where calving occurs almost immediately, reaching its peak in early June.

The herd migrates to the north slope to take advantage of the rich tundra vegetation in the brief but fertile Arctic summer; to avoid its natural predators, who seldom venture onto the slope; and to gain respite from the hordes of mosquitoes in the winds off the Arctic Ocean. Beginning in late summer the herd makes its way once again south of the range and disperses across Gwich'in lands to endure the winter.

For centuries the herd has been the primary source of food for the Gwich'in's subsistence economy. The Gwich'in have harvested animals from the herd in substantial numbers and developed a culture closely bound to the herd and its migration patterns. The herd continues to do well in this habitat. The Gwich'in, in turn, have survived as a people, though not without considerable hardship.

To prepare himself for the trip, Ron had read scientific reports on the potential effects of petroleum development in ANWR and an anthropological study that described the ancient ways of the Gwich'in. The scientific reports on the Porcupine Caribou Herd were inconclusive, Ron thought. Its numbers had declined in recent years due to natural causes, not oil production. Thirty years of oil drilling at Prudhoe Bay had apparently done no harm to the smaller Central Arctic Herd, whose range included the production facilities. In fact, the herd's numbers had increased in recent years for reasons that eluded scientists. Nevertheless, scientists were concerned. The parts of ANWR slated for drilling, the so-called 1002 lands, were among the best feeding grounds for the caribou. Would the caribou of the Porcupine Herd seek other, less nutritious feeding grounds more populated with predators? One thing the reports made clear was that reproductive success depends on summer weight increase and avoidance of predators. The scientists urged caution.

From the anthropological study Ron learned about the traditional nomadic way of life of the Gwich'in, their main food sources, and their relation to the caribou. He understood intellectually their concern for the loss of both their primary food source and their traditional culture. He was not prepared by his study, however, for the degree to which their traditional culture already seemed to be in jeopardy, something he learned after arrival at the clan gathering. He was not sure he understood enough about these people, the technology of oil, or the ecology of the north slope to make a recommendation on drilling in ANWR. To make any recommendation might well be an exercise in disinformation, harmful to meeting the nation's energy needs, or worse, harmful to these people who had so kindly hosted him for five days.

Throughout his stay during the clan days, Gwich'in tribal elders had been eager to recount the old days and their experiences. Barbara Frank, whose age was difficult to judge, but who looked to be in her seventies, told about the old days and of summer movements in small family groupings. The warm days added nuts, berries, and fruit to their steady diet of moose and small animals. In winter she remembered a harsh life in crude shelters and a diet of caribou and whatever other animals trapping produced. She expressed in deeply spiritual terms the close relationship of her people to the caribou. Although she spoke with nostalgia, she never once urged that the modern comforts of the village be abandoned for a return to the wilderness.

Another elder, John Christian, remembered the coming of the missionaries and the schools they established. He related how his parents and grandparents were attracted to the village that grew up around the church and school. They were fascinated by the new technologies that added a margin to subsistence in the Arctic and by the amusements that brought variety and diversity. His family was subsequently baptized. They abandoned their given names for Christian names and assumed the superiority of the new and the inferiority of the old.

Alongside these private conversations were daily public gatherings with starting times that baffled Ron. It was confusing to have no schedule, no appointed time to begin. Things just happened. The sessions began when the spirit moved and ended when there were no more speakers. Other more experienced visitors dismissed his confusion as "Gwich'in time." There was no set agenda. An elder kept order and transferred to each speaker the large decorative staff that conferred the right to address the assembly.

The general topic for the first public gathering was oil exploration in ANWR. Moses Peters, an important tribal elder, spoke in English and presented his assessment of the situation. He reviewed existing production procedures at Prudhoe Bay and the shipment of oil through the Alaska pipeline. He claimed that operations at Prudhoe Bay had adversely affected the smaller Central Arctic Caribou Herd that summered in the vicinity. He acknowledged the increase in the size of the herd but dismissed it as normal fluctuation. The herd, he asserted, was reluctant to cross the pipeline and did not graze in the vicinity of the wells.

Moses went on to say that the oil companies expect their next big find will be in ANWR. He feared that the one hundred miles of pipeline, four hundred miles of roads, the gravel pits, the production facilities, and the air strips would seriously disturb the migration routes of the Porcupine Herd at a crucial time in its annual cycle. "Caribou survival," he insisted, "depends on being born in the right place at the right time, and all of the caribou depend upon these summer months on the north slope to rest and restore food reserves. It is this period of predator-free resting and feeding that prepares the caribou to reproduce and to survive the winter. I know the oil companies have improved their drilling techniques, but I am still worried."

Moses handed the staff to his daughter, Mary, who added: "Oil waste and the burn-off of natural gas would contaminate the tundra. The caribou would not be able to eat." She concluded with alarm: "We will starve again, as it happened before, but this time it will be worse."

Mary returned the staff to her father, who concluded by saying that they needed to continue to press for the permanent protection of ANWR. "The refusal of the US Congress over the past few years to pass energy legislation that includes developing ANWR for oil is not enough. The oil companies are keeping the pressure up. They are arguing that terrorism and dependency on foreign sources of oil, especially in the unstable Persian Gulf, necessitate opening ANWR. Now that the price of oil has increased, as supply dwindles in coming years, gas-hungry Americans will make known their demands for new sources of supply. Environmentally conscious Senators may not be able to withstand all this pressure, and even if they do, the increased Republican majority in the Senate may be able to pass legislation without them. We must get permanent protection now. The caribou is our main source of life, our very survival. We can't live without the caribou. All our traditional skills, our whole way of life, will be lost if there are no caribou."

Ron was impressed by the sincerity of these appeals and the efforts of the Gwich'in to secure reliable scientific evidence. He was troubled, however, by some of their conclusions. He also recalled his conversation with Glen Stone, a friend who worked as an engineer at Northern Oil. They had discussed the issues prior to Ron's departure for Alaska. Glen had talked about his own involvement on the north slope at Prudhoe Bay. He painted a rosy picture of the benefits of oil production to all Alaskans. "Oil money," he said, "builds schools, roads, and other public works projects. It keeps personal taxes low and enables the government to pay each resident a yearly dividend. The Native Americans benefit too, perhaps most of all."

Glen went on: "Production at Prudhoe will not continue forever. We need ANWR to maximize our investment in the pipeline and to keep those benefits rolling to Alaskans. Northern Oil geologists say they can technically recover sixteen billion barrels of oil. The US Geological Survey, basing its numbers on what is economically recoverable, has much lower, but still considerable, estimates. There is a lot of oil there, enough for nearly a year's worth of US consumption. Why lock up such a valuable resource? As for ecological concerns of the environmentalists and Gwich'in, I think they are wrong about the effects at Prudhoe. The Central Arctic Herd is in fine shape. Modern construction and containment techniques minimize negative environmental impacts. Believe me, we take great precautions. The Gwich'in have little to worry about."

Glen continued by pressing one of his favorite themes, the coming energy crisis. "Oil, gas, and eventually even coal will be so expensive in the future that we will have to switch to alternatives. Appropriate alternatives are not in place and will require considerable development. In the meantime, we will need all the fossil fuels we can get our hands on. Otherwise, production of goods and services will decline and unemployment increase. It won't take long under those circumstance to unlock ANWR. We can be patient; it's just a matter of time."

Glen ended the discussion by pointing out that other native groups in Alaska, in particular the Inupiat on the north slope, have far fewer problems with exploration than do the Gwich'in. He wondered aloud why the Gwich'in were so troubled but offered no opinion since he had not been in contact with them. Ron wondered too, especially about Glen's evaluation of the scientific evidence at Prudhoe and his claim that oil revenues had benefited groups such as the Gwich'in.

As the days of talk continued, Ron thought he detected something deeper at work. Oil exploration seemed to be symbolic of the invasion of modern technology and the threat it presented to traditional Gwich'in culture. It was an obvious enemy: alien, capitalist, consumer-oriented, and potentially destructive to the environment. What really seemed at issue was Gwich'in identity.

The little that was said about oil exploration after the first day seemed to support this conclusion. Instead, the question of identity dominated public sessions. Speaker after speaker decried the erosion of Gwich'in culture. Some in prophetic voice condemned the erosion outright. Others reflected their own personal struggle to preserve the best of the traditional culture while adopting chunks of modern life.

The speakers focused their concern on language. Mary Peters reported through a translator that in some villages only 20 percent of the children understand the Gwich'in language. She was troubled that the local schools taught English as the primary language and, worse, that some schools ignored native language altogether. For the most part she herself did not speak in English, believing that speech in her native tongue was a mark of integrity.

As he thought about it later, Ron certainly agreed that language was crucial. But the matter seemed to run still deeper. He reflected on the one school in the village that was hosting the clan gathering. It was by far the largest, best-equipped, and most modern structure in the village. Built by the state of Alaska with money from oil royalties, its facilities were state of the art. Villagers could not avoid making comparisons between it and their own humble dwellings.

Even Ron, a total stranger, made the comparison, although he had not taken the time during the meeting to explore the implications. As he thought about it later, it seemed odd that Gwich'in from other villages and non-Gwich'in like himself were not housed in the school but were put up in make-shift tents. He thought about his own backpacking tent and the mosquitoes that were so big villagers were said to build bird houses for them. How much easier it would have been to lay his pad on the floor of the school, away from the swarms of mosquitoes and in easy reach of flush toilets and showers. How much easier indeed! He too could understand the attractions of modern technology.

Ron's reflections returned to the village itself and the things he had observed while hanging out and wandering around. Snowmobiles, while out of use for the summer, were everywhere in storage. Satellite dishes for television reception were common. The table in the laundromat was covered with glamour magazines. The teenagers roamed the village in groups without apparent direction, much like teenagers roam malls throughout North America. Joy riding and kicking up dust on big-tired, four-wheeled vehicles was a favorite pastime.

Perhaps the most obvious symbol of all this was the five-thousand-foot gravel runway that ran like a lance through the center of the village. As the place where visitors, fuel, mail, and supplies entered, it was the symbolic center of town, he reflected.

Although wary of his untrained eye, Ron concluded that the matter of oil exploration on the north slope was also a matter of the invasion of an alien culture and ideology. Yes, saving the caribou herd was important. Yes, teaching the kids the language was also important. But the deeper questions in these deliberations seemed to be, How can caribou and language survive the onslaught of modern technology and thought? How can a traditional people maintain its identity when much that is attractive to them comes from a more powerful and alien culture and seems to make life easier and more interesting? The problem for the Gwich'in was not just the oil on the north slope. It was also the school, the runway, the motorized vehicles, the glamour magazines, and maybe even the churches.

The Gwich'in gave the last days of their gathering to stories of flight and return. A procession of witnesses including Mary Peters testified to the horrors of migration to the outside. Lost identity, alcoholism, drug addiction, a final bottoming out, and then a return to roots were common experiences. For each witness, Ron wondered, how many were lost in the bars of Fairbanks?

Ron had been impressed with the integrity of those who testified. They were no longer innocent about modern culture. They seemed to have returned much stronger for their trials and with a healthy respect for their traditions, the land, and the ambiguities of their situation. Perhaps these survivors and their children were the hope for a future that would be both easier and more satisfying. Maybe a new and stronger identity was being forged right before his eyes. He was moved to tears by Mary Peters's concluding remarks, this time in English:

"It is very clear to me that it is an important and special thing to be Gwich'in. Being Gwich'in means being able to understand and live with this world in a very special way. It means living with the land, with the animals, with the birds and the fish as though they were your sisters and brothers. It means saying the land is an old friend and an old friend your father knew, your grandmother knew, indeed your people have always known. . . . We see our land as much, much more than the white man sees it. To our people, our land really is our life."

Ron's attention turned to the present and his report and recommendations to the church and society committee. Should he merely report what he had seen and write in pious, uncritical generalizations? Despite his ignorance as an outsider, should he try to state his misgivings about what is happening to this alien but very rich culture? Should he accept Glen's optimistic assurances about environmental impacts and the benefits or mention the Fairbanks taxi driver who condescendingly observed that the controversy over ANWR was so much Indian smoke and mirrors to exact higher royalties from the oil companies? Should he recommend that the church support further oil exploration on the north slope or take up the cause of the Gwich'in, feeling as he did that more was going on with these people than the dispute over exploration? And how should he factor in his own strongly held attitudes about social justice for traditional peoples and his conviction that Americans were consuming far too much energy in the first place?

Commentary

Oil and the Caribou People

Under similar conditions fifty years ago North Americans would have ignored this case. Led by oil companies and backed by federal, state, and local governments, they would have moved in to tap the resource with little hesitation. They might even have done to the caribou herd and the Gwich'in what they did to the buffalo and the Plains Indians. The Gwich'in would have been silent, and observers such as Ron would have noted little out of the ordinary, much less questioned their powers of discernment.

Today corporations and government are often more sensitive, a new breed of environmentalist is crying for the preservation of species and ecosystems, the Gwich'in are speaking out, and observers are questioning their own assumptions. Oil demand remains high, however, and with the depletion of reserves this demand may have the last word.

AN ETHIC OF INTEGRITY

To understand this case, a new appreciation of an old virtue, integrity, is helpful. The word *integrity* comes from the Latin *tango*, meaning "to touch." The past participle of *tango* is *tactus*. Add the preposition *in*, and the English word *intact* emerges. Further consideration yields other relevant related words such as *integration* and *integer*.

The Christian tradition speaks of the immanence of God, of the God who is revealed in Jesus Christ and continues to relate to the world through the Spirit. In an ethic of integrity, God is the power of integrity that creates and sustains in three distinct but related dimensions of existence: (1) personal integrity, (2) social integrity, and (3) nature's integrity. Jesus Christ is the embodiment of God's power of integrity and points to the experience of inner wholeness or integration that is God's primary work with humans.

Personal integrity, the first dimension, involves an inner harmony that is the foundation and source of inspiration for an outer harmony that seeks a consistency between act and intention. God's integrating power of love creates internal harmony in the self when the self is receptive. This internal harmony also creates the spirit and will to respond with love and justice.

The relationship of God and the self that produces internal harmony is called faith. It empowers and frees the self to act in accordance with intentions.

For Christians, intentionality is informed by norms derived from the Bible, the traditions of the church, and the personal experience of the Spirit. Sin is the power of disintegration that blocks integrity. Sin results from the refusal of the self, others, or the community to receive the power of integrity and is experienced as something done to a person or something the person does willfully. The continuing power of sin prevents the full realization of integrity. The presence of God in the midst of sin provides the resources for partial integrations and the assurance that the full realization of integrity is God's final aim. Integrity is dynamic, something that is partially realized, lost, to be hoped for, and received again.

Personal integrity is part of Mary Peters's reluctance to speak English in the public gatherings. She apparently sees speaking in her native tongue as an important element in the reinvigoration of Gwich'in culture and wants to match her words and deeds.

Ron Blanchard's personal integrity is also an issue in this case. Given his limitations as an observer, how is he to report his experience and make recommendations so that his intentions for the well-being of the Gwich'in, his own society, and the Porcupine Caribou Herd are realized?

Finally, personal integrity is a matter for everyone. In this case it involves knowledge of the issues, accurate understanding of the history of Native Americans, and sensitivity to finding one's way in a different culture.

Social integrity, the second dimension, is the harmony of act and intention in a community. Communities have integrity when peace and justice are foundational ethical concerns. While communities have fewer resources than individuals for receiving and acting on the power of God's integrity, peace and justice are deep wellsprings. To the Greeks, justice was the harmony of a well-ordered community where equals were treated equally, unequals unequally. For the Hebrews, *shalom* and righteousness resulted from keeping the covenantal relation with God and following the guidelines of the law. They included a special concern for the poor. For both Greeks and Hebrews, peace and justice fed on each other and together nourished social integrity.

Christians melded Greek and Hebrew traditions, emphasizing basic equality in Christ and seeing in the person of Jesus the model and the power for both peace and justice. These understandings of peace and justice have developed further in Western traditions with the norms of equality and freedom. Persons should be treated equally and left free unless some ethically justifiable consideration justifies a departure from equality or freedom. Such departures, when adequately justified, are called equity.

From the seventeenth and eighteenth centuries came the notion of rights as a further development of the norm of justice. Rights are a human way of giving greater specificity to equality and freedom. One of the best examples

is the Bill of Rights found in the US Constitution. At first only a few enjoyed rights. As time went on, rights were extended to ever more groups,
for example, minority groups and women. Today some would extend the
concept of rights to animals and plants. So, for example, animals have a
right to be treated with care and the right to have a clean habitat. In the
thinking of those who maintain that animals have rights, the caribou in the
case have a right to their feeding grounds in ANWR.

While peace and justice are the spiritual and ethical foundation of social
integrity, they presuppose the provision of sufficient consumption. The equal
sharing of poverty can be as disintegrating as war and injustice. The definition of basic sufficiency is notoriously difficult, of course. Clear in the extremes of absence and excess but vague at the margins, the concept of sufficiency is useful for setting floors to poverty and discriminating about levels
of consumption. As the commentary on the case "Rigor and Responsibility" makes clear, the norm of sufficiency establishes a floor below which a
just society does not let its members fall. On the up side, it calls into question nonsustainable consumption and efforts to justify environmentally
destructive consumption. Sufficiency applies to plants and animals as well.
They too need what is necessary to sustain their evolutionary trajectory.

Basic also to peace and justice are elements of a common culture. No
society can long remain integrated without some minimum of shared understandings, symbols, values, and traditions. A culture can become so frag-
mented by invasion from without or conflict within as to lose its identity.

A consideration of social integrity is central to this case. From the side of
the Gwich'in, the integrity of their culture appears to be in jeopardy. Their
way of life depends on the land and their subsistence on the Porcupine
Caribou Herd, which needs its special summer habitat in order to flourish.
Their identity as a people depends on the maintenance of their language
and respect for their traditions. Sensitivity to their situation calls for an
understanding of the difficult changes they are facing, changes from the
outside that may be too rapid for them to preserve that basic minimum of
common culture.

From the side of the wider North American society, the Gwich'in and
other native peoples deserve respect. In Christian perspective, this respect
stems from the love of neighbor that stands at the center of the tradition
and the norm of justice. There is also a need to address the dependency of
industrial societies on the consumption of copious amounts of energy. Can
such consumption be justified on grounds of economic sufficiency? Is it
sustainable? Is it really integral to North American identity? These are questions North Americans should address before drilling begins in ANWR.

The third dimension is the integrity of nature. While human integrity
and nature's integrity are separated in many people's minds, they are related because humans are a species in nature like any other species. All
species must use nature as a resource to survive. The human species and
other species are distinct because other species do not exercise intentionality,

at least not in the same way or to the same degree. Therefore, it is incorrect to speak of a harmony of act and intention, justice, or sin in the rest of nature. These terms apply to humans. Still, the concept of integrity may be even more relevant to nature, considering the root meaning of the word.

The integrity of an ecosystem or species is its intactness, its capacity to evolve dynamically or sustain itself so that a variety of individuals and species may continue to interact or fit together. What comes first to mind is a pristine (untouched) wilderness. This is too static a concept, however, and today a rare exception as humans have made themselves at home in an ever greater number of earth's ecosystems. Rather than some abstract, pristine ideal, it is better to speak in terms of the norm of sustainability. This norm allows for human participation in and use of nature without endorsing activities that cause the disintegration of systems and species. Such activities should be named for what they are—sin.

Maintaining the integrity of ecosystems is not solely a prudential matter for humans. Nature in biblical understandings has more than use or utilitarian value. It also has intrinsic goodness, at least in the understandings of the writers of Genesis 1, where God sees nature as good independent of humans, and in Genesis 9, where God makes a covenant with all of creation. In Christian perspective, nature is much more than a resource, or backdrop, or something to be overcome. Nature is to be cared for ("till it and keep it" in Genesis 2:15) as Jesus himself cared for others and sought their fullest realization. Humans are called to be good stewards in the image of God as that image is revealed in Jesus Christ. God will eventually redeem the whole creation (Rom 8). Nature's integrity is represented in this case by the Porcupine Caribou Herd. Oil drilling in its summer range has the potential to degrade habitat critical to the herd. The integrity of the herd is threatened and with it the social integrity of the Gwich'in.

ENERGY AND AMERICAN INTEGRITY

The era of cheap and abundant energy is almost over. The fossil fuels (oil, gas, and coal) that currently support industrial societies are being depleted rapidly and are not renewable. Oil and gas will be in short supply and very expensive sometime in the next century. Already production at Prudhoe Bay adjacent to ANWR is declining and will be a mere trickle of its former self by 2015. Coal reserves are sufficient to last several hundred years, even with increased consumption. Of great concern with fossil fuels, however, are their serious drawbacks, notably air and water pollution, degradation of the land, global climate change, and eventual depletion.

Global climate change is particularly troublesome. Fossil fuels are decomposed organic matter that grew millions of years ago. When burned, fossil fuels produce a variety of gases that pollute the air. They also produce nontoxic carbon dioxide (CO_2), the levels of which in the atmosphere have increased 20 percent in the past forty-five years. They continue to rise rapidly. The vast majority of scientists think that increasing levels of CO_2 and other so-called greenhouse gases will result in a temperature rise of four to ten degrees Fahrenheit by 2100. They say average global surface temperatures have already risen over one degree over the past century.

Evidence of warming is now available, including retreating mountain glaciers, a thinner arctic ice pack, animal and plant shifts, rising ocean levels, and heat-damaged coral reefs. Scientists are not altogether clear what will happen if this increase continues unabated, but some predict the inundation of low-lying areas, more extreme weather events, hotter summers with more drought, and more heat-related illnesses and deaths. A minority of scientists disputes the theory of global climate change and dismisses the evidence as natural variation.

In terms of supply, the prospects for nuclear energy are brighter, but the environmental impacts of present technology are as bad as or worse than those of coal. Energy from the fission of heavy atoms is more or less on hold because of economic costs, continuing concerns about safety, the threat of terrorist attack, and the vexing problem of waste storage. Energy from the fusion of hydrogen atoms holds great promise but may never be commercially available due to the difficulties and dangers of containing the great temperature and pressure necessary for a sustained reaction to take place. It is also likely to be very expensive.

Unless fusion is harnessed at a reasonable cost, nations will eventually need to meet their energy needs from sources that are sustainable over a long period of time, essentially renewable resources. Solar power is frequently mentioned is this regard. Conservation, the name given efforts to save energy either by cutting back or by producing with greater efficiency, will also be essential.

The realm in which renewable sources of energy and conservation reign will be markedly different from the present realm where economic growth, as measured by the Gross Domestic Product, governs. Sustainability and sufficiency will necessarily guide energy decisions, not growth, at least not growth of energy and resource-intensive production and consumption.

Between this realm and the one to come there will be a difficult period of transition that is already beginning and whose duration is difficult to predict because the rate of technological innovation cannot be known. The realm to come can be delayed if limits to growth are aggressively attacked with the so-called technological fix, that is, a commitment to find technological solutions to resource constraints.

Certainly new technology will have a role to play, but if the shape of human communities and the distribution of costs and benefits are disregarded in the rush for technological solutions, the new realm will hardly be worth inhabiting. Groups like the Gwich'in, if they can continue to exist in such a climate, will be peripheral. Social scale will be large and structure complex, with hierarchical, centralized, and bureaucratic administration.

Materialism accompanied by great disproportions of wealth will continue as the reigning philosophy. In short, social integrity will be under severe pressure from the demand to find "fixes" and to pay those who can.

Alternatively, a society geared to renewables and conservation will bring pressure on everyone to live sustainably and to be satisfied with basics. It will be a society where appropriate scale, simplicity, a greater degree of decentralization, and greater equality will prevail.

Energy choices are social and value choices. If a critical mass of North Americans decides on lives that consume large amounts of energy and natural resources, or alternatively, to live sustainably, it will simultaneously choose the economic and political structures to organize and sustain such decisions.

The decision to explore for oil in ANWR is thus much larger than meets the eye when technological and economic calculations are the only factors. In its largest dimension the question is, What kind of society do present stewards of the earth want for themselves and their children? And beneath this lurks the basic question of social identity and character. Who are North Americans as a people? What should be the center of their common culture?

The question of basic identity goes even deeper. In the commentary on the case "Rigor and Responsibility," two normative Christian traditions governed the analysis—rigorous discipleship and responsible consumption. The amount and style of energy consumption currently enjoyed by North Americans are difficult, if not impossible, to justify in terms of either tradition. Energy sufficiency can certainly be endorsed and a case made for oil as necessary in any transition, but the unnecessary and wasteful consumption of the present not only violates the norm of sustainability but also the model of frugality and simplicity seen in the person of Jesus Christ.

In sum, Christians will have difficulty justifying exploration in ANWR even before they consider environmental effects. Yes, oil will be needed in the transition to a more sustainable society, but until North Americans reduce their high levels of consumption and consider their identity in a world of limited resources, all the oil in ANWR will make little difference. The worst possible outcome stares them in the face: further depletion of oil reserves, no long-range alleviation of supply problems, and the possible loss of the Porcupine Caribou Herd with its consequent impact on Gwich'in culture.

THE CURRENT ENERGY DEBATE

Today, two primary visions of energy futures vie with each other to dominate the direction of US energy policy. The traditional vision behind recent Republican Party initiatives calls for increasing the supply of energy and would assign large corporations the primary task of finding new sources and generating power. Advocates of this vision assume technological innovations and market mechanisms will overcome resource limits and pollution problems. Willing to entertain a few conservation measures and endure limited environmental regulation, these advocates hold out for a minimum of government intervention in markets. Their vision of the future is largely economic. In their vision economic growth will provide ample wealth for every person as long as the nation stays the course of market capitalism. Drilling for oil in ANWR follows easily because human economic good takes first priority.

In contrast, a new vision of a sustainable energy future with broad support in the environmental community has emerged. Its proponents see government and the corporate sector cooperating to provide sufficient energy supplies while protecting the environment. They recommend dispersed and less intrusive technologies and a more equitable distribution of income, wealth, and power. They are more ecocentric as opposed to anthropocentric and focus on environmental limits to continued economic expansion. They would not drill for oil in ANWR.

GWICH'IN INTEGRITY

The view of the Gwich'in in this case is through the eyes of a non-native on a short stay who is unfamiliar with their culture and has no formal training as an observer. Any one of these limitations might skew his observations.

While caution is warranted, a few things are clear. First, the Gwich'in are deeply concerned about the Porcupine Caribou Herd for reasons of subsistence and social integrity. Their history is tied nutritionally and spiritually to the herd. Were the herd to lose its integrity, the Gwich'in would receive another rude shock to their identity.

Second, Gwich'in culture, like most native cultures in the Americas, is in jeopardy. Ron wonders whether there is enough common culture left to maintain social integrity. The Gwich'in worry about this too but also express words of hope and show signs of reinvigoration.

One way to approach the situation is to advocate closing ANWR to exploration and to pursue a policy of disengagement, leaving the Gwich'in to work out their own future. Such an approach has its attractions, given past injustices. The perceived need for oil, the many linkages between cultures in Alaska, and the intermingling of peoples on the land, however, make disengagement all but impossible.

Alternatively, policymakers could continue to pursue the two patronizing approaches that have governed US policy in the past. The first of these two approaches pictures Native Americans as backward savages in need of superior Western technology, social institutions, and culture. While still widely held, this picture must be dismissed outright and confession made for the expropriations, massacres, and deceptions it has promoted. The chapter on the domination and elimination of Native Americans by people of European origins is one of the ugliest in the annals of world history.

The other traditional approach is to idealize Native Americans as "noble savages." This idealization, while more sensitive than the first, leads to confusion about native care of the land, the moral superiority of native peoples, the ease and comfort of nomadic life in a harsh climate, and the place of native religions in modern technological society and in the environmental movement.

The Gwich'in have a different—not a superior or inferior—way of life. They are a shrewd and politically interested community of people who have learned how to negotiate from strength. They know of the potential monetary rewards of oil production in ANWR. They know that the Porcupine Caribou Herd is resilient and that the environmental consequences of oil production at Prudhoe Bay are not altogether clear. They know they have political support in the rest of North America, and they know how to use it. They know as sub-Arctic people that they have different political interests than the Inupiat on the north slope. They know that northeastern Alaska is no Eden.

How then should North Americans view the Gwich'in? Most appropriate is a perspective that begins with respect and exhibits a concern for their social integrity. Included should be a frank recognition that a conflict continues between two cultures, the one closely linked to a subsistence way of life on land, the other more powerful, linked to modern technology and capitalistic economic organization.

Traditionally, the Gwich'in were hunter-gatherers who long ago migrated from Asia and settled in the sub-Arctic south of the Brooks Range in Alaska and the Yukon and Northwest Territories in Canada. They subsisted directly off the land, primarily on the Porcupine Caribou Herd, which they harvested in sustainable numbers. Life was difficult, but the people were resourceful. They relied on sharing, the extended family, and respect for the wisdom of others, especially elders.

Necessarily, they had a special relation to the land and to its flora and fauna. To the Gwich'in, the land is sacred. It is inalienable. It cannot be bought or sold but is held in common as the basis of subsistence. Subsistence is much more than a way of securing food. It is a productive system that entails living directly off the land and demands the organized labor of practically everyone in the community. There are countless tasks in a subsistence economy, each requiring specialized skills. Subsistence is also a system of distribution and exchange that operates according to long-established rules. It links the generations and knits the community into a common culture. It is the material basis for Gwich'in values and underlies the relation of the Gwich'in to the land.

Modern industrial society is obviously different, perhaps most obviously in how it relates to the land. Those in modern society are not as close to the land. They do not see it as sacred. They buy and sell it and encumber it as private property. They view it through the eyes of the economist as a factor of production and obtain its produce by selling their labor and purchasing the means of subsistence in markets far removed from the land.

The traditional Gwich'in way of life persists in spite of deep inroads by modern industrial society. Cultures are never static, of course, but the rapidity of the changes, many of which have been imposed, not chosen, have the Gwich'in worried about their future. Imported goods and food; movement into villages under the influence of Christian missionaries; the introduction of schools, welfare payments, and wage labor; and the acceptance of labor-saving and recreational technologies have brought unprecedented and swift changes. With them have come values and methods of social organization quite foreign to native peoples and a sense of inferiority and powerlessness.

That identity and alcoholism are problems is not surprising. The imports from modern society form a barrier separating Native Americans from their traditional cultures. The words of Inupiat Polly Koutchak express this sense of being walled off that also seems to characterize the lives of many Gwich'in:

> I always feel deep within myself the urge to live a traditional way of life—the way of my ancestors. I feel I could speak my Native tongue, but I was raised speaking the adopted tongue of my people, English. I feel I could dance the songs of my people, but they were abolished when the white man came to our land. I feel I could heal a sick one the way it was done by my ancestors, but the White man not only came with their medicines—they came with diseases. What I'm trying to emphasize is that I am one in the modern day attempting to live a double life—and, from that my life is filled with confusion. I have a wanting deep within myself to live the life of my ancestors, but the modernized world I was raised in is restricting me from doing so.[1]

The future of the Gwich'in's subsistence way of life is in jeopardy. Ron Blanchard's account, however, reveals considerable evidence of continuing social integrity. The Gwich'in have organized themselves to defend their interests. A spirit of resistance is expressed in the refusal by some to speak English and in opposition to oil production in ANWR. The Gwich'in recognize shortcomings in their school system and the importance of language to a cultural identity. Younger people are returning to the villages to raise their families. Many seem determined to overcome the ravages of alcoholism. Skeptics might view this evidence as staged by the Gwich'in to impress unsophisticated observers or as a failure to assimilate to a superior culture. In contrast, eyes of respect will interpret this evidence as a triumph of the human spirit.

Nor should the Gwich'in's subsistence way of life be dismissed. Granted the Gwich'in have purchased tools to make that way of life easier and as a result must resort to wage labor. Granted also, they have supplemented their diets with food from the outside, thereby improving nutrition. These actions are not decisive, however. Their subsistence way of life will continue as long as they choose to live in rural Alaska, for the simple reason that a market economy will never produce a sufficient economic base to support them in this setting. Except for the oil, which is not on Gwich'in lands, there are not enough commercially valuable resources in rural Alaska.

Respect for the Gwich'in in their subsistence way of life is important in this case. From the outside it is a matter of justice and recognizing the legitimacy of Gwich'in concern about identity, the land, and the caribou. From the inside it is a matter of economic sufficiency and the maintenance of a common culture.

The Porcupine Caribou Herd is central to Gwich'in integrity. The caribou are the means of continued subsistence. Cultural identity is bound up with the land and the herd. Oil exploration is viewed as a threat to the herd and as another one of those barriers that wall the Gwich'in off from their identity. Respect in this case means listening to what these people are saying.

NATURE'S INTEGRITY

When anthropocentrism dominated discussions such as this, a commentary would have ended with the preceding section or with a short statement of the value of the Porcupine Caribou Herd as a resource for Gwich'in subsistence. Utilitarian considerations dominated analysis. The intrinsic value of landscapes, species, and ecosystems was left out or separated off into the realms of philosophy or theology. This is no longer the case. Analysis needs to be fully integrated and nature's systems viewed as having value of their own.

The issue for the integrity of nature in this case is the sustainability of the Porcupine Caribou Herd, whose survival depends on the preservation of summer habitat on the north slope of the Brooks Range in ANWR. On the one hand, the need to preserve this habitat is symbolic of a more general problem: the worldwide degradation of land and ecosystems that causes the extinction of species and the reduction of biodiversity.

The causes of this wider degradation are complex, but certainly an increased human population that consumes more and uses more powerful technologies is principal among them. Oil exploration and development in ANWR on fragile Arctic tundra is simply another example of behavior that degrades the natural environment, Glen Stone and his safeguards notwithstanding. In some cases, and this may be one, any intrusion whatsoever can be destructive, and humans should probably stay out.

On the other hand, the issue is quite specific: the impact of oil exploration and development on the herd and other species that inhabit the Arctic ecosystem. Exploration itself may be innocent enough if all it means is looking around, overturning a few rocks, probing the ground here and there, and then leaving. Who could object? Producing oil is another matter.

The case itself offers important information about the herd, not all of which bears repeating. The herd numbers about 130,00 animals, down from a recent high of 180,000. Critical to the herd is its summer calving and feeding in areas believed to have the greatest potential for oil discovery. If the herd is displaced from its richest feeding grounds to others where the vegetation is less nutritious and predators are more numerous, the herd may suffer. Less nutrition means less weight gain. Weight gain is critical for the females and is directly related to calf survival and birth rates the following summer. Predators are found in greater numbers to the south in the foothills of the Brooks Range. Presumably the herd would move in that direction with displacement, since this is what occurs in years of heavy snowfall in the prime feeding areas. In good weather years, displacement might have little effect, but scientists are concerned about other years where displacement would add to already bad conditions and put the herd under stress.

The more than thirty years of experience with the Central Arctic Herd at Prudhoe Bay is the only evidence that scientists have to predict effects on the Porcupine Herd in ANWR. The Central Arctic Herd numbers about 27,000 animals. It appeared to grow rapidly in the late 1970s and early 1980s. After 1985 the ratio of calves per one hundred cows dropped, more so in areas in the herd's western range near oil production at Prudhoe Bay. Recently, the herd's numbers increased rapidly. Scientists are cautious about these data, however. There is no long-range information on numbers or calf/cow ratios. The estimates of herd size are based on aerial surveys. Natural fluctuations in ratios and size are to be expected, and without baseline date, causes of short-range fluctuations are difficult to determine. The data suggest little impact but are not conclusive. Until more data are gathered, scientists are reluctant to make predictions on the basis of trends in the Central Arctic Herd.

Scientists have arrived at several significant conclusions, however. The Central Arctic Herd avoids humans, roads, and production facilities at Prudhoe Bay, the females more than the males. In other words, production facilities displace the herd. Also, the herd as measured by calf density is in worse shape the closer its animals are to production facilities. This is the evidence that worries scientists and the Gwich'in, for displacement in ANWR would drive females to less favorable calving and feeding grounds.

PERSONAL INTEGRITY

Mary Peters's reluctance to speak English in public gatherings is probably difficult for most North Americans to understand. English is, after all, the main language of international communication, not to mention the language of common culture in the United States. If Mary's first priority is to get the Gwich'in's message out to observers such as Ron, it would behoove her to communicate directly instead of through an interpreter.

Mary is, however, speaking to her own community as well, and it is probably more important for her to establish her own integrity within the community before she speaks to outsiders. Whatever else, her reluctance to speak English should not be viewed by outsiders as a snub or as culturally backward. To expect Mary to give up what is central to her culture and her own identity is the epitome of cultural imperialism. Mary's act is in keeping with her intention to reinvigorate Gwich'in culture.

As for Ron Blanchard, he must decide how to word his report and what to recommend concerning oil exploration and production in ANWR. Personal integrity depends on receiving God's power of integrity. Ron's first act should be a prayer for openness and discernment.

Ron might next reconsider his intentions. The case makes clear that he is troubled by the threats to Gwich'in social integrity. The disintegration of the Porcupine Caribou Herd would threaten their subsistence way of life and arrest efforts to reinvigorate old traditions. Ron is no doubt aware of the tortured history of Native Americans in post-Columbian North and South America. Under the norm of justice with its concern for the poor and oppressed, he might well give the Gwich'in the benefit of the doubt about their motivations, their reading of the scientific evidence, and the political nature of their appeal. He should be careful not to cloud his judgment with patronizing illusions about Gwich'in nobility, however.

The case also reveals that Ron has convictions about excess energy consumption. He listens carefully to Glen Stone, who is convinced that energy sufficiency for North Americans is at stake, but does not appear to be swayed.

The evidence on the threat of oil production to the integrity of the caribou herd should also be a consideration. If he is perceptive, Ron will pick up the caution of scientists who have studied the possible consequences. The lack of conclusive evidence should lead him to be cautious himself. No longer, he might conclude, can an ethic that considers only human integrity control outcomes. He should also remember that the Porcupine Caribou Herd has intrinsic value as part of God's good creation.

Finally, Ron will want to bring a special awareness to his decision, an awareness that applies to any visitor to a different culture. Ron is not alone in his lack of understanding of Gwich'in ways or training in methods of observation. In such situations humility about one's own capacities and respect for the integrity of others are paramount virtues. He should be careful to qualify his recommendation with an admission of his own limitation. He should also be prepared to do more studying and listening and to look at his own consumption of energy.

What Ron decides to do with his observations is finally his responsibility, as it is the responsibility of every visitor to other cultures. Ethical analysis can pave the way to good decisions, but good character and personal integrity are needed to translate analysis into good actions.

CONCLUSION

The case against exploration and production in ANWR is strong. It rests on three pillars: (1) respect for Gwich'in social integrity, (2) respect for nature's integrity, and (3) the failure of North Americans to curb their energy appetites. The case may not be as strong as it seems, however. ANWR is not on Gwich'in lands or even in the same ecosystem. The main link of the Gwich'in to ANWR is the Porcupine Caribou Herd. If it can be demonstrated beyond a reasonable doubt that oil production represents little or no threat to the herd, then Gwich'in integrity is not threatened and the first two pillars fall. Should North Americans curb their demand for energy and thereafter use the oil in ANWR to fuel the transition to sustainable energy consumption, then the third pillar crumbles.

For the moment, however, the three pillars stand. The effects on the herd are not clear, the herd is central to Gwich'in integrity, and North Americans have yet to make a determined effort to change their habits.

NOTE

[1] Polly Koutchak, quoted in Thomas R. Berger, *Village Journey* (New York: Hill and Wang, 1985), 13.

ADDITIONAL RESOURCES

Bass, Rick. *Caribou Rising*. San Francisco: Sierra Club Books, 2004.
Berger, Thomas R. *Village Journey*. New York: Hill and Wang, 1985.
Brown, Joesph Epes. *The Spiritual Legacy of the American Indian*. New York: Crossroad, 1993.
McFague, Sallie. *Super, Natural Christians*. Minneapolis: Fortress Press, 1997.
Martin-Schramm, James A., and Robert L. Stivers. *Christian Environmental Ethics: A Case Method Approach*. Maryknoll, NY: Orbis Books, 2003.
Madsen, Ken. *Under the Arctic Sun: Gwich'in, Caribou, and the Arctic National Wildlife Refuge*. Englewood, CO: Earthtales Press, 2003.
Matthiessen, Peter, and Subhankar Banerjee. *Arctic National Wildlife Refuge: Seasons of Life and Land*. Seattle: Mountaineers Press, 2003.
Nash, James A. *Loving Nature*. Nashville, TN: Abingdon Press, 1991.

Nash, Roderick. *Wilderness and the American Mind.* 3rd ed. New Haven, CT: Yale Univ. Press, 1982.

Osgood, Cornelius. *Contributions to the Ethnography of the Kutchin.* Yale Univ. Publications in Anthropology, No. 14. New Haven, CT: Human Relations Area Files Press, 1970.

Rolston, Holmes, III. *Environmental Ethics: Duties to and Values in the Natural World.* Philadelphia: Temple Univ. Press, 1988.

Websites

American Petroleum Institute
http://www.api.org
American Wind Energy Association
http://www.awea.org/
Center for Renewable Energy and Sustainable Technology
http://www.crest.org/index.html
Gwich'in Steering Committee
http://www.alaska.net/~gwichin
National Energy Policy: Bush Administration
http://www.whitehouse.gov/energy/
National Resources Defense Council
http://www.nrdc.org

Case

Using Gene Therapy?

"Hello, I'm Dr. Wales, Ms. Greenville. Have a seat." He motioned her from her stance at the door of his office to a leather chair in front of his desk and took a seat behind the desk. "What brings you to see me today?" asked Fred Wales, the director of the Genetics Center at Memorial Hospital.

"My younger brothers and sisters and I were just recently informed that our father has Huntington's Chorea," confided Myra Greenville. "We were advised that we should be tested. The result of the testing was that I am a carrier. Ever since I found out I've been reading everything I can about Huntington's. I have always wanted to get married and be a mother. In three months I graduate from engineering school, and I already have a job. My boyfriend and I have been together for almost a year, and I think he is giving me a ring for graduation," said Myra Greenville, sniffing as she tried to stop the tearing in her eyes.

"This must be very hard for you," murmured Dr. Wales. "I'm so sorry. But you have already been tested. So what can I do for you?"

"I came to Memorial because I understand that you are doing experimental work in gene therapy. I want this gene removed, so that I can't pass it on to my future children. I thought I would be a good subject because I am willing to take any risk to protect children of mine from this disease. My father is only forty-one years old, but he goes back and forth between periods when he is as normal as ever, and periods when he is out of his mind, even violent, and those periods are getting longer and more frequent. When he is lucid, he cries to think what he has passed on to us. He's consumed with guilt. And he didn't even know he was a carrier. There is no way I want to feel that kind of guilt," insisted Myra. "Please help me!"

Dr. Wales hesitated, and then, leaning forward over his desk, spoke slowly and solemnly: "Ms. Greenville, the cure you want doesn't exist now, and

This case was prepared by Christine E. Gudorf. Copyright © The Case Study Institute. The names of all persons and institutions have been disguised to protect the privacy of those involved.

may well never exist in the form you want. Let me explain. What you want is to alter the germline, to change the identity of some of the genes that get passed on from one generation to another. There are many unknowns in such a path, and many problems both technical and moral. It may never happen. What is much more likely to happen in the near future is that we will have gene therapy for affected individuals that will either turn off disease-bearing mutant genes, such as the one for Huntington's, or otherwise alter it so as to ameliorate the disease. While such gene therapies are just beginning to be researched, some will probably be available within the next decade or so. Whether they will include therapies for Huntington's I don't know. Huntington's Chorea, because of its seriousness, has a high degree of researcher interest. It is likely that were you to have an affected child, there would be treatment for Huntington's before the disease manifested itself in your child's thirties or forties, but no one can promise that we will have successful therapies by the time you yourself will need them. The gene therapy experimentation at Memorial that you have seen references to involved arthritis, are on a very limited experimental scale, and are inconclusive as yet."

Myra Greenville did not seem surprised by Dr. Wales' speech, but her shoulders slumped noticeably, and her eyes teared again. "So I have to tell Ted that if he marries me, in fifteen years or so I will go insane and need to be institutionalized. Even more, in order to have children who won't become insane when they are still in their thirties, we would have to be willing to abort any fetus that tests as a carrier. Or else only adopt. That's it, isn't it, Doctor?"

"Yes, Ms. Greenville. Huntington's is a devastating disease, for those affected and all those around them. We don't have better options yet. I'm very sorry."

As he concluded the appointment, Dr. Wales asked whether she was receiving counseling help. At her negative answer he urged her to maintain a counseling relationship over the next years, and offered to have his secretary send her a number of names and telephone numbers for local genetic counselors. She thanked him but explained that until she graduated and began her new engineering job, she had no health insurance, so genetic counseling would have to wait. As he closed the door behind her, Dr. Wales crossed to his desk, leaned back in his chair with his head against the headrest, and closed his eyes.

Three days later Fred Wales was in Sydney, Australia, at a conference of genetic researchers discussing the ethics of gene surgery. The topic was germline therapy, and as he spoke, Dr. Wales thought of Myra Greenville and her request: "I am a little impatient at the constant cautions that we do not know enough always to recognize the beneficent functions of what seem to us 'bad' genes. While that is true in general, and should prevent us from turning off or replacing all genes that seem deleterious, there are some cases that are clear. With Huntington's, for example, what could we discover that is beneficent about this gene that would outweigh the costs of carrying it? Since the vast majority of the population do not carry it, it cannot perform any exclusive, necessary function. On the other hand, the very early and often rapid onset of serious dementia, which is frequently violent, requires institutionalization, and yet takes many years to kill the patient, can hardly be painted too negatively. Deciding that Huntington's is a bad gene that should be removed from the human gene pool is not like deciding that genes for brown eyes, freckling, or short stature are bad genes to be eliminated." And then he told them about Myra Greenville, omitting her name.

"Dr. Wales," said Erik Nelson, a young Danish researcher, "we have all been touched by such patients. It is because of people like her that we became scientists, to alleviate human misery. And as scientists, we have a duty to continue to push the envelope, to discover cures, and not to be deterred by the nay-sayers who want to stop all research and condemn people like your patient to madness and death because they fear dealing with the unknown. Science is not reckless; it proceeds one step at a time, through experimentation. We should trust the scientific process and not let obstacles be put in the path of progress against killer diseases."

But Elena Weiss, a German geneticist, impatiently retorted: "Dr. Nelson, it was science that was the great god of the Nazi medical experiments, too, and of the team that developed the atomic bomb. What scientific safeguards protected the world from them? There are real risks in what we are considering doing, and we need to weigh those risks responsibly. Science does not replace the need for morality and conscience; it only gives us more tools, and those tools can be used for good or ill."

The room erupted into a buzz of local responses and a dozen hands waved, waiting to be recognized. The chairperson recognized Dr. Yamaguchi, a researcher from Tokyo, who responded: "We do need to weigh risks and benefits in science, and only experimentation can tell us where they lie. In my lab we have been working with ways to turn off the Huntington's gene, and a major problem that we have had is that we have as yet no laboratory test to detect when we are successful. We cannot simply wait years to see if a treated patient develops Huntington's. But we know so little about the function of the normal gene in the pair that we are having difficulty determining some way to test for the disabling of the Huntington's gene. It is difficult to predict how long this step will take. For myself, I would like to see fuller discussion of turning to the germline, but I do think that that process must wait until we know more about the normal function of that gene pair. Otherwise, we are taking risks of damaging the human gene pool, damage that could entail great human suffering and moral dangers to redress." Dr. Yamaguchi concluded with a shallow bow of his head.

Marsha Logan, a researcher from the UK, volunteered: "Many of us would agree that therapy to the germline should wait until we have more information about the internal workings of all the parts of the genome. But it seems to me that many of us are operating on different basic assumptions that necessarily lead to different conclusions. For example, many conversations on the subject seem to treat germline alterations as if this would be the first intervention by modern medicine into the human gene pool. This is simply not true. We can differ on whether or not further intervention, in particular this intervention, is justified, but we should all acknowledge that modern medicine has drastically altered the human gene pool. We have only to look at treatment for diseases such as diabetes, especially childhood diabetes. In the past these children all died long before they were of an age to reproduce. Today, they routinely reproduce in developed nations. There are a host of people with genetically linked diseases today who pass on their susceptibility to disease instead of dying before they can reproduce. And there are other genetic problems as well. There is speculation that both Viagra and the new fertility drugs for women will increase the prevalence of birth defects by allowing older people with higher rates of gene mutations, who otherwise would not be reproducing, to reproduce. Every time we prevent an epidemic, inoculate against disease, or treat individuals of reproductive age, we intervene in the gene pool. There is no way to avoid such interventions and still cure disease and prolong life.

"With respect to susceptibility to some diseases, it has been suggested that those saved from early death be advised not to reproduce. But this, too, is an artificial intervention, since if nature were left alone, some patients would recover from many of these diseases and conditions and live to reproduce, and in some cases might be conveying resistance to the disease. We can never know what the human gene pool would be like without our interventions. So we have to decide what the guidelines for further intervention should be, given that we have not only already begun to alter the gene pool but see no moral way that medicine can do its duty to individual patients and at the same time refrain from further alteration."

David Mottahedeh from Paris responded: "Yes! Of course there have already been many interventions. And the number and effects of those interventions continue to increase. It is the scale of interventions, not the fact of interventions, that we must address. But surely the danger in germline therapy is that once it is doable, the scale may be uncontrollable. Look at the development of plastic surgery, from fixing birth defects and gross damage from accidents to preoccupation with bigger breasts, faces without wrinkles, and prettier noses, or the developments in pharmacology that took us from aspirin and antibiotics to Viagra and Rogaine. We people in medicine understand ourselves as responding to human suffering, and people do suffer from being too short, fat, thin, bald, freckled, and some practitioner is going to respond to their cry, especially if there is money in it. This is what I see as the problem—controlling the scale of interventions. So far, what has controlled the scale of intervention in the world has been massive poverty; most people on the face of the earth do not have the means to afford medicines, and some do not get even the simplest inoculations."

He concluded, "But we have to assume that global poverty can be ameliorated, and that therefore we must assume that whatever interventions we introduce will in the future be utilized by all persons afflicted with the condition the intervention addresses."

Victoria Derby from Perth added: "I think we have to look beyond the scale question to a difference in kind as well. The kinds of interventions we have had in the past have perhaps increased what we might call 'bad' genes in the overall pool, but they have not restricted diversity within the pool. In fact, some of them might even have increased diversity. The threat of the new interventions, such as germline therapy, is to diversity. Cloning, like germline therapy, also has tremendous theoretical potential to reduce diversity. We cannot just assume that new interventions will balance the older ones; resistance to a number of diseases is not 'balanced' by fewer body types or a narrower range of intelligence."

Richard Luttstein of Vienna objected: "I am not sure I agree with the direction of this conversation. Perhaps it is because I am primarily a clinician and only secondarily a researcher. But it seems to me that I answer principally to my individual patients. I cannot think that it is compatible with the doctor-patient relationship for us to decide that we cannot cure a patient who is suffering from disease because some time in the future there may or may not be consequences for the larger society from this cure. It is not my job to plan the future of the human race; it is my job to restore my patients to full lives. That is why I am also a researcher." Dr. Luttstein finished to a smattering of applause.

"So each of us should fulfill our narrow little roles and let the future of the planet work itself out, huh?" asked Dr. Derby. "So fishermen around the globe say it is their job to provide people with fish, and if in the process fish populations are too depleted to recover, earth simply will have no fish. Isn't there a problem with this? Don't we all have obligations to the whole of the species, to the whole of the planet?"

Dr. Luttstein responded tiredly: "It is as much as I can do to fulfill the obligations that my mother, my wife, my children, my patients, my professional colleagues, my office staff , my neighbors, and my nation place on me. There is no way I can handle obligations to everything on the planet now and in the future."

At that moment, the chairperson declared that time had run out, and the session was called to a close.

As they walked out of the meeting, Dr. Wales remarked to Dr. Derby: "I often feel like Luttstein, that it is impossible to be responsible to so many different constituencies, that I am only human. On the other hand, I wonder if we are ever responsible to any of these individuals if we do not take into account the future of the species as a whole."

"Yes, I know," responded Dr. Derby. "And yet it is so easy to avoid that responsibility in clinical practice, because the patients we see are focused, understandably, on the real suffering and threats facing themselves and their families. And their focus becomes ours. Perhaps it would be easier to deal with these moral questions if it were possible to separate clinicians, who treat affected patients, from researchers, who work on future interventions and are better able to see the larger picture. But practically, researchers need to be involved at the clinical level, too, in order for the interventions they develop to address real needs safely."

"But," Dr. Wales added, "while clinicians may be reinforced in an individual focus because of their involvement with suffering patients, that is not the source of the narrowness of their vision, if we can call it that. How many researchers do you know who became researchers on breast cancer, Parkinsons, MS, or other diseases because a parent, a child, or a sibling has been devastated by that disease? We are all susceptible to developing narrow vision due to our emotional response to suffering. And, of course, the "pioneer" model of researcher out there on the margins, heroically cultivating new territory, defying the odds and believing that science alone has all the answers, does tend to support such a focus. We all have to battle with that image of ourselves; it has been a part of our Western culture. We all need to be brought down to earth occasionally and reminded that we are only one part of a huge, interconnected universe."

Dr. Derby nodded her agreement. But despite his words and Dr. Derby's agreement, Dr. Wales could not help wondering how the arguments would sound to Myra Greenville if she were there to hear them.

Commentary

Using Gene Therapy?

What is this disease that Myra Greenville wants gene therapy for? Huntington's, often called Huntington's Chorea, is a hereditary, degenerative brain disease. Usually in mid-life, cells in the caudate nucleus of the brain begin to die, initiating a relentless deterioration of intellectual ability, emotional control, balance, and speech. Chorea—involuntary movement—is usually a symptom as well. Huntington's is caused by a single dominant gene. Every child of an affected parent has a 50 percent chance of inheriting the gene that causes Huntington's. Although ultimately fatal, Huntington's patients can live decades after the onset of the disease. Many become difficult, even violent, and must be institutionalized as they lose control of their lives and emotions. Huntington's can destroy families; children often watch a parent disintegrate with the disease and then spend the next decade or two waiting to develop the disease themselves if, like Myra, they have tested positive for Huntington's.

Some argue against testing family members of Huntington's patients, but most counselors, as in this case, advise testing, both so that potential sufferers can prepare themselves and their family for the onset of the disease and to counsel affected persons to avoid creating affected children. Christians have different responses to the question of testing, especially testing of the unborn, with one factor in the difference being attitudes toward abortion. If abortion is seen as an option, then it is possible for carriers of Huntington's to have children without risking passing on the disease. For Christians for whom abortion is not a moral option under any circumstances, however, having the test done on an unborn child may be seen as creating a strong temptation to abort if the fetus proves positive for Huntington's.

The subject of gene therapy has been widely discussed in bioethics for the last few decades, and within that discussion the issue of alteration in the gene pool has been one aspect among many others. Many of the questions in bioethics about gene therapy involve considerations of a range of questions about experimentation on human subjects that are crucially important to consider for human ethics but do not have implications for environmental ethics. This is true, for example, of issues of respect for the welfare and dignity of human subjects in research. But the issue of directly altering the gene pool of succeeding generations (as opposed to the indirect alterations that have occurred as the result of human efforts at treating disease and controlling epidemics) must be a central one for environmental ethics as well as for bioethics. This means that Christian ethics needs to address this question with an eye to both human responsibilities to other humans, and human responsibilities to all of creation.

ENVIRONMENTAL ETHICAL CONCERNS

Environmental ethics is aimed at human stewardship of creation, a stewardship that effectively makes humans co-creators with God. Humans, then, are stewards charged with the preservation of diverse forms of life and their habitats, including the preservation of diversity in human beings, since diversity is critical for the adaptations that allow human life to continue under changing conditions. Too often Christians interpret the Genesis command to "be fruitful and multiply, and fill the earth and subdue it" (Gn 1:28) to mean that the world belongs to humans to use as they like; they use terms like *the environment* to mean *the environment of humans,* as if it were somehow only the setting for the human drama, as if we humans were not really part of that environment. But attempts to alter human biological makeup are as relevant to environmental ethics as attempts to alter any other part of the environment. This is true not only theoretically but practically. We know that while some diseases seem to be specific to a certain species, other diseases move between species. That is why humans are affected by swine flu, rabies, malaria, and yellow fever. Most HIV researchers believe that HIV, too, crossed to humans from animals, in this case African monkeys. The second Genesis creation story reminds us just how closely connected we are to other living creatures. In that story God originally created these living creatures to be companions for the first human. Altering the epidemiological reactions of humans could have unknown impact on our companion species.

At the same time, when environmental ethics considers subjects such as gene therapy, it cannot ignore that the preservation of the human species is more than the preservation of human biology in its diverse forms. Just as environmental ethics aims at the preservation of animal species within their natural habitats, and not merely within zoos and laboratories, because it is the community life of the species that is valuable and not just its biology, so the preservation of the human species must look beyond human biology to the entire life system that makes humans human. Suffering, empathy for those suffering, and altruistic effort to ameliorate the suffering of others, even at some cost to oneself, are not only central commands of the gospel but are also all intrinsic to what it means to be human. Our psychology and relationality are important parts of our human nature, increasingly understood to be important aspects of human development. It would be wrong to ignore the Myra Greenvilles of the world in deciding what conditions should be researched and which treatments and cures pursued, even if they do constitute a small minority. Yet at the same time, the benefits to the Myra Greenvilles must be balanced against the benefits and sufferings to future individuals that might be wrought by the development and use of the planned interventions. This weighing of costs and benefits must be an inclusive, broadly conceived process in which the interests of all the stakeholders are considered. The decision made should safeguard the common good of all of creation, because, as Genesis tells us, God not only made all of creation, but God pronounced all of creation good and pleasing.

Christians often think of morality and ethics in terms of personal morality, of whether individual acts are right or wrong, or whether they accord with scripture or church teaching. They are often stymied when forced to face social policy issues that are not directly addressed by scripture or historical teaching. But Christian ethics is not necessarily based on extracting from the tradition a set of rules to follow. Christian ethics can also be understood as extracting from the Christian faith tradition values to be protected. One basic value is the common good. In the public life of Jesus a great deal of emphasis was placed on lifting up various marginalized groups in Jesus' own society so that their needs were considered within the common good. The poor, the sick, the outcast, women, and children—the common good, Jesus' teaching insisted, included the good of all of these groups that were distinguished by their powerlessness.

In this case most of the major stakeholders in the issue of germline gene therapy are unborn generations of humans who cannot speak for themselves. They share the powerlessness of the marginalized in Jesus' society. Part of the ethical task in such a case is to use our own experience, our imagination, and our capacity for empathy to understand the interest of these not-yet-existing stakeholders. We feel empathy for the Myra Greenvilles of the world, for the many millions of people afflicted with diseases and medical conditions that restrict and shorten life, for the families whose physical and emotional capacities are exhausted in the care of these loved ones, and for the societies that carry the burden of providing their medical care. We need to ensure that when we are weighing the risks that germline therapy may entail, that when we discover the likely biological and medical forms of those risks to future humans, we also consider the toll in suffering that living with those results will also entail for those persons and all their relationships. The failure to use our imagination and empathy within the process of proportional reasoning can, and has, resulted in great tragedy. This was Jesus' point in the parable of the Good Samaritan. Instead of simply asking what kinds of people we should recognize as neighbors with claims on us, he asked who in that story was the neighbor of the injured man—who would we want to claim us as a neighbor if we were in need? This reversal inserts a wholly new and imaginative perspective into the issue of neighborliness.

DO NO HARM

For physicians the primary ethical norm should be clear. Their Hippocratic oath demands that they do no harm. They are to exercise their skills in efforts at beneficence, not malevolence. Historically, the beneficence demanded of physicians has applied both to their intentions and to the foreseeable consequences for their individual patients. This is one of the tension points at the meeting. Physicians doing clinical work with individual patients understand themselves as obliged to obtain the best results for the individual patient, while those who understand themselves as research scientists aim at benefits for humanity as a whole. Clinicians' primary virtue is an undivided loyalty to each patient, which sometimes entails ignoring ways in which promoting the welfare of one patient can conflict with the interests of the larger society, as when over half of the health-care budget in the United States is spent on elderly people in their last year of life.[1] Research scientists, on the other hand, are committed to pushing the boundaries of scientific knowledge in service to humanity as a whole, but sometimes they are too quick to assume that every new piece of knowledge or technique advances the common good. Many new reproductive technologies, for example, *in vitro* fertilization, somatic cell transfer, and embryo transfer, have created situations that, even after twenty years, societies do not know how to handle at the legal or the familial level. Children can now have three genetic parents, for example. Sometimes pushing the envelope in science creates social and ethical chaos, which entails a great deal of human suffering.

SOMATIC AND GERMLINE GENE TRANSFERS

This case discusses both somatic and germ cell transfers. Both involve using a vector, often a virus, to deliver a new therapeutic gene to the appropriate target cell. The difference is that the target cell can be a germ (sperm or ovum) cell, in which case the change is passed on to the next generation, or it can be a non-germ (somatic) cell, in which case the therapeutic gene affects only the individual patient and not his or her offspring. At the present time there are hundreds of studies being conducted in somatic cell transfer in both humans and animals in the United States, as well as many studies in germ cell transfer in animals. Both kinds of studies have had mixed results, with one of the two principal problems involving vectors. Most vectors are viruses, because viruses already have a way of encapsulating and delivering their genes to cells in a pathogenic manner. Scientists have tried to remove the disease-causing genes and replace them with therapeutic ones. But viruses can introduce other problems, including toxicity and immune and inflammatory responses. Some vectors have been found to cause mutations, others work only on growing, dividing cells. A major concern is that the known viral vectors are able to carry only a few small genes.

Some nonviral vectors are based on synthetic chemicals. Most of these have relatively good rates of delivering the therapeutic genes to the target cell, but few consistently deliver the genes to the nucleus of the cell where it would be effective. Scientists are experimenting with possibly introducing a forty-seventh artificial human chromosome alongside the normal forty-six, as this vector would be capable of carrying substantial amounts of genetic code, and the body's immune system would probably not attack it because of its similarity to the normal chromosomes. But it is yet unknown how this extra chromosome would affection mutation or functioning in the other forty-six chromosomes. While an individual who consents to somatic gene transfer would voluntarily accept the risks that would accompany such therapy, offspring who would be affected by those risks in germline gene transfer, or if natural processes spread somatic gene therapy to germ cells, would have no opportunity to consent to these risks.

COMPLEXITY
IN GENE FUNCTIONING

The mapping of the human genome that was roughly completed at the end of the twentieth century offered scientists the capability to study the full range of inherited conditions we call disease by isolating specific genes and examining their function. Scientists have learned that the functions of many genes are not crudely deterministic. That is, many genes do not act independently; rather, their effects depend upon a host of other factors, including the presence of other genes. Thus, while gene transfer was originally developed to deal with monogenic diseases, the majority of trials now under way involve the treatment of diseases known to have a number of genetic causes, such as cancer, vascular disease, and infectious diseases. This knowledge has severely dampened early hopes for quick cures for many genetically linked diseases and complicated the research task for somatic as well as germline gene therapy.

All of the above problems plague somatic gene transfer. But there are additional problems. Many scientists think that a major risk of somatic gene transfer is that there is so little certainty about where the therapeutic gene will end up. There seems to be considerable risk that a vector will introduce the therapeutic gene into a cell other than the targeted one (for example, a sperm cell or ovum), or that the somatic cells that have successfully accepted the therapeutic gene will through some natural process transfer the gene to a germline cell.

PROSPECTS FOR GERMLINE GENE TRANSFER

Gene transfer to germ cells raises many new and even graver issues. As in somatic gene transfer, a problem is that some cells do not receive the gene, or receive multiple or partial copies of the gene. No one knows what the effects of multiple or partial copies of the gene might be. They could well be severe, even lethal, and they might not become known until adulthood, when the errors could be passed on to future generations. Some insertion techniques could interfere with other important genes, and this, too, could cause severe health problems. It is for these reasons that germline transfer has been considered ethically impermissible. In animal studies of germline transfer, embryos with detectable problems can be detected and "selected out." Adult animals that develop problems can be eliminated. Human subjects cannot be treated in this way.

This is why Dr. Wales was so pessimistic in responding to Myra Greenville's plea—it is very unlikely that germline intervention will be available within the next decade or even two decades. As we saw in the case itself, Dr. Yamaguchi, the Huntington's researcher from Japan, reported two problems in his attempts to "turn off" the Huntington's gene: the lack of understanding of the function of the normal gene in the pair, and the inability to tell whether the gene had in fact been turned off by the intervention. Since Huntington's does not usually manifest itself until the mid-thirties or in some cases the mid-forties, even if researchers only chose subjects in their thirties, they might have to wait a decade to see if the gene had been successfully turned off and if the patient remained symptom free. From an environmental point of view, the significant problem here is the lack of knowledge about the function of the normal gene, or, by implication, about the interaction between the two. What if the turned off gene has other important functions that we don't yet know? Or what if the normal gene requires some activity of the "diseased" gene in order to work? Research into Huntington's is paradigmatic for other germline research as well: there have been no breakthroughs in any research to eliminate disease in animals through germline therapy.

The problems posed by inadequate understanding become profound when one contemplates interventions in the germline, permanent alterations in the gene pool passed on to the next generation. We know of a few of the genetic adaptations that have occurred in human evolution over the millennia. West African communities developed a mutant recessive gene (sickle cell) that conveys resistance to malaria, the single most threatening disease in their world. Persons who had only one such mutant sickle-cell gene had malarial resistance without sickle-cell disease, but those who carried two such genes had the debilitating and often fatal disease. If the original carriers of sickle cell had had gene surgery centuries ago, millions more West

Africans would have died of malaria in the intervening centuries, compared to the fraction of deaths that actually occurred from sickle-cell ane-
mia. How many more such double functions will be discovered in the human gene pool?

SCIENCE AND CHRISTIAN ETHICS

Dr. Weiss is right to insist that science is a tool, not a system of morality.
But even more, science is aimed at gaining facts, which are one type of
knowledge. But they are not the only type of knowledge or even the most
important type of knowledge. Facts should be used in the service of values.
Values can be ends, or ultimate values, or they can be instrumental values,
values whose importance depends on the ends they promote. To the extent
that science has values, they are instrumental values. Science can be useful
in obtaining human ends, but science cannot tell us what ends should be
pursued, what ends are in the best interests of the biosphere, much less of
humans themselves. Christian ethics is about values, the kind that are ends
in themselves, such as life, justice, love, mercy, and community. Dr. Nelson
is naive to think that humans can take ultimate values from science.

At the same time, there is a problem with Dr. Weiss's use of examples,
especially of the Nazi doctors. For while the Nazi doctors were certainly an
example of science gone amok, the use of this kind of example does not
help us to see the most dangerous—because so much more common—situations where evil is not so blatantly chosen and obvious. Evil is at its most
dangerous when it is prosaic, because then it is ignored. Dr. Weiss's example of the atomic bomb is better chosen, in that during the development
of the bomb, the justification for the project was to save lives by forcing a
Japanese surrender without the need for an invasion that would entail hundreds of thousands of casualties. But circumstances changed, and by the
time the bomb was ready to use, the Japanese had already offered to surrender. The bomb was dropped twice for a variety of reasons: to extract an
unconditional surrender, to demonstrate American might to the USSR, and
to test the power of the bomb that had been developed. Such cases can be
illustrative of the moral dangers in scientific experimentation. The intention of the developers of the bomb was good, and the use they foresaw was
acceptable in terms of proportional reason, but the actual use was more
morally problematic.

The same thing can easily be imagined of cloning. One of the clearest
dangers of cloning is shrinking of the gene pool. Hundreds of persons who
heard the National Public Radio spoof about the Ted Williams DNA Bank
after the athlete died called local radio stations wanting to know where the
Bank was. The callers had not understood that the program was a satire;
they actually wanted to buy Williams's DNA for cloning purposes. There is
a market for cloning. We can also think of the numerous scandals involving

owners and employees of sperm banks and fertility clinics around the world who substituted their own semen for that from couples and anonymous donors. The more technologies we have that provide the proliferation of a few genetic makeups over many other diverse ones, the greater is the danger to the human gene pool.

While even the most dedicated of individual scoundrels could not hope to spread more than a few hundred or perhaps thousand copies of himself or herself, a universally available germline therapy that eliminated all tendency to inheritable disease, from breast cancer, sickle cell, diabetes, and Huntington's to asthma, heart disease, and allergies, would drastically affect the diversity in the gene pool. As Dr. Mottahedeh mentioned in the case, what has kept the scale of genetic interventions from medicine so modest thus far has been global poverty—only a few have been able to afford the benefits of modern medicine. But Christians must hope and work for an end to global poverty for the majority of the world's population. Kant was wise when he insisted that we should not propose any action that could not be universalized to all without causing harm.

As should be clear from the discussions in the case, gene therapies are in the works, though it will be some years before many are ready for large-scale experimentation on humans. But *germline* therapies for humans are not yet on the horizon. At the moment, it is the scientific, not the moral, hurdles that prevent their development. This means that we have some time for the human community to debate this issue, to learn what the risks may be in more specific terms, and to evaluate the risks against the likely, not just the desired, benefits. One of the questions that will undoubtedly arise is: Why take the risks of germline therapy if we can successfully treat a genetic disease by simply turning off the gene that causes it, so that there are no symptoms of the disease? We might prefer not to pass on that gene to our children, but if the therapy is available and effective for them too, why take the risk of great harm to the gene pool?

Inevitably, some people's answer to that question will revolve around a particular way of seeing humans in the world—as strong, in charge, invincible. We are often uncomfortable thinking about the human species in terms of limitations, especially limitations accepted as permanent. Modern humans have projected a self-image of the human species as progressing toward infinite knowledge and control of the universe. From a Christian or any truly religious perspective such an attitude is idolatry, a worship of humanity in place of God, a refusal to accept the status of finite creatures in God's world. It is moral hubris, a refusal to accept the claims on us of future generations.

And yet, to take the opposite point of view, that God alone is ruler over all, and that therefore we have no overarching responsibility for the world and the welfare of its species' lives, is to deny the very qualities that God instilled in humanity at creation, the very nature that God graced in the incarnation.

NOTE

[1] Daniel Calahan, *Setting Limits: Medical Goals in an Aging Society* (Washington, DC: Georgetown Univ. Press, 1995).

ADDITIONAL RESOURCES

Adams, Jean. "Competition in Medical Ethics: Confidentiality and Huntington's Chorea." *Journal of Medical Ethics* 16, no. 4 (December 1990).

Daniel, Edwin. "Can We Survive the Biotechnology and Genetic Engineering Revolutions?" *Peace Research Abstracts* 37, no. 5 (2000).

Evans, John H. *Playing God? Human Genetic Engineering and the Rationalization of Public Bioethical Debate.* Chicago: Univ. of Chicago Press, 2002.

Hackett, Perry B. "Genetic Engineering: What Are We Fearing?" *Transgenic Research* 11, no. 2 (2002): 97–99.

Hein, Peter Ulrich. "Human, Mutant, Machine: On the Relationship of Body Cult and Genetic Engineering." *New Genetics and Society* 19, no. 3 (2000): 317–29.

Jeffreys, Mark. "Dr. Daedalus and His Minotaur: Mythic Warnings about Genetic Engineering from J. B. S. Haldane, François Jacob, and Andrew Niccol's *Gattaca.*" *Journal of Medical Humanities* 22, no. 2 (2001): 137–52.

McCormick, Richard A. "Moral Theology and the Genome Project." In *Controlling Our Destinies,* edited by P. R. Sloan. Notre Dame, IN: University of Notre Dame Press, 2000.

Parens, Erik. *Enhancing Human Traits: Ethical and Social Implications.* Washington, DC: Georgetown Univ. Press, 1998.

Peters, Ted. *For the Love of Children: Genetic Technology and the Future of the Family.* Louisville, KY: Westminster/John Knox Press, 1996.

Rixecker, Stefanie. "Genetic Engineering and Queer Biotechnology: The Eugenics of the Twenty-First Century?" *Journal of Genocide Research* 4, no. 1 (2002): 109–26.

Weiner, Charles. "Drawing the Line in Genetic Engineering: Self-Regulation and Public Participation." *Perspectives in Biology and Medicine* 44, no. 2 (2001): 208–20.

Wright, Susan. "Legitimating Genetic Engineering." *Perspectives in Biology and Medicine* 44, no. 2 (2001): 235–47.

PART V

BUSINESS

Case

Big Business and the Boys' Club

Pastor Michael Hopkins stepped off the elevator and through the carved mahogany door into the quiet elegance of the Chicago Men's Club. He was struck by the contrast between this environment and the recent images of the Jamaican slums that had prompted his request for this luncheon meeting. After giving his name to the club's host, Mike was courteously informed that he was several minutes early; he was welcome to wait in the bar until Mr. Palmer and the rest of his party arrived.

Mike Hopkins's mind sifted through the events of the past four weeks as he considered how he would share his Jamaican experience with Frank Palmer and George Delaney, executives in transnational corporations with interests in the Caribbean as well as members of his affluent North Shore congregation. Harold Atkins, a management consultant to the travel industry and a good friend of George's, was also expected to join them. The previous month while Mike and his wife, Carol, were vacationing in Jamaica, they had unexpectedly run into Anthony Robinson, a Jamaican pastor who had done his seminary field education in the United States under Mike's direction. When Mike and Carol saw Tony for the first time in four years, he was playing the piano in their hotel's cocktail lounge. They spoke briefly during Tony's break; he invited them to come with him the following morning to his new "parish."

After serving as associate pastor in a large Jamaican congregation—unsuccessfully, according to Tony—Tony had requested and been granted by his conference an unsalaried, three-year leave from regular pastoral duties to work in the slums of Montego Bay. Tony worked primarily with the

---

This case was prepared by Alice Frazer Evans and Robert A. Evans. Copyright © The Case Study Institute. The names of all persons and institutions have been disguised to protect the privacy of those involved.

boys' club during the day and supported himself and his ministry by playing the piano at night in the lounge of a fashionable tourist hotel.

Mike remembered vividly the events of the next morning as they drove through Montego Bay in the Hopkins's rented car. At the time Mike expressed his astonishment at the contrast between the extreme poverty of the great mass of people in the area and the plush tourist zone and the homes of affluent business and government leaders. In Tony's "parish" Mike and Carol saw hundreds of crude palm shanties, many with seven and eight occupants. There were no plumbing facilities, and the only available water, as much as a half-mile away from some huts, came from a single faucet put in by the city. Tony explained that most of the adult population was uneducated with little or no hope for employment in an increasingly urban-oriented nation.

Tony was convinced that "the very presence of the concentrated wealth—the fruit of an economy largely based on the tourist industry—is essentially destructive and explosive. Although it is primarily the product of the natural tropical setting of our island, it is not shared with the nation." Tony continued: "The young people with whom I work have virtually no public education available. They see the contrast between the haves and have-nots and are understandably bitter and frustrated. My boys turn to gangs, drugs, and stealing out of desperation and a lack of self-worth. The human tragedy in this slum is a crime against God's good creation and is contrary to Christ's mandate to love our neighbors as ourselves. In Luke 4:18 Jesus declares his mission, part of which is 'to bring good news to the poor' and 'to let the oppressed go free.' We are called by Christ to be in solidarity with the poor and oppressed of our world. This is not only my parish, but, as a Christian, it is also yours."

In his spare time while with his former congregation and now full time, Tony worked with a gang of young boys. He used his gifts as a musician to teach them to play the few instruments he could gather. They had slowly formed a band. Now Tony felt there was real competition among the boys to belong to the band. "For most of these boys playing an instrument gives them the first feeling of accomplishment they have ever experienced. It is only with a concept of pride and self-worth that these young men can even begin to hope for a different life."

Tony's plea to Mike Hopkins still rang in his ears. "Reverend Hopkins, I've got over a hundred boys and twelve instruments. My church is struggling in Jamaica. It simply has no funds to work in the slums, and most of the church members place no priority on this kind of ministry. Through your congregation and your contacts in the United States, can you get support for my club? God has empowered these boys to fight for human dignity. Join us in this struggle for liberation. I know from my time with your congregation that you have influential and powerful businessmen who could help us.

"Bauxite, exported to the United States, is Jamaica's primary source of foreign exchange. But the US-based tourist industry is second and more directly affects our economy. Tourism annually grosses millions of dollars through the exploitation of our beaches and the cheap labor of our people. I know well-educated people with solid hotel management skills and no jobs. A number of hotels folded in the tourist crash following 9/11. The industry has recovered, but the foreign owners continue to bring in their own nationals. Virtually no Jamaicans are in management positions.

"Day laborers, with visions of North American dollars, come from coastal villages and small farms up in the mountains to work in the hotels. With limited skills and no job security, they are at the mercy of fluctuating tourism trends and more often than not end up homeless and unemployed. Whole families try to survive by begging tourists to buy shells, fruit, or straw hats. These factors directly contribute to the growth of the slums. Tourism has also corrupted our culture by its presence, producing assembly line handicrafts and phony festivals. You should see what happens when the cruise ships pull in.

"Small and even larger businesses are also suffering because US companies undersell our local merchants by flooding our markets with overstocked and outdated items. Don't your Christian executives who benefit from the social and market structures created here by their businesses have some responsibility for their brothers and sisters in Jamaica who are negatively affected by those structures?"

Mike Hopkins snapped back to the present as Frank Palmer put his hand on Mike's shoulder and said: "Welcome again to the club. Our table is waiting." After the men had ordered lunch, Mike sketched the essence of his morning in Montego Bay and put Anthony Robinson's questions to his friends.

Frank Palmer, now sixty-six, recently retired from the vice-presidency of Consolidated International Beverage Company, turned to Mike with a grin. "When the church urged you and Carol to take that vacation, I should have known you couldn't just go and escape for a week! Well, to deal with the issues Tony put to us, we may first need to sort out why we have any responsibility. I personally believe that I *am* my brother's keeper. As a Christian, I find it impossible to observe conditions such as you describe and not seek a responsible way to help. Revolting conditions of hunger and health address not only company executives but also boards of directors and stockholders. There is a minimal but increasing sense of corporate responsibility in many companies. Tony is right. We get a profit; we must give in return. As the Bible says, 'From everyone to whom much has been given, much will be required' [Lk 12:48]. The issue then goes from rationale to strategy."

At this point George Delaney cut in, "Frank, as corporations we already give in terms of salaries for individuals, opportunities for small local businesses, and taxes to the government, all of which provide funds a country had no access to prior to our arrival. As you know, I am in the hotel business, and Tony has got to face some realities. He speaks of US companies grossing millions in the Caribbean. This is true, but he has a superficial view of gross operating profit. The return on investment is frequently very poor. The initial risk of building a hotel is increased by political instability and even the danger of eventual expropriation of property. For months following 9/11 the Jamaican tourist industry lost revenue of over a million dollars a day from canceled reservations. After the tremendous expense of building in a developing country, the management then has to continue to import at great expense the luxuries our customers expect. Most tourists want to feel at home with familiar cuisine. They want to live in the air-conditioned comfort of a hotel that provides a secure base for controlled exposure to an alien culture in the streets and markets.

"To provide that US-like retreat center in another culture is expensive. In fact, the percentage of operating profit in the Caribbean is one of the lowest of any major overseas operation, largely due to some of the highest employee salaries and benefits. We return a tremendous amount of income to those people. Good Calvinists like us acknowledge we're all sinners, but a significant number of Jamaicans benefit from US corporate presence.

"Look, Frank, for me to say I'm against helping the less fortunate is like saying I'm against motherhood. But as you have said in the past, you don't sell a moral attitude on its own merits. You've got to convince a company that it's in its self-interest to create a good working environment in order for its business to prosper. That's not only good business, it's sound policy based on human nature. Frank, while we may disagree on the rationale, we seem to agree on the conclusion. The long-term view of stability and profitability call for a controlled, careful strategy for corporate involvement in international issues."

"But, George," Mike Hopkins responded, "aren't we called as Christians to serve the world and not to attempt first to maximize our own benefits? I've seen you personally take a strong stand in the community on issues you felt were morally correct, even when this might jeopardize your image or result in a personal loss in the view of some people. Why must a corporation's assumption of social responsibility always be based on self-interest in contrast to an individual's responsibility? And as Tony indicated, what about the self-interest of the vast majority of Jamaicans who don't benefit from those statistically high employee salaries? While acknowledging our own sin, don't we also have to see the sin of an elite group of Jamaicans who link their self-interest to US corporate profit?"

Harold Atkins, thirty-eight, head of one of the largest travel-consultant firms in the Midwest, had been silent up to this point. Harold now spoke clearly and firmly: "Self-interest or not, I frankly don't think there is *any* premise for a business to become involved in the social concerns of a host country. Just as our country is based on a clear separation of church and state, so should our economic institutions function independently. Our

Lutheran friends have it right when they speak of two realms, one secular and one religious.

"A corporation is not an individual. A business has one responsibility—to create customers. If it does this well, the profit benefits host and guest. If not, both are out of business. An individual can afford to act responsibly in relation to his or her moral commitments. There is no corporate moral commitment in a business. Corporations do not have the luxury of being responsible in the same way. I may personally give money or time to some world social agency, but I'm not about to counsel my clients to do the same thing. The primary responsibility of my clients is to their stockholders, who have invested in a business, not in a philanthropic organization."

Frank Palmer slowly turned to Harold. "I used to operate with a similar logic in executive decisions, although I don't think I was ever asked to articulate it. Now, I am less persuaded. That logic appears, so my children argue, to divide one's life into neat compartments that don't correlate with one another. Why should a company be released from moral responsibility simply because it's a corporate institution? A business has several levels of obligation, only one of which is to its stockholders. True, you can't sell being a 'do-gooder,' but I am accountable for my employees because they are my employees, and I am accountable for those in need because they are in need. Somehow I must assume responsibility for my influence in my private and corporate life—even for my sins. This is at the heart of any sense of stewardship for the natural and human resources of the world. I'm not thinking simply about myself; I'm worried about the world my grandchildren and the Jamaicans' grandchildren will inherit."

As the lunch arrived, Mike Hopkins joked that judging by the intensity of the conversation, he certainly didn't need to encourage his friends to express their opinions. Mike noted that he was struck by the genuine ambiguity and complexity of the problem and needed to focus the concern he felt. "If we all agree that *some* moral responsibility exists—whether personal or corporate—how, for example, could an influential individual or hotel chain in the Caribbean go about effecting change for those in need? How can we respond, if at all, to Tony's request for help?"

"I've learned from experience," responded George Delaney, "that it is a mistake to sidestep the established channels. Governments, even of developing nations, tend to thrive on the status quo. We must convince them that economic stability depends on a solid middle class. It's in both our best interests to establish technical-training programs. Through supervised grants that use the resources of our money and our people, we should also seek to support health and education projects as well as indigenous crafts and music. This helps maintain the original culture; it also protects the reasons the tourists go to places like Jamaica. Mutual self-interest is the key."

Harold Atkins retorted: "But how do you justify any immediate return to your stockholders? The hotels I advise pay fair wages by local standards.

This is income for people who wouldn't otherwise have jobs. These people appear content with their lives. You're making paternalistic assumptions that it is in the best self-interest of Jamaicans for their country to become a copy of our society. My hotels pay high taxes. It's the local government's responsibility to channel the taxes into social programs as it sees fit. But the ultimate use of taxes is not my client's business. Personally, however, I would be willing to give Mike money to send to Tony's boys' club."

"Now, here's where I have to back off," interposed George. "Tony is not working through channels. It is my understanding that he was given that leave of absence from the church after a dispute with his conference over priorities. Lack of local support for his program also seems to indicate alienation from his former congregation. I remember Tony as a responsible young man, but to give him money without some form of control is another matter. To ask a hotel or a corporation to sponsor such a charitable project could jeopardize its relationship to the established middle class and possibly to the government. If these boys reach a point of 'self-realization' in which they put on pressure to evict my hotels, or worse, expropriate the investment, a project without supervision would be self-destructive. We must face the fact that our businesses are parasites on another culture. We need to work for the most symbiotic relationship possible between a parasite and its host. We don't seek the death of the host or the extermination of the parasite. Both organisms can survive and flourish through negotiated mutual interest and respect."

Frank Palmer shook his head. "Each of us and our corporations are involved in risks every day. We must respond in a way that is not demeaning. We can't offer assistance to Tony and then show him we have no confidence in his vision for his own people. A semi-paternalistic attitude is perhaps inevitable, but the overly paternalistic style of the 'company mill' will corrupt our humanity and theirs. We need more than bigger mission gifts—strings or no strings attached. The request from Tony, our former pastor and student, is to assume some responsibility for those who are in need based on Christian concern. I'm reminded of Christ's repeated call to Peter to 'feed my sheep.' Tony points us to children who are hungry for human dignity. A strategy for development ought to involve business, government, and church interests in Montego Bay and Chicago. Our church never touched me in this area, or perhaps I never listened. I feel called—I just don't know where."

George Delaney responded, "Frank, your vision is that of a retired corporation executive who has leisure and security. I wish you luck. Project-oriented mutual-interest programs are what Tony really needs, and if my competitors were to concur, we could make some headway here. A low-profit region like the Caribbean may be a place to try out such an approach. We have less to lose there."

Harry Atkins countered, "As a consultant, I don't think you have weighed properly the pressures of profit and growth at home or of instability and corruption in Jamaica. Are you willing to make the necessary payoffs? A corporation advisor would counsel, 'Don't exceed your corporate responsibilities for involvement.' However, as an individual I will make a pledge and write a check to Tony for his work. I always wanted to play a flute; this way I can at least buy one."

"The meal is almost over," Mike said. "We seem to have gone in so many different directions I'm wondering if there is any way we can consolidate our efforts in response to Tony."

Commentary

Big Business and the Boys' Club

Jesus Christ ministered to the poor and the politically powerless and lived in their midst. For centuries this man and his ministry have confronted his rich and powerful followers with the scandal of relating poverty and powerlessness to the wealth, might, and indifference of Caesar in his various ecclesiastical, political, and military configurations. In this case the destitution and muted desperation of Jamaican youth joined in a boys' club confront the confidence born of power of businessmen gathered in the quiet elegance of the Chicago Men's Club. Are these two all-male clubs destined to remain alienated from each other and the women of the world until the Lord returns in glory? Or has the power of Jesus Christ trickled down to all the clubs of this world?

This is a case first about corporate responsibility and second about poor countries and the place of transnational corporations (TNCs) within them. Since the latter is more appropriately the subject of other cases in this volume, this commentary will focus on corporate responsibility. It will assume that there is a Christian call to assist the poor.

The surface questions in the case are whether and how to assist Tony Robinson and the boys in his club. The deeper question is whether corporations have social responsibility beyond their economic responsibilities to produce goods and services, hire workers, and realize a profit.

This is a complex case. The characters may at first glance seem easy to understand, but their positions are a maze of assumptions, strategies, and theological understandings. Exploring this maze is the primary order of business. Four routes through the maze are offered by Tony Robinson, Frank Palmer, George Delaney, and Harold Atkins. Each route provides a way to assist Tony and thereby to exercise corporate responsibility. Each has theological foundations. And each is open to criticism.

TONY ROBINSON

Tony is the first of the four to make an appearance. Mike Hopkins and his wife run into him in the cocktail lounge of their Jamaican hotel where

Tony is playing the piano at night to support his work in a Montego Bay slum during the day. Tony recounts the ups and downs of his ministry in the four years since their last meeting. Tony uses the term *unsuccessful* to describe his service in a large Jamaican congregation. Later George Delaney reminds Mike that Tony was given a leave of absence from the congregation after a dispute over priorities. George is not sure what the dispute was about, although he concludes that Tony does not work through channels. Almost unnoticed is the further information that Tony worked with a gang of young boys in his spare time at this former congregation. Apparently this gang and its slum environment are Tony's new, self-selected parish.

From this sketchy information and his obvious sympathies, it is safe to assume that Tony feels squeezed between rich and poor worlds inside Jamaica and between North and South global perspectives outside. He is not playing the game according to the rules; as a result he finds himself isolated and without resources except for his music.

Tony is outraged at the conditions in the slums of Montego Bay and blames the tourist industry and its confederates in the Jamaican government, whose "generosity" has meant the slum has all of one water spigot. Tony clearly takes the side of those who live in the slums and probably represents their views. His approach to relieving the inhumane conditions of the slums is to jump into the thick of the fray and to empower the poor to provide their own relief. Specifically, he is using the vehicle of a musical band to drive the boys to a new consciousness based on an awareness of their own self-worth. He seeks the support of TNCs in order to empower the boys. This is explosive stuff, and George Delaney is correct to recognize it as such.

Tony seems ambivalent about TNCs. He lays at their feet the ills of Jamaican society. The conclusion would seem to follow that they should get out and take along the "phony festivals" and "controlled exposure to an alien culture" they have created. But Tony does not follow through to this conclusion. Furthermore, he draws pay from his adversaries and even asks them, through Mike, to support his work with the boys. He apparently believes that corporations have a responsibility to help pick up the pieces of the shattered Jamaican culture.

Liberation is the foundation of Tony's perspective. He cites Luke 4:18, a favorite text of liberationists. He makes use of liberation themes and methods as he tries to create a new awareness among the boys. His criticism of TNCs echoes themes articulated by other advocates for the poor in Latin America. He explicitly urges Mike Hopkins to join the struggle for liberation.

George Delaney insinuates that Tony is a dangerous radical. This is understandable, for whether or not Tony actually deserves this label, his ideas and actions are clear threats to TNCs and to George as an executive in the tourist business. "Who knows," George must be thinking, "those kids might rise up and burn the hotels. And if they stop short of that and just cause local riots, Jamaica will be dead to tourism overnight." To the supporters of TNCs and the form of development they bring to poor countries, George's insinuation and thoughts will seem well founded. To supporters of liberation they will seem self-serving.

FRANK PALMER

On the surface of things Frank seems to be the "good guy" in the discussion at the men's club. He is so willing to help. A retired executive of a beverage company, Frank leads off the discussion with his versions of helping the poor and corporate responsibility.

According to Frank, the way to help the poor is to involve business, government, and church interests in a coordinated development effort. He seems to assume that such a coordinated development plan is on the drawing boards and that the interests he mentions can be harmoniously drawn into such an effort on behalf of the poor. Unfortunately, there is no plan, harmony is nonexistent, and he admits a lack of direction.

On the matter of corporate responsibility, however, Frank is clearer and more direct. The wretched conditions of the poor in Montego Bay cry out for correction. TNCs have been among the forces that have generated these conditions and profited from them. TNCs have a social responsibility beyond making a profit that in no way differs from that of an individual. They are called to respond to Tony's request.

Theologically, Frank anchors his position in the biblical concern for the poor, repentance, stewardship, and the integration of all life under the lordship of Jesus Christ. He cites Jesus' summons to "feed my sheep." He mentions Cain's response, "Am I my brother's keeper?" to God's query regarding the whereabouts of Abel, Cain's slain brother. Frank emphatically rejects Cain's implication that he is not responsible for his neighbor.

Frank insists that a corporation is responsible on several levels for its acts, and especially for its sins, suggesting that TNCs have been shortsighted in poor countries and need to change their ways. He links this responsibility to the grand theme of stewardship. Individuals and corporations are God's stewards and are responsible for passing on to future generations what they have inherited from the past in no worse and preferably in better shape than they received it. Finally, he rejects Harold Atkins's separation of reality into individual and social spheres with different moralities. For Frank, there is one world in Christ. Corporations cannot claim release from social responsibility just because they have characteristics and functions that distinguish them from individuals.

Several criticisms are directed at Frank's position. George calls him paternalistic, a charge that has some foundation. Frank advocates corporate responsibility but links it neither to substantive social change nor to the participation of the poor. His coordinated development effort is not coordinated with the poor he would help. Business, government, and church leaders will presumably do all the work, then descend on the poor with their grand schemes. He also appears satisfied with responding to the symptoms of poverty with repentance and charity.

Harold Atkins refuses to budge from his distinction between individual and social realms and its implied rejection of Frank's argument for corporate social responsibility. In so doing he follows a long and honorable tradition in Christianity that makes this distinction. This tradition holds that groups have different functions and fewer moral resources than individuals and sometimes must act in ways that cannot be justified on ideal grounds. Violence—and the just-war response to it—is only one instance of this.

Left unmentioned is Frank's optimism that responsibility can be exercised easily and a harmony of interests be established. His sense of sin is almost nonexistent or at least not explicit.

GEORGE DELANEY

George is engaging because of his hard-headed realism. An executive in a TNC with interests in the Caribbean, he looks at corporate responsibility in dollars-and-cents terms and with a careful calculation of interests. His position may not be as hard-boiled as it at first seems, however. He does not subscribe to an unvarnished version of Adam Smith's "invisible hand," which guides the pursuit of self-interest toward the social good. He does not agree with Harold Atkins that corporations discharge all their social responsibilities in making a profit. His dogged pursuit of mutual self-interest is hard-headed in its understanding of sin but leaves the door open for TNCs to do more than just pursue profit.

For obvious reasons George is very cautious about helping the poor. He argues that Mike and Frank are overlooking the many ways in which TNCs already assist the poor through salaries, purchases in local markets, and taxes to governments. He assumes that these expenditures represent new money for Jamaica, an assumption that may be true in the case of his firm but is not generally true in poor countries where TNC investment funds often come from local sources.

George goes on to give details about the Caribbean region and its travel industry, which he depicts as being on the brink of disaster. The purpose of all his realism about social unrest and costs might be to persuade his colleagues that the travel industry can afford neither social change nor social responsibility.

To Jamaicans of Tony Robinson's persuasion, however, George's other details about luxury, familiar cuisine, air-conditioned comfort, controlled exposure, and alien cultures send a different message. These Jamaicans will automatically compare these details to their experience of poverty and conclude that George is arrogant and insensitive. Mike Hopkins softens this conclusion a bit when he points out George's involvement on moral issues in his own community.

The essence of George's position on assistance to the poor and the role of TNCs can be summarized in the words "mutual self-interest through established channels." What he appears to be advocating is a TNC-led model of development that stresses rapid economic growth. Eventually, or so the logic of this perspective goes, the poor will be best served by a careful strategy of corporate involvement with local governments that slowly lets the gains of economic growth trickle down to the poor. Stability and a solid middle class are essential ingredients.

George understands self-interest to be the motivating force in economic decisions and reasons from this to an accommodation of interests in mutually beneficial projects. He is not naive about harmonious accommodation, however. He recognizes that Tony's view cannot be included. Negotiations should go on between established powers with radicals such as Tony excluded.

Theologically, George's perspective rests on his view of sin. More precisely, it rests on the good that results from containing sin, especially the sin of those who threaten the established order. He refers to the tradition of Protestant reformer John Calvin and its heavy stress on sin. He returns again and again to self-interest as the primary human motivator. He speaks of a "sound policy based on human nature." Finally, his anxiety about instability and revolution suggests a strong fear of anarchy. Order must be maintained even if it means a measure of repression.

George has historical evidence to support his case. The tortured course of human history offers ample grounds for realism. But for his colleagues Frank Palmer and Mike Hopkins, George's realism is too thoroughgoing. For them, mutual accommodation of self-interest, particularly when it refuses to accommodate a majority of the population, cannot be the limit of human creativity and morality. Mike even protests George's realism by citing his involvement in the community. Still, George makes reference to no positive norms. Jesus Christ does not seem to make a difference for him in social affairs. Corporate social responsibility for its own sake is apparently too much to expect.

For all his consistency on sin, George is not particularly consistent in apportioning it. While he assumes corporations are motivated by self-interest, he is not nearly as worried about their sin as about Tony's. He overlooks entirely the well-documented evidence of TNC contributions to oppressive conditions in the poor world. He is oblivious to the failure of TNC-led development to make much of a dent in poverty. He ignores altogether the sin of the "solid middle class" that partially controls most governments. Indeed, in most poor countries the middle class George refers to is a small, wealthy elite protecting its own interests. Witness the one water spigot in the Montego Bay slum. In short, George's prescription is to protect the rich and constrain the poor, however much he might appeal to "trickle down" theory and the virtues of market capitalism.

HAROLD ATKINS

Harold is the youngest of the trio of businessmen and head of the largest travel consulting firm in the Midwest. The strength of his conviction that corporations have no place in the social welfare business or interfering in Jamaican internal politics may suggest an uncaring attitude. Such a suggestion would be wide of the mark, for Harold makes quite clear his willingness to give as an individual.

The division of individuals and corporations into separate spheres is the driving conception in Harold's scheme of things. Harold, unlike George Delaney, expresses no reluctance to assist Tony. He almost writes a check on the spot out of his personal account. He would not, however, approve a request from the treasurer of his company to issue a check on the corporate account. Individuals may give, but corporations may not.

This division of things into separate spheres is deeply ingrained in Western ways of thinking. It stems from, among other places, ancient Greek thought with its dualisms of light and dark, mind and body, and good and evil. It informs the US Constitution with its separation of powers and its distinction between church and state. In religious terms it is expressed in the two-realms understanding to which Harold refers.

Harold argues that corporations have one and only one social responsibility—to make a profit. Profits are the lifeblood of any business enterprise. Without them a business must shut its doors, and when it does, it fails in its ancillary responsibilities to shareholders, employees, customers, and even the public through its incapacity to pay taxes. Profits are also an important signaling device. They tell investors where to put their money so that resources will be efficiently allocated. Harold is certainly correct in one respect. There is little room for romanticism about profits and their link to the production of goods and services. Profits are the first priority of any business in a market economy.

The question, however, is not really about the priority of profits. No one at the lunch table would disagree with that. Even the absent Tony would probably concur. The question is whether corporations have other social responsibilities. Harold seems to think not.

His full argument, were he to make it, would probably go something like this. The moral responsibility of corporate executives is to produce goods and services and in so doing to serve the interests of the owners. Investors entrust their funds to executives and become owners or shareholders with the expectation of a return. Executives are stewards of these funds and break trust with the owners when they use corporate profits for their own self-selected causes. In effect, they levy a tax on the shareholders without giving them representation in the decision. Morally, executives must respect the wishes of shareholders and abstain from trying to do good for them. It is the owners who should be the ones to exercise moral responsibility as they allocate their corporate dividends and capital gains among competing claims.

Harold might also argue on pragmatic grounds. Using hard-won earnings on extraneous social concerns reduces profits and makes a company less attractive as an investment. In the case of environmental protection, it can also make a company less competitive. If managers act responsibly to clean up their company's pollution while competitors continue to pass pollution costs on to the public in dirty air and water, they incur higher costs. The same goes for paying higher wages and increasing safety measures. A highly competitive market system puts great pressures on managers to keep such costs to a minimum.

On pragmatic grounds Harold might also question Frank Palmer's knee-jerk advocacy of corporate social responsibility. Would Frank really want powerful corporations paternalistically mucking around in the affairs of nations and individuals? The days of the company town are over. Corporations are not well situated to set priorities for governments or to decide complex moral and social issues. More than likely they will set directions in their own narrow self-interest and bungle tasks they have assigned themselves. Thus for a host of philosophical, moral, and pragmatic reasons Harold would urge corporations to stick to production and money making and let individuals and governments set social priorities.

Theologically, Harold bases his perspective on the call to give, which he would answer individually with personal good deeds and socially with government activity. He also cites the two-realms understanding first articulated by Augustine and later developed by Luther. This perspective divides reality into sacred and secular spheres that are governed by God's right and left hands, respectively. The right hand of God, exercised in the church, is the hand of faith, hope, and love. Grace, forgiveness, charity, and nonviolence abound in this realm. The left hand of God, exercised by governments and other social institutions, is the hand of order, pragmatic calculation, and justice. Punishment, coercion, and even justifiable violence (the so-called sword as a symbol of the ordering function) have important roles to play. These two spheres are distinct, if not separate, and should not be confused, in Luther's thought. They are held together by the two hands of one God and by individuals who are free to live in both spheres while recognizing their differences.

Corporations as economic institutions are part of the secular realm and are governed by different norms than individuals. The function of corporations is not to love people, which they cannot do anyway, but to order economic life so there are sufficient resources for basic necessities. For corporations to get mixed up in charity or non-economic social concerns is to confuse the way God has ordered human life. This confusion will lead to disorder and in the end accomplish little. Charity is the province of individuals and groups organized to provide it.

This perspective is well established in Christian tradition. Yet a too rigid separation of realms, of which Harold may be guilty, misses the subtleties of the traditional two-realms formulation. The realms are not separate. To repeat, they are held together by God and by individuals who carry motives of love and intentions to serve ethically from their personal faith into the social realm. Faith, hope, love, grace, forgiveness, charity, and nonviolence are not irrelevant to the primary economic function of corporations. At the very least corporations can act justly, obey the law, and refrain from causing injury.

Frank Palmer counters Harold's tendency to separate by distinguishing levels of responsibility. He makes a good point. Corporations have different functions and priorities, but God's realm of love, though distinct, is relevant to every level of Harold's work and to the business of his firm. The thorny issue is discerning relevance and deciding what is the appropriate exercise of corporate social responsibility.

CORPORATE RESPONSIBILITY

Actually, a number of mediating possibilities stand between Frank's "either" of full social responsibility and Harold's "or" of limited responsibility. George Delaney articulates one position in spite of its problems. He advocates social responsibility as long as it is consistent with the overall interests of the company, with long-term profit presumably high on his list of interests. Another position would allow for social responsibility if it enhances profitability and would give managerial discretion if it does not.

Harold Atkins's perspective shorn of its theological wraps is usually associated with economist Milton Friedman. In a now classic 1970 essay entitled "The Social Responsibility of Business Is to Increase Its Profits," Friedman set the case for profits as the exclusive responsibility of corporations. Friedman made many of the same arguments as Harold Atkins. Corporations are not persons. Managers have a moral responsibility to serve stockholders with profits. Individuals and social institutions other than corporations are better situated to set and carry out social priorities.

But even Friedman stepped back from an extreme interpretation of this view. In a little-noticed sentence of his essay, Friedman spoke of profit seeking "while conforming to the basic rules of society, both those embodied in law and those embodied in social custom." Conforming to the law does not substantially change his position, but his openness to social custom certainly makes a difference.

The fact is that most North Americans expect corporations to be ethical. The best run and most profitable firms are often ones in which values and social responsibility are woven deeply into the corporate fabric. In other words, there is such a thing as corporate character, and ethics flow out of character.

In fact, corporations cannot avoid social responsibility. They are so large and powerful today that their activities inevitably spill over into non-economic realms. It is really not so much a matter of yes or no to social responsibility as it is of being responsible or irresponsible. Being a responsible corporation does not mean becoming a flag-waving social activist promoting each and every social cause. Profits are primary in a market system. Corporations cannot meet all the claims placed on them and certainly should not fool themselves about moral purity. Harold Atkins is correct about the exercise of corporate social responsibility. It can cause competitive disadvantage and injustice and lead to the setting of wrong priorities and to poor execution. All these are considerations that constrain the capacity, if not the imperative, to be moral.

How managers should act in pursuing corporate responsibility is open to debate. There are at least two moral minimums: to act according to the law, and to avoid and correct injury. To follow the law is self-explanatory, however ambiguous it may be at times. To avoid injury and to rectify past injuries may be as simple as adequate on-the-job safety precautions or as complex as pulling investments out of places where human rights are abused. Included in this second minimum is certainly the just treatment of employees and customers.

Beyond this minimum the debate begins. The call to charity and the obligation to lend assistance are strong parts of Christian tradition, more so when there is a critical need, proximity, capability, and no one present who is better able. The distinctions encountered in the two-realms understanding give pause and to a degree constrain but do not finally limit this obligation. Jesus Christ is the lord of both realms, and the Christian is called to live ethically as an individual and as a member of social institutions. Life is of a piece, not separated into exclusive spheres.

The forms that corporate responsibility can take are infinite, but four general categories stand out:

1. Self-regulation to avoid or to correct injury.
2. Affirmative action to correct internal corporate abuses and to improve conditions internal and external to the corporation.
3. Leadership in moral causes.
4. Developing corporate character and managing values so that morality permeates the corporation.

The fourth, in particular, should receive greater attention than it has.

Should Tony be assisted? It would be a small matter and generous for the three businessmen to open their pockets and give individually. As for a corporate gift, that would also be in order, easily accomplished, and a matter for objection only to those purists who deny any social responsibility for corporations.

In the larger context, however, this apparently simple question raises fundamental and perplexing dilemmas. In terms of Christian tradition the dilemma is how to connect the poverty and powerlessness of Jesus and his followers to the wealth and might of the modern corporation. In terms of poor countries the dilemma is how to bring poor peasants and urban slum dwellers into a just relationship with TNCs and local elites. The three solutions proposed in the men's club in typical power-broker fashion all rely on charity, although Frank talks vaguely about a coordinated development effort and George about mutual assistance projects. None includes a shift of power and privilege. Tony's overall orientation has seeds for fundamental change, but little is said about power.

Is charity all rich Christians can do to link the worlds of poor and rich? Perhaps corporate responsibility means something more daring: either to take the poor as the point of departure or to get out. To take the world's poor as a point of departure would be difficult for TNCs. They have little expertise in meeting the needs of the poor, and, with self-interest as a given, little inclination. The poor have no money to buy their products, and TNCs make high profits with things as they are.

To pull out of poor countries might then be the responsible path. Jamaica might be better off without the tourist industry. But try to tell Jamaicans that. A few might listen, but whatever else they do, TNCs provide jobs and thereby infuse or at least generate income. They may not be the right kind of jobs, and taking them may mean serving the status quo, but Jamaicans have few alternatives. Few institutions are waiting in the wings to infuse large amounts of capital while taking the poor as their point of departure.

This more daring either/or of corporate responsibility is an indictment of TNCs. It is not, however, an indictment of TNC executives as mean-spirited and uncharitable. They are part of a system that has been tremendously productive and meets the material needs of many people. They must be self-interested. The problems they face are systemic. At present, TNC-led market capitalism is not adequately meeting the needs of the world's poor. Sensitive executives feel squeezed between the forces at work. Perhaps one thing they could do is to pay Tony a visit and learn firsthand about conditions in Jamaica and the view from the vantage point of the poor.

For the time being the two worlds of poor and rich remain alienated and apart. The power of Jesus Christ has not been allowed to trickle down. This leaves Christians themselves squeezed between conflicting perspectives and wondering which alternative is the best one to act on in an imperfect world.

ADDITIONAL RESOURCES

Beauchamp, Thomas L., and Norman E. Bowie, eds. *Ethical Theory and Business.* 7th ed. Englewood Cliffs, NJ: Prentice-Hall, 2003.
Bowie, Norman. *Business Ethics: A Kantian Perspective:* Oxford, UK: Blackwell, 1999.
Friedman, Milton. *Capitalism and Freedom.* Chicago: Univ. of Chicago Press, 1962.
―――. "The Social Responsibility of Business Is to Increase Its Profits." *The New York Times Sunday Magazine* (September 13, 1970).
Green, Ronald M. *The Ethical Manager: A New Method for Business Ethics.* New York: Macmillan, 1994.
McCoy, Charles S. *Management of Values.* Boston: Pitman, 1985.
Mount, Eric, Jr. *Professional Ethics in Context.* Louisville, KY: Westminster/ John Knox, 1990.
Niebuhr, Reinhold. *Moral Man and Immoral Society.* New York: Charles Scribner's Sons, 1932.
Peters, Rebecca Todd. *In Search of the Good Life: The Ethics of Globalization.* New York: Continuum, 2004.
Simon, John G., Charles Powers, and John P. Gunneman. *The Ethical Investor.* New Haven, CT: Yale Univ. Press, 1972.
Stackhouse, Max L., and Dennis McCann, eds. *On Moral Business: Classical and Contemporary Resources for Ethics in Economic Life.* Grand Rapids, MI: Eerdmans, 1995.

Case

Klamath Conflicts: Limited Water Resources

Amanda Anderson felt the vibration of her cell phone. Clicking it on, she heard the familiar voice of Matthew Howe, pastor of a Methodist church in the Klamath Falls region of southern Oregon. They had worked together when both served churches in Portland. Amanda had moved on to Oregon Associated Ministries as director of environment and justice concerns, and Matthew had moved to southern Oregon and a new church.

Matthew wanted her to come down to the Klamath Falls area to preach in his church and to lead a workshop on conflict resolution. He talked about needing help in the polarized atmosphere that continued to hang over the region. "The issues," he said, "are still the same: limited water resources in the Klamath River Basin and their equitable distribution. I continue to be pinched between opposing sides and between my own environmental concerns and the entrenched views of my parishioners, many of whom are farmers who feel threatened by the continuing uncertainty over the availability of water for irrigation." Matthew had tried the path of mediation, without success in his estimation, but was not willing to give up quite yet. He was convinced that the only way to resolve the continuing disputes was for the parties involved to work out their differences through negotiation and compromise. "Perhaps you could help where I have failed," he added. "I know you are well versed in the issues and good at conflict resolution."

Amanda hesitated because she knew the situation in the Klamath River basin. It was no exaggeration to speak of water wars. "But," she thought to

---

This case was prepared by Robert L. Stivers. Copyright © The Case Study Institute. The names of all persons and institutions have been disguised to protect the privacy of those involved.

herself, "what Matthew is asking for is part of my vocation. How can I not at least try to help." So Amanda agreed to come, and they set a date.

As she thought about the sermon and the workshop, three things were certain. First, environmentalists were right that the Klamath River Basin, especially the upper basin above Iron Gate Dam in northern California, was in deep trouble ecologically because there were simply too many demands being placed on its water resources. This was especially true in late summer, when demand for irrigation is high, precipitation low, and snow melt all but gone. Low river levels combine with degraded habitat and water pollution to put pressure on fish and other species native to the basin.

Second, leaders at the local, state, and national levels had neglected the interests of Native Americans in the basin. Leaders had ignored their rights to water under treaties negotiated in the nineteenth century and even for a time eliminated their status as a tribe.

Third, the farmers who irrigate have legitimate grievances and should not be left alone to bear the costs of a newfound environmental awareness. Other groups were also responsible for the environmental damage and low water levels.

HISTORICAL OVERVIEW

The upper basin of the Klamath River is not exceptional in terms of limited water resources. Water managers have over allocated water resources in many basins in the dry, intermountain west and, for that matter, in many semi-arid regions of the world. Amanda understood these things in a general way and had read a lot about the Klamath situation.

Just to make sure about details and recent developments Amanda called Professor Carl Robbins, who was doing a study of conflicts over water in the upper basin. "Irrigation in the basin began in the late nineteenth century," he told her, "but the big push came with the Klamath Project, one of the largest land reclamation and irrigation projects ever undertaken by the US Bureau of Reclamation. Begun in 1902, it took fifty years to complete. Water managers encouraged farmers to homestead, and after World War II allotted new lands by lottery to returning veterans. Today approximately 130,000 acres in Oregon and 70,000 acres in California on fourteen hundred farms are watered by the project. The ecological impacts have been considerable, involving the controversial conversion of wetlands and wildlife refuges to productive farmland and the runoff of herbicides, pesticides, and fertilizers into the region's waterways.

"In April 2001 drought conditions prevailed and water managers for the Klamath Project, acting under the mandate of the Endangered Species Act, were forced by court decisions and new biological opinions from the US Fish and Wildlife Service and the National Marine Fisheries Service to curtail water for irrigation. At issue were two species of endangered sucker fish that had once been abundant in the basin and a run of threatened wild Coho salmon. During the years 1995–97 massive fish kills had decimated the sucker fish for reasons that were not well understood but probably involved excessive algae that reduced oxygen levels in Upper Klamath Lake. The Coho had long been in decline as a result of over fishing and degraded habitat. The curtailment involved 170,000 acres and 1,200 farms in the project. Summer rains permitted some release of water, but in the end farmers received only 22 percent of their average annual allocation. The situation was incendiary.

"Farmers and those they support blamed environmentalists and Native Americans. Environmentalists, Native Americans, and those who fished downstream blamed the farmers. Everyone blamed the government. Outside groups took advantage of the situation to pursue political agendas. Farmers were outraged that the needs of fish would be put before their right to the water. Old animosities toward Native Americans who claimed prior water rights were rekindled.

"The farmers took matters into their own hands and on four occasions forcibly opened the head gates to the Project before federal marshals were called in to stop them. Farmers, already under economic pressure from corporate farms and foreign growers, suffered considerable financial loss, even though some governmental assistance was forthcoming. More important, perhaps, they lost the security they had so long enjoyed. Uncertainty with all of its anxieties replaced confidence. They demanded just compensation for their losses under the 'takings' clause in the Fifth Amendment to the US Constitution, claiming that the government had taken their property through its enforcement of environmental regulations. Now, several years later, little has been resolved, and wounds still fester.

"While the farmers' claims sometimes seem a bit exaggerated," Carl added, "they need to be put in perspective. Irrigators are not the only ones making demands on the limited water supply. Nor are they the only ones affecting critical fish habitat. Yet they are being forced to bear a disproportionate financial burden of enforcing environmental regulations. Loggers have changed stream ecology by clear cutting to the banks of watercourses and poor road building. Ranchers in the upper basin graze and water their livestock near streams, altering riverbanks and depositing manure. Municipalities continue to withdraw more water to satisfy growing populations that also demand that electrical utilities build dams to generate power and provide recreational opportunities. Dams change the nature of rivers by changing flow patterns and temperatures. Over fishing downstream and in the ocean has significantly reduced wild salmon runs that also must put up with degraded habitat in the upper basin where they spawn.

"Responsibility extends even further," he went on. "Managers of the Klamath Project and legislators encouraged farmers to till the land and gave them assurances that there would be ample water. They even entered into compacts with the farmers that established irrigation as the number one priority for water use. They ignored treaties the US government had negotiated in the nineteenth century that reserved water for local Native American tribes in all accustomed places for subsistence and ceremonial purposes. Needless to say, in the rush to meet human demand managers and legislators disregarded birds, fish, and other wildlife. The marshland of the upper basin is one of the most important wintering grounds for migrating birds on the Pacific flyway. Numbers are in serious decline, now only a fraction of what they used to be. Fish species, as I have indicated, are also in trouble.

"As the 1990s wore on, the decline of these species became obvious. Environmental groups called for enforcement of the Endangered Species Act and other environmental laws. The US Fish and Wildlife Service listed the two sucker fish species as endangered and the National Marine Fisheries Service listed a wild salmon run as threatened. Such listing is supposed to prevent further degradation of the habitat, but what it means exactly is hard to say. Scientists who must determine such things are only beginning to understand the complexities of the basin's ecology. There is ample opportunity to make mistakes that cause financial hardship, but to pursue a course of inaction based on scientific uncertainty is not good stewardship.

"Two years of drought in the early 1990s exacerbated the situation. In most years there is ample water to meet demand in the basin. In years of drought this is not the case. And when drought coincides with the late summer dry season and peak crop production, water reductions lower stream and lake levels, raise temperatures, and concentrate pollutants. This is not good for in-stream species and those who depend on them." Carl went on to fill in the details and ended by telling Amanda she could feel free to call him at any time.

A FARMER'S PERSPECTIVE

After talking to Carl, Amanda decided she needed to speak with those directly involved in the conflict. First, she called Peter Oldridge, a farmer in the region who was suggested by Pastor Howe. He was not in but returned her call about an hour later. He seemed eager to talk. He began by describing farming as a way of life, expressing a vision of the yeoman farmer coming west, working hard, and providing for his family. He related the trek west of his grandfather, who settled on a parcel of land in the Klamath Project, farmed it, paid his full share of irrigation costs, and upon retiring, passed the farm on to Peter's father. "What we are about," he said, "is preserving a way of life and providing food for a growing world population. We think the first priority for water use in the Klamath River Basin should be irrigation, as it has been for over a century. Over the years federal, state, and local officials have recognized this priority, provided water, and encouraged us to use the land beneficially for growing food crops. We have responded by fulfilling our end of the bargain and exercising good stewardship of the land.

"What is happening now amounts to a conspiracy by environmentalists, Indians, and other outside forces to take control of the government and take our water away. Environmentalists are the worst. They come from all over the country and complain that farmers are degrading animal and fish habitats by lowering water levels, raising stream temperatures, and releasing pollutants in the runoff of irrigation water.

"We are good stewards of the environment and are getting better at it every year. Their accusations are unfounded, and their science is unsound. In 2001, with little knowledge of the basin, they persuaded the Bureau of Reclamation that water levels in lakes and stream would be too low for those sucker fish. Later studies showed that this was not true. Water levels are now higher than they were before the Klamath Project was begun. The fish do not need more water. Their decline is due to natural causes.

"In all this the environmentalists used the deeply flawed Endangered Species Act to dupe water managers in order to gain power for themselves and remove farmers from the land. The law is badly flawed because it makes the farmers pay all the costs. It is unconstitutional because it deprives us of our property. Its implementation has been arbitrary because of the poor science on which decisions are based.

"Environmentalists are successful because they are better organized and, unlike farmers, their organizations don't pay any taxes. As they plot our ruin they make this big deal about saving the fish. They want nature to come first, even before human need. Don't they know that God made humans in his own image and gave us dominion over the fish? In Genesis 9 the Bible tells us that it is all there for us. How can they claim that fish take priority over humans? What counts is human well-being. We need to be fed, and farmers hereabouts do a good job growing food.

"The Klamath Indians are not much better. We have had good relations with them, but they have been poor stewards. Years ago they readily accepted the government's money to end their status as a tribe. They squandered their settlement money. Now they claim a prior right to substantial amounts of water based on some out-of-date nineteenth-century treaty. The courts seem to have been taken in by their claims. So the farmers get moved further down the line. We get less water, and our rights are taken.

"We think all this constitutes a grave injustice. We have rights to the water. These rights were granted to us in order to protect our investments in land, equipment, and water-delivery systems. These rights are attached to our property. They are perpetual as long as we make beneficial use of the land. They insure that water will be available on a first in time, first in right basis. When the government takes our water away, it ought to compensate us fully for our losses.

"The injustice gets worse. We don't know when managers will withhold the water next to comply with environmental regulations. This uncertainty leads to higher levels of anxiety and lower property values. They made a compact with us to provide water and are failing to keep their end of the bargain."

ENVIRONMENTAL PERSPECTIVE

Next Amanda called Emily Williams, a close friend and executive director of Citizens for Healthy Habitats, a statewide environmental group that was part of the Klamath Task Force that had formed in 1999 to address environmental problems in the Klamath River Basin. Emily was a committed environmentalist who often spoke about newly emerging biocentric attitudes toward nature. Instead of the anthropocentric, dualistic, hierarchical, and dominating attitudes of the farmers and water managers, she urged thinking in terms of the whole biosphere. She referred to the biocentric attitudes of connection, equality, and cooperation. Instead of looking at ecological systems solely in terms of economic value, she liked to think in holistic terms. She appealed to the social policy of her church, whose ethic of ecology and justice was guided by the four norms of sustainability, sufficiency, participation, and solidarity. Amanda reflected on Emily's perspective and how far it was from Peter's. They seemed to live in different worlds. How could she ever get them to talk to each other?

Emily picked up the phone after only one ring. She repeated much of what Carl Robbins had said. The Klamath River habitat, in her opinion, was badly degraded, with extinction a looming reality for a number of species. She placed a good deal of the blame on the misguided Klamath River Project. She did not blame the farmers directly, but she gave Amanda an earful about the design and management of the project. She claimed the engineers and managers had unwisely allocated the land and water without regard for other species and for Native Americans. "The project," she said, "takes by far the biggest share of the water that users remove from the lakes and streams. The project makes its greatest demands at the time of lowest flow. The negative impact on habitats has been enormous. Farming on the present scale in the basin cannot coexist with other species. In my opinion the needs of declining species and the reserved water rights of Native Americans take priority. The farmers are unable to see this and will not sit down to negotiate.

"As for the farmers' takings claims, they do not know the law. They do not own the water in the basin as they claim. The public owns the water. In addition, the law is by no means settled, especially when it comes to regulatory takings. Nor have water rights in the basin been fully adjudicated by the courts, which means that no one is quite sure about quantities and priorities. The courts must decide this basin by basin, and the task, while it has been going on since 1975 in the Klamath River Basin, is still not finished. Invoking takings is also a cumbersome process. It's like cutting butter with a chain saw. The courts will be tied in knots by the claims, and in the end the farmers will not succeed. And, if by chance they do, you can say goodbye to environmental laws, not to mention zoning and historical-preservation laws. They will be too expensive to enforce.

"I am sympathetic to the farmers' plight. All of us are responsible for the overuse of a limited resource. The farmers are being required to pay the largest share of the cost to protect the fish. They deserve help, but as long as they are so stubborn, we will never resolve this conflict."

OTHER CONVERSATIONS

A few days later Amanda called Johnny Frank, who spoke for the Klamath Tribe. In contrast to the rosy picture painted by Peter Oldridge, he told her about a tortured history of repression and continuing racism against Native Americans in the region. "They took our land, forced us to live on a reservation, and then tried to take what was left by terminating our status as a tribe," he said bitterly. He related the hatred directed at Native Americans during the summer of 2001, which he claimed was still very strong. "It is not a pretty picture," he went on, "but now that the courts have recognized our reserved rights to water under the 1863 treaty signed by Abraham Lincoln himself, things look better. Once the courts adjudicate the allocation of water in the basin, we should at least get our fair share."

Amanda also talked to Bob Blanchard, a water manager in the Klamath Project. He related in graphic terms the tightrope he was walking between the warring parties. He admitted that water managers in the past had paid little attention to anything except irrigation. "It is an easy hindsight judgment to make now that the science of ecology is more sophisticated," he added. "Back then managers had little sense of what might eventually happen. They were flying blind."

The next call went to a rancher friend of Amanda's, Roberta Blanchard. Roberta acknowledged the damage to fish habitat caused by livestock, especially in the area above Upper Klamath Lake. She and her husband were now practicing what she called sustainable ranching. They were keeping their livestock away from the banks of streams and trying to grow natural vegetation.

Finally, Amanda contacted Adam Carter, a lawyer in the Portland area who was acquainted with court decisions on water rights and regulatory takings. He first noted that the last clause in the Fifth Amendment to the US Constitution says: "nor shall private property be taken for public use without just compensation." He was fully aware of the takings claims made by farmers in the Klamath River Basin in 2001. "This is a complicated matter," he added. "Let me tell you a few things you need read up on before you can evaluate these claims. I will also send a recent paper on the subject that fills in the particulars. Here is my list.

1. The evolution of rights language to give specificity to the ethical norm of justice.
2. The extension of rights in the form of water rights to govern the allocation of water in arid regions.
3. The relation of rights to responsibilities.
4. The tension between protecting the common good, as in preserving species, and protecting the individual against arbitrary seizure of property.
5. The conflicts between rights holders, for example, Native Americans and irrigators.
6. The cumbersome nature of adjudicating water rights.
7. The relation of water rights to property rights.
8. Court decisions on regulatory takings.
9. The financial and political consequences of accepting takings claims and demands for compensation.
10. The political agendas of outside groups that further inflamed both sides in the 2001 conflict.

"I hope that isn't too much to chew on," he concluded. "It's complicated but not impossible to grasp. Be prepared, however, for the conclusion I have reached. The complications, the unsettled nature of the law, the consequences of accepting claims and demands, and the politicized nature of the debate make the use of the takings clause a very poor instrument for redressing the losses of the irrigators. Litigation will take years, tie up the courts, and prolong the conflict. What those folks need to do is sit down and reach an agreement on what is a just allocation. No other process will work."

Several days later the paper arrived. Amanda studied it until she grasped the basics. She would never be a legal expert, but at least she would be able to understand the discussion.

CONFLICT RESOLUTION

As a final task, Amanda reviewed her extensive notes on conflict resolution. Two years before she had taken a workshop with the Plowshares Institute of Connecticut. She had used her skills on several occasions in local churches and even in a few environmental disputes in the Portland area. She was surprised to find she had natural ability as a mediator and often had been called to assist.

In her mind, however, she was still not sure of the most effective approach for intervention in Klamath Falls. She agreed with Adam Carter's conclusion that the people most involved in the conflict needed to work out a resolution. Matthew Howe, whose congregation included a number of leaders representing a wide spectrum of positions, was a good place to start. But as an outsider, Amanda also needed to build trust in the wider community in order to encourage and support the diverse parties to begin to talk to one another, especially when feelings on all sides were so strong. Even as she struggled to decide how she personally felt about the issues raised by the complex dispute, Amanda knew that she must be completely unbiased in speaking with the parties. Amanda's experience had also convinced her that to reach a sustainable resolution, the process that was developed was likely to be more important than the specific agreements the parties made.

Commentary

Klamath Conflicts:
Limited Water Resources

The Psalmist praises God's good creation with its seemingly unlimited water resources.

> You make springs gush forth in the valleys;
>   they flow between the hills,
> giving drink to every wild animal;
>   the wild asses quench their thirst.
> By the streams the birds of the air have their
>   habitation;
>   they sing among the branches.
> From your lofty abode you water the mountains;
>   the earth is satisfied with the fruit of your work.
>   (Ps 104:10–13)

One wonders how the Psalmist would speak today were he plunked down in the Klamath River Basin and given a few days to poke around. The situation there has changed dramatically in less than a century. Amanda Anderson might well start her sermon with this text and point to the changes that have occurred.

Limited fresh water resources are a problem not only in the Klamath River Basin but also in river basins throughout the world. The problems result not from any reduction in the overall supply of water, but rather from the degradation of watersheds and a dramatic increase in human demand. The increase in demand is a product of an expanding human population, higher per capita consumption in wealthy countries, and the enhanced technical capability to extract water from lakes and streams. Local and regional climate variations and more or less effective management of the water supplies amplify or modulate these causes from place to place. Problems are particularly acute in arid regions with sizable human populations and places with significant seasonal fluctuations in rainfall.

In the United States the landmass between the 100th meridian and the Pacific Ocean is generally dry with the exception of mountainous regions and the coast. Seasonal fluctuations with especially dry summers characterize much of the region. In most of the region's river basins humans have withdrawn so much water and so altered the character of watercourses that aquatic dependent species, especially fish, are threatened with extinction. Legislators have responded to this situation with new laws to protect species and their habitats. Water managers have a mixed record of enforcing these new laws and in the process of enforcement have occasionally withheld water allocations to certain users, in particular farmers who irrigate. The withholding of water supplies is a serious problem for farmers and has occasioned intense conflict in several locations.

In the Klamath River Basin in southern Oregon and northern California, irrigators, using water-delivery systems built by the US Bureau of Reclamation, the state of Oregon, and local water districts, annually divert a significant portion of the water from the Klamath River and its tributaries to produce food crops. Irrigators are the single largest group of users to take water out of the stream in the watershed.

The basin is normally well watered by rain and snow in the Cascade Mountains, but periodic droughts and seasonal fluctuations can severely limit the supply of water. During the late summer months, after the snow pack has melted, lake and stream levels become dangerously low, water temperatures rise, and pollutants from agricultural runoff and other sources are concentrated in what water remains. The situation is more complex than this, of course. Stream degradation and species decline have multiple causes. Overlapping political jurisdictions, conflicting laws and regulations, differing ways of perceiving the actual situation, and diverse attitudes toward nature complicate things even more. In spite of these complexities, irrigators are the primary focus of attention because they divert so much water.

The year 2001 was a drought year in the Klamath River Basin, not the worst on record but serious nonetheless. In April 2001 the US Bureau of Reclamation announced there would be little or no water available for irrigation. Federal water managers had concluded that three threatened species of fish would be seriously jeopardized if normal diversions were allowed. Since these officials controlled water allocations to about 50 percent of the irrigated land in the region, including the most fertile land, the decision promised a huge impact. Some farmers were threatened with at least a year's loss of income and substantial loss of property value due to the uncertainty of future allocations. Farmers rose up in protest. They organized large demonstrations at the point where water is diverted from the river to their fields in the city of Klamath Falls, Oregon. They even took matters into their own hands and illegally opened the gates to release the water.

Since 2001 the situation has not improved markedly, although water is again flowing to the farmers' fields, and public protest has ceased. The various groups mentioned in the case are still pitted against one another. The war of words continues.

THE ETHIC OF ECOLOGICAL JUSTICE

Ethically, the situation calls for a reconsideration of traditional Christian attitudes toward nature. While anthropocentric attitudes toward nature once sufficed to maintain the human species without endangering entire ecosystems, this is no longer the case. Increasingly the biosphere must be considered along with the human sphere. No longer can nature be separated from culture, considered inferior, or dominated. Connection to and cooperation with nature are now in order lest humans degrade the very basis of all life.

In addition, a new ethic is needed. Christians have many resources to meet this need. For over twenty years what is here called the ethic of ecological justice has been emerging in ecumenical circles. It offers a Christian perspective to guide decision-makers on important environmental and social issues.

Justice

The norm of justice used in the title of this ethical perspective is an inclusive concept. Its full meaning is given greater specificity by the four norms of sustainability, sufficiency, participation, and solidarity. Justice is, however, a norm in its own right with a distinct history in Christian ethics and Western philosophy.

The biblical basis for justice with its special sensitivity for the poor starts with God's liberation of the Hebrew slaves in Egypt and the establishment of a covenant, one of whose cardinal features is righteousness (Ex 22:21–24). The biblical basis continues in the prophetic reinterpretation of the covenant (Mic 6:8; Am 2:6; 5:11; 8:4–8; Is 10:1–2; Jer 22:13–17).

In the Christian scriptures the emphasis on justice is muted in comparison to the prophets, but the concern for the poor may be even stronger. Jesus himself was a poor man from a poor part of Israel. His mission was among the poor and directed to them (Lk 4:16–20). He blessed the poor and spoke God's judgment on the rich (Lk 6:20–26; Mt 5:1–14).

The early church carried on this tradition. Paul's concern is frequently for the weak members of the community. This is his concern as he addresses a question that now seems quaint—eating meat sacrificed to idols (1 Cor 8). He affirms the new freedom in faith that is one important foundation for political freedom. Freedom is not license, however. It involves concern for the neighbor and the common good.

Paul is even more emphatic on equality, which with freedom is the backbone of the modern concept of justice. His statement on the ideals of freedom and equality is among the strongest in the entire biblical witness: "There is no longer Jew or Greek, there is no longer slave or free, there is no longer male and female; for all of you are one in Christ Jesus" (Gal 3:28).

For the Greeks justice meant treating equals equally and unequals un-equally. This simple statement of the norm of justice hides the complexities of determining exactly who is equal and who is not and the grounds for justifying inequality. It leads in modern interpretations of justice, however, to freedom and equality as measures of justice. It also leads to the concept of equity, which is justice in actual situations where a degree of departure from freedom and equality are permitted in the name of achieving other social goods. So, for example, most societies give mentally and physically impaired individuals extra resources and justify this unequal treatment in the name of greater fairness. This is a departure from equal treatment but not from equitable treatment. The problem, of course, is that self-interested individuals and groups will always ask for departures from freedom and equality and use spurious justifications. This is one reason justice needs love as its foundation and careful scrutiny of claims for justice in practice.

The Bill of Rights in the US Constitution and more generally the various declarations of human rights that have appeared from time to time over the past two hundred years are ways to spell out justice and equity in greater detail and to protect individuals and minority groups against the arbitrary power of the state. Rights are not God-given or inherent in the natural or-der of things. They are tentative social expressions of justice and a histori-cal testimony to the concern for balancing the well-being of both the com-munity and individuals. They are hard won and express cultural lessons developed over a long period that should be respected.

In a situation of limited water resources where available supplies can-not meet the demands of all users, the state also has the responsibility to allocate the water it ultimately owns in an equitable fashion to serve com-munity and biotic goods. In some places in some years this may mean with-holding the water implied in water rights. The withholding of water should always be a reluctant decision based on calculations of equity, the best sci-entific knowledge, and applicable laws. It should never be a matter of po-litical expediency, even though there are numerous examples where bias and political pressure have been determining factors.

Communities should never ignore the hardships that result from diffi-cult decisions about the allocation of limited water. Justice calls for an equi-table distribution of costs and pays special attention to pain and suffering. Communities should support those who lose the most, both human and other species. The exact nature of this support, however, should be deter-mined locally in dialogues among those in positions of responsibility and those affected, or, in the case of other species, those who defend the inter-ests of other species.

Sustainability

Sustainability may be defined as the long-range supply of sufficient resources to meet basic human needs and to preserve intact natural communities. It expresses a concern for future generations and the planet as a whole and emphasizes that an acceptable quality of life for present generations must not jeopardize the prospects for future generations.

Sustainability is basically good stewardship and is a pressing concern today because of the human degradation of nature. It embodies an ongoing view of nature and society, a view in which ancestors and posterity are seen as sharing in present decisions. The present generation takes in trust a legacy from the past with the responsibility of passing it on in better or at least no worse condition. A concern for future generations is one aspect of love and justice. Sustainability precludes a shortsighted stress on economic growth that fundamentally harms ecological systems and any form of environmentalism that ignores human needs and costs.

There are several significant biblical and theological foundations for the norm of sustainability. The doctrine of creation affirms that God also sustains. The creation is also good independently of human beings (Gn 1). The goodness of matter is later picked up in Christian understandings of the incarnation and the sacraments.

Psalm 104, part of which is quoted at the beginning of this commentary, is a splendid hymn of praise that celebrates God's efforts at sustainability. Similarly, Psalm 145 rejoices in the knowledge that God gives "them their food in due season . . . [and] satisfies the desire of every living thing" (vv. 15–16). The doctrine of creation also emphasizes the special vocation of humanity to assist God in the task of sustainability. The first creation account in Genesis describes the responsibility of stewardship in terms of "dominion" (Gn 1:28); the second creation account refers to this task as "to till it and keep it" (Gn 2:15). In both cases the stress is on humanity's stewardship of *God's* creation.

The covenant theme is another important biblical and theological foundation for the norm of sustainability. The Noahic covenant (Gn 9) celebrates an "everlasting covenant between God and every living creature of all flesh that is on the earth" (v. 14).

Sufficiency

The norm of sufficiency emphasizes that all forms of life are entitled to share in the goods of creation. To share in the goods of creation in a Christian sense, however, does not mean unlimited consumption, hoarding, or an inequitable distribution of the earth's resources. Rather, it is defined in terms of basic needs, sharing, and equity. Sufficiency repudiates wasteful and harmful consumption and encourages humility, frugality, and generosity.

This norm appears in the Bible in several places. As the people of God wander in the wilderness after the Exodus, God sends enough manna each day to sustain the community. Moses repeats God's instructions to the people: "gather as much of it as each of you needs" (Ex 16:16). The norm of sufficiency is also integral to the set of laws known as the Jubilee Legislation in Exodus 23.

In Christian scriptures sufficiency is linked to abundance. Jesus rejected the notion, however, that the good life is to be found in the abundance of possessions (Lk 12:15). Instead, the good life is to be found in following Christ. Such a life results not in the hoarding of material wealth but rather in sharing it so that others may have enough.

The norm of sufficiency is also supported by biblical and theological understandings of wealth, consumption, and sharing. Two general and not altogether compatible attitudes dominate biblical writings on wealth and consumption. On the one hand, there is a qualified appreciation of wealth; on the other, there is a call to freedom from possessions that sometimes borders on deep suspicion. (For more on these two attitudes, see the case "Rigor and Responsibility" in this volume.)

The biblical witness on consumption follows much the same pattern. The basic issue has been between self-denial and contentment with a moderate level of consumption. The way of moderation is expressed well in 1 Timothy: "There is great gain in godliness with contentment; for we brought nothing into the world, so that we can take nothing out of it; but if we have food and clothing, we will be content with these" (1 Tm 6:6–8).

Sufficiency and sustainability are linked, for what the ethic of ecological justice seeks to sustain is the material and spiritual wherewithal to satisfy the basic needs of all forms of life. They are also linked through the increasing realization that present levels of human consumption, especially in affluent countries, are more than sufficient and in many respects are unsustainable.

Participation

The norm of participation likewise stems from the affirmation of all forms of life and the call to justice. This affirmation and this call lead to the respect and inclusion of all forms of life in human decisions that affect their well-being. Voices should be heard, and, if not able to speak, which is the case for other species, then humans will have to represent their interests when those interests are at stake. Participation is concerned with empowerment and seeks to remove the obstacles to participating in decisions.

The norm of participation is also grounded in the two accounts of creation in Genesis. These accounts emphasize the value of everything in God's creation and the duty of humans to recognize this value by acting as good stewards.

The prophets brought sharp condemnation upon the kings and people of Israel for violating the covenant by neglecting the interests of the poor and vulnerable. They repudiated actions that disempowered people through the loss of land, corruption, theft, slavery, and militarism (Am 2:6–7; Is 3:2–15; Hos 10:12–14).

With Jesus comes a new emphasis, the kingdom or community of God (Mk 1:14–15). The nature of this community is visible in the person of Jesus, who resisted the purity laws of his time that excluded whole groups of people. He sought out the poor and oppressed.

The concern for the poor evident in the gospels is another support for the norm of participation. Without some semblance of justice there can be little participation in community. Equality of worth, rough equality of power, and political freedom are prerequisites for genuine communities.

Achieving rough equality and freedom as well as participatory communities is difficult, and more so in conflict situations. Decisions requiring expert technical judgments and having wide-ranging consequences must be made in a timely way. Popular participation in making decisions can paralyze essential processes. Expedience often results in the exclusion of certain voices and interests.

Finally, there is the difficult problem of how to bring other species and ecosystems into human decision-making. In one sense they are already included because there is no way to exclude them. Humans are inextricably part of nature, and many human decisions have environmental consequences that automatically include other species and ecosystems. Beyond this, it helps to see plants, animals, and their communities as having interests that humans should respect. They have a dignity of their own. They experience pleasure and pain. The norm of participation should be extended to include these interests and to relieve pain, in effect, to give other species a voice.

Solidarity

The norm of solidarity reinforces the inclusion of all forms of life as well as adding an important element to the inclusion of marginalized human beings. The norm of solidarity emphasizes the kinship and interdependence of all life forms and encourages support and assistance for those who suffer. The norm highlights the communal nature of life in contrast to individualism and encourages individuals and groups to join in common cause with victims of discrimination, abuse, and oppression. Underscoring the reciprocal relationship of individual welfare and the common good, solidarity calls for the powerful to share the plight of the powerless, for the rich to listen to the poor, and for humanity to recognize its fundamental interdependence with the rest of nature. The virtues of humility, compassion, courage, and generosity are all marks of the norm of solidarity.

Both creation accounts in Genesis emphasize the profound relationality of all of God's creation. These two accounts point to the fundamental social and ecological context of existence. Humanity was created for community.

This is the foundation of solidarity. While all forms of creation are unique, they are all related to each other as part of God's creation.

In their descriptions of Jesus' life and ministry, the gospels provide the clearest examples of compassionate solidarity. Jesus shows solidarity with the poor and oppressed; he eats with sinners, drinks from the cup of a Gentile woman, meets with outcasts, heals lepers, and consistently speaks truth to power. Recognizing that Jesus was the model of solidarity, Paul used the metaphor of the body of Christ to emphasize the continuation of this solidarity within the Christian community.

Conclusion

The problems associated with limited water resources and their equitable distribution are part of a larger whole. In the past two hundred years humans have developed powerful technologies to wrest resources from nature to improve the material conditions of human life. Improvements have been spectacular.

Now, on the back of this good, ride increased materialism, ecological degradation, and new forms of injustice. The present task is to orient these technologies to sustainable and sufficient ends and to balance the power of those who own and manage these technologies. Issues of limited water resources, water rights, and takings are only one part of this larger task.

LIMITED WATER RESOURCES

Christians should be sensitive to conflicts over limited water resources. Family farmers, agriculture-related business people, and agricultural workers are the core of many rural congregations. Family farms and businesses and a way of life are threatened not only by weather and market fluctuations but also by the economic squeeze caused by the shift from family farms to large-scale, often corporate-dominated, agriculture. Farmers have a legitimate concern to preserve a way of life that contributes substantially to the world's food supply, the US economy, and American culture.

Farmers' sense of entitlement to water is increased by historical patterns of water allocation. In some cases farmers have paid for the construction of facilities to store water in seasons of high flow. This is generally a sustainable practice that should be encouraged. In other cases federal, state, and local water managers have encouraged farmers to use limited water resources and all but ignored other users. Water managers granted farmers liberal water rights during the twentieth century and in some places entered into compacts with irrigation districts to provide water. For years farmers were first in line for water and grew accustomed to having their water needs met. Some of them came to think of their annual allocation as a right with one primary responsibility, the production of food for other human beings. Worldwide about 70 percent of the water taken out of rivers is used for irrigation. Of this, about two-thirds is consumed by growing plants and not return to river basins.

In the process of food production farmers have also put pressure on limited water resources and contributed to habitat degradation and species decline. They are not alone. Other human users have contributed significantly; for example, those who have over fished and urban users who have demanded water with little concern for conservation. Power producers have erected dams that alter habitats and impede fish runs. To add pressure, these groups are sometimes in conflict with one another. Those who fish, for example, are in conflict with farmers over stream flows. Municipalities covet the water that goes to irrigation.

Christians also have responsibilities to nature and other groups of water users. The four norms of sustainability, sufficiency, participation, and solidarity give considerable weight to the interests of other species. Environmental laws and regulations and their enforcement support the common good.

The legitimate claims of Native Americans under treaties negotiated with the US government in the nineteenth century are also important and have been recognized by the courts. In a 1983 decision (US v. Adair) the Ninth Circuit Court held that treaties negotiated in the nineteenth century implied a reserved water right to preserve traditional hunting, fishing, and gathering. The court also held that Native American farmers owning land on a former reservation are entitled to water for agricultural needs with the date the suit was brought as their priority date. These claims have and continue to be neglected in water-allocation decisions, a neglect that excludes Native Americans from participation.

In addressing these issues legislators and water managers need to be responsive to the appeals of all those affected. Justice calls for an equitable distribution of both costs and benefits. For farmers, voluntary land or water-rights buybacks, disaster relief, the development of alternative water resources, the provision of new technologies to conserve water and to protect threatened species and aquatic habitats, funds for retraining and relocation, and mediation processes to resolve disputes are appropriate governmental and community responses. While the enforcement of environmental regulations supports the common good, the costs of environmental preservation should not be forced on one group alone.

The task of scientists is to determine what it takes to sustain and preserve ecological systems. The best science available should be the basis for policy decisions about specific streams and lakes. The term *best science* is ambiguous, however, because scientists are not always in agreement on a given topic, and scientific studies are frequently used selectively by the advocates of alternative positions. Scientists cannot solve political and ethical debates. Nevertheless, scientific grounding is essential to wise decision-making. Without it, environmental debates degenerate into partisan wrangling.

Christians have a different role to play. They are called not only to be advocates of justice but also to respond to those who suffer from the difficult decisions of water managers and the courts. They are called further to a ministry of reconciliation (2 Cor 5:18), offering themselves as vehicles for peaceful conflict resolution.

WATER RIGHTS AND TAKINGS

Rights language is one way to speak about justice and equity. The concept of rights came to the fore during the Enlightenment and was given prominence in Europe and the Americas by an emerging commercial class that sought to limit feudal privileges, balance the power of monarchs, and secure political participation for itself. As time passed, other groups claimed rights for themselves and were also included as participants. Today, the process of extending rights to marginalized groups continues. Some environmental philosophers and theologians would even extend rights to other species and speak of biotic rights, for example, the rights of other species to a healthy and whole habitat and to satisfy their basic needs.

Rights are intended to protect the legitimate interests of individuals and groups over against the state and other groups. Rights are not absolute. Rights do not give unlimited privilege to the individuals who hold them. Rights are limited by the responsibilities of each right holder to respect the same rights in others and to self-limit his or her own claims. They are further limited by the community's responsibility to promote the common good and to restrain those who seek individual gain at the expense of others and the community as a whole. Finally, different rights occasionally come into conflict and must be adjudicated. In other words, rights limit each other.

In the process of extending rights to ever more groups, water rights were established in the late nineteenth and early twentieth centuries to prevent conflicts and to protect investments in farms and irrigation systems. According to Rick Bastash, an authority on water rights in Oregon:

A water right is the legal authorization given by the state to a party to use a specific amount of public water in a specific way at a specific location for a specific purpose. It is not a title to the water itself. Only the public owns the water.[1]

Certain rules with local variations govern water rights in the western United States. They include:

1. The water granted in a water right must be for beneficial use.
2. The right attaches to the property and may be sold with it.
3. "First in time, first in right"; that is, earlier rights have priority over rights granted later.
4. "Use it or lose it"; the right is forfeited in most states after five years of no use.
5. Rights are forever.
6. The water in a right is free.

Court decisions to uphold the treaty rights of Native Americans and legislation such as the Endangered Species Act have in effect extended water rights even further. The treaties reserved to the tribes certain uses of water. While these reservations were not described as rights, in the present context they are the equivalent of rights. The same principle applies to legislation to protect species and their habitats.

Conflicts over water rights, Native American treaty rights, and environmental legislation have also raised the issue of "takings." The last clause in the Fifth Amendment to the US Constitution, the "takings clause," reads: "nor shall private property be taken for public use without just compensation." The intent of this clause is to limit the power of the state to seize property arbitrarily and to protect the interests of property owners. Until the twentieth century the courts applied the clause only to the physical seizure of property through the government's power of eminent domain.

In 1922, however, the Supreme Court ruled in *Pennsylvania Coal Co. v. Mahon* that some forms of regulation could effectively qualify as a taking of property. This decision narrowly opened the door to what has been called regulatory takings. The courts have held that a taking has occurred only if the enforcement of a regulation permits little or no economic use. Thus, according to the Supreme Court, a taking is a government action that either physically occupies property or removes nearly all its economic value. Short-term loss of income or partial loss of economic value do not usually qualify as a taking under existing court rulings.

In the 1990s property-rights advocates and those who wanted to revise or reverse what they considered to be intrusive laws and regulations began lobbying legislatures to open the door wider. These groups sought to understand takings to include compensation to property owners for any possible financial loss from the enforcement of a regulation.

The Klamath River Basin is a good example of this. Farmers who lost significant income and property-rights activists claimed regulatory takings. The farmers' claims for compensation were bolstered not only by a loss of income but also by a compact between the Bureau of Reclamation and local irrigation districts to provide water.

Were these claims of takings to be accepted by the courts or a wide-open takings provision enacted by legislatures, the cost of preserving critical ecological systems would certainly increase. In an unlikely, worst-case scenario the state might not have sufficient funds to compensate all claims. Added bureaucratic costs would be incurred figuring out the legitimacy of claims. Government officials would at a minimum be reluctant to enforce laws and regulations with such expensive price tags. Such a scenario would effectively eviscerate environmental laws and regulations, not to mention zoning, safety, and historic preservation laws.

These claims involve other problems. They view land and other species in economic terms and measure their value in terms of money. They assume that economic value should take precedence over other values. They overlook the intrinsic value of the land and other species as creations of God. Then there are the legal questions involved in these claims. The arena of water rights does not provide a good venue for considering the extent to which government regulation of the use of property should require compensation to the owner of the property. When, for example, zoning regulations prohibit a landowner from building a strip mall on a parcel of land, the issue is clearly whether the regulation has taken away all or nearly all value of the land. When the government physically appropriates the land to build a road or a post office, the issue is much simpler. The government has physically taken or occupied the land, and compensation generally must be paid. If the government, however, restricts an owner of water rights from using water that the owner claims, is that a mere regulation of the water rights? Or is it a physical taking of water to which the water right's owner had an entitlement?

Even if it should be treated as a mere regulation, there is the further question whether the regulation eliminated all or nearly all value of the property. Further still, it would not be clear whether "the property" is the water right as a whole, the water rights for a given year, or the land to which the water rights may be attached. That choice could determine the outcome. Finally, it is not clear that any one approach to the issue of water rights and takings is appropriate given the many situations in which such an issue might arise.

Given all these problems, the lawyer in the case, Adam Carter, reached the conclusion that claims of takings are a cumbersome instrument for redressing the losses of the irrigators. They also do not get at the real problems of the equitable distribution of limited water resources and the preservation of habitats. This may be true, but it leaves the farmers with only three options: (1) to bear the financial burden of environmental regulation; (2) to press their claims in court; or (3) to enter an uncertain negotiating process.

CONFLICT RESOLUTION

While conflicting Christian perspectives can be serious sources of conflict, the church can also play a significant role in facilitating cooperative processes. Congregations can provide a safe place to build relationships, share information, and offer compassionate listening. Paul entrusts Christians with the message of reconciliation: "All this is from God, who reconciled us to himself through Christ and has given us the ministry of reconciliation" (2 Cor 5:18).

This challenge calls Christians to initiate processes where those in conflict can come together in non-threatening ways to work out their differences. While reaching a mutual agreement on specific issues dividing a community is important, many Christian peacebuilders see as equally or more important long-term goals in deepening mutual understanding, building positive relationships, and equipping parties to better address future disputes.

Matthew Howe's invitation to Amanda to preach and possibly to lead a workshop in Klamath Falls offers her a way to enter the community and begin to build trust, a critical component for becoming a peacebuilder. By building a process to bring disputing parties together for constructive dialogue, she would also be responding to Adam Carter's advice: "Litigation will take years, tie up the courts, and prolong the conflict. What these folks need to do is sit down and reach an agreement on what is a just allocation." Finding mutual agreement in Klamath Falls about fair and equitable water allocation among members of the congregation and even in the wider Klamath Falls community would not end the competition over water rights in Oregon or California. However, better understanding of the historical background of water rights and claims, deeper understanding by the parties of one another's needs, and the process of working together on agreements all parties are willing to support would equip the citizens of Klamath Falls to address future conflicts and would offer a powerful model for constructive resolution in other communities.

While reviewing her notes on addressing community conflicts, Amanda would be reminded that she is only a possible mediator. She would initially enter the situation as an "intervenor"—an unbiased person who acknowledges the conflict, seeks to learn more about it from the parties, and is willing to assist the parties in considering a number of approaches to address their differences. An authentic mediator or mediating team must be asked for and accepted by all the parties.

Some intervenors recommend convening a community-wide discussion on a divisive topic. Without a process to build skills of objective analysis and listening, develop clear goals and guidelines, and build a level of trust among participants, such meetings may lead to even deeper division. Entering the situation more slowly through trusted local leaders within a community of faith could provide a solid base for long-term resolution. If Amanda's worship leadership shows her to be a person with empathy for the pain people feel when they are caught in difficult conflicts and a person with skills and experience to help members of congregations deal more effectively with their own conflicts, she and Matthew Howe would have a base upon which to introduce a workshop on conflict resolution.

Congregational support for such a workshop could be developed through meeting with lay leaders and other members of the congregation. The effect of the workshop would be significantly expanded if the congregation were to choose to open it to the wider community, with a clear goal of seeking out diverse perspectives.

A primary focus of a one- or two-day workshop would be skill building, with a strong emphasis on "deep listening" to one another and the realization that to convey genuine understanding of another person does not necessarily mean agreement with that person. Only the concluding hour or two of the workshop would need to be devoted to discussing possible approaches to the deep divisions about water allocation. A concrete plan would be unlikely to emerge from this discussion, but the selection of a trusted and diverse committee and suggestions of invitations to others not present would be a major advance toward this group building, a process, with Amanda's support, that the wider community could accept.

Amanda must bring to her role as intervenor or eventually mediator understanding of the issues at hand, openness to learning from the participants, a commitment to protect those who are most vulnerable, and the self-awareness to guard against showing bias to any specific perspectives. She must also be aware that this is only the beginning of a long process of careful listening; feeling the pain, frustration, and often anger of the parties; and constant prayer for the wisdom, patience, and strength to be a trustworthy bridge between the parties. Her vision, with God's grace, is to help build a fair and just process for this community to move toward respectful relationships and sustainable agreements.

NOTE

[1] Rick Bastash, *Waters of Oregon: A Source Book on Oregon's Water and Water Management* (Corvallis: Oregon State Univ. Press, 1998), 48.

ADDITIONAL RESOURCES

Bastash, Rick. *Waters of Oregon: A Source Book on Oregon's Water and Water Management.* Corvallis: Oregon State Univ. Press, 1998.

Bates, Sarah F., et al. *Searching Out the Headwater: Change and Discovery in Western Water Policy.* Washington, DC: Island Press, 1993.

Blake, Tupper, et al. *Balancing Water: Restoring the Klamath Basin.* Berkeley and Los Angeles: Univ. of California Press, 2000.

Bouma-Prediger, Steven. *For the Beauty of the Earth: A Christian Vision for Creation Care.* Grand Rapids, MI: Baker Academic, 2001.

Brueggemann, Walter. *The Land: Place as Gift, Promise, and Challenge in Biblical Faith.* 2nd ed. Minneapolis: Fortress Press, 2002.

Czech, Brian, and Paul R. Krausman. *The Endangered Species Act: History, Conservation Biology, and Public Policy.* Baltimore: The Johns Hopkins Univ. Press, 2001.

Lichatowich, Jim. *Salmon without Rivers: A History of the Pacific Salmon Crisis.* Washington, DC: Island Press, 1999.

Martin-Schramm, James A., and Robert L. Stivers. *Christian Environmental Ethics: A Case Method Approach.* Maryknoll, NY: Orbis Books, 2003.

McFague, Sallie. *Life Abundant: Rethinking Theology and Economy for a Planet in Peril.* Minneapolis: Fortress Press, 2001.

Meltz, Robert, et al. *The Takings Issue: Constitutional Limits on Land Use Control and Environmental Regulations.* Washington, DC: Island Press, 1999.

Shogren, Jason F. *Private Property and the Endangered Species Act: Saving Habitats, Protecting Homes.* Austin, TX: Univ. of Texas Press, 1998.

Shogren, Jason F., and John Taschirhart, eds. *Protecting Endangered Species in the United States: Biological Needs, Political Realities, Economic Choices.* New York: Cambridge Univ. Press, 2001.

Websites

American Rivers
  http://www.americanrivers.org/mostendangered/klamath2002.html
Fishers
  http://www.pcffa.org
Klamath Basin Water Crisis
  http://www.klamathbasincrisis.org
Klamath Coalition
  http://www.klamathbasin.info
Oregon Natural Resources Council
  http://www.onrc.org/programs/klamath/onrcposition.html
US Fish and Wildlife Service
  http://klamathbasinrefuges.fws.gov/lowerklamath/lowerklamath.html

PART VI

HEALTH

Case

Baby Boy Hernandez

Mary Flemming closed her office door, trying to shut out any more interruptions to her morning. She had a difficult staff meeting in thirty minutes and wanted to finish the outline for a paper she was presenting as an incoming officer of the State Hospital Administrators Association.

As the associate administrator for medical care at Oglethorpe Memorial Hospital, Mary was responsible for oversight of one of the five regional neonatal intensive-care units in the state. In light of increasing fiscal problems, Mary had been asked to address issues of funding for neonatal care.

Mary glanced through her notes, aware of the dramatic changes in care for newborns after the hospital had been designated a regional neonatal center. As a matter of fact, the excellent neonatal program at Memorial had been a significant factor in luring Mary from her previous position. The State Department of Human Resources, in collaboration with the Council on Maternal and Infant Health, had identified and awarded federal funds to select hospitals for renovations, equipment, staff, and newborn transport vehicles. Mary was convinced that under the direction of Dr. Sam McBride, Memorial had one of the best neonatal units in the South.

The effects of the program had been dramatic. Although it was still the state's number-one health problem, infant mortality had dropped 25 percent after the system was established. There was a parallel drop in the number of premature infants with permanent mental and physical handicaps. When Mary had first come to Memorial, it was a thrill for her to see those little babies survive. The whole unit rejoiced with the families, and Mary remembered the heartwarming letters she and members of the staff had received from grateful parents. Memorial was saving an average of seventy-five babies a year who would have died without specialized care.

This case was prepared by William P. Bristol and Alice Frazer Evans. Copyright © The Case Study Institute. The names of all persons and institutions have been disguised to protect the privacy of those involved.

But in the past few years Mary felt that problems with the unit had begun to outweigh the benefits. As the technology had improved, smaller and smaller babies began to survive. And as the birth weight went down, the incidence of long-term complications and the cost of care went up.

Mary checked back over her files for the previous year. During that year Memorial had admitted over fifty infants weighing less than seven hundred grams (less than a pound and a half). A few years ago, Mary estimated, the full cost of care for some low-birth-weight infants was as high as $500,000, with an average cost of $150,000. Today the figures would be much higher. The real squeeze came because a disproportionate number of mothers with SGA (small for gestational age) babies sent to Memorial from Comstock and other county hospitals were indigent, with no medical insurance. In the early years of the program the $5,000 per infant state subsidy for these babies was significant; today it hardly seemed to make a dent. On top of that, state funds available to Memorial ran out completely a little more than halfway into the fiscal year. With the present state budget squeeze, Mary had little hope that additional funds would be allotted to neonatal care. With the skyrocketing cost per infant, the end result was a cut in state funds.

In the past Mary could have charged some indigent cases to the Department of Children Services. She knew her predecessor had even charged some to the old migrant-worker program that the state had run a decade ago. When she had first come to Memorial, Mary had been able to elevate costs in some areas to absorb the losses, but both federal and insurance programs designed regulations to prevent cost shifts. Increasingly, patients of independent means were going to the smaller, private hospitals for maternal care. Last year, counting overhead costs, Memorial's neonatal intensive care unit lost over a million dollars. In an earlier study of twelve children's hospitals, neonatal care consumed 25 percent of hospital expenses but represented only 8 percent of the admissions. Mary was sure the statistical imbalance was even greater in general admissions hospitals like Memorial. Mary knew the hospital, specifically her department, was faced with some serious decisions. And, she ruefully realized, she had been dumb enough to agree to address the issue before her colleagues at next week's association meeting. They were all aware of the problem; she had to come up with some answers.

Mary glanced at her watch and realized she was due at the neonatology staff meeting. Twice a week various members of the staff gathered for what was called "the patient planning meeting." More often, Mary mused, it could be described as a battle royal. Baby Boy Hernandez was today's topic. Mary muttered to herself as she hurried down the hall, silently swearing at Comstock County Hospital for dumping another non-paying obstetric case on Memorial. The Hernandez baby alone had run up a bill approaching $125,000, and Sam McBride still didn't have the kid off the respirator. Migrant workers such as Anita Hernandez had always been a problem in this part of the state. They had no money, no insurance, and rarely spoke English.

Most of the staff showed up on time, although two nurse representatives had just been called away to respond to a code. As they gathered around the coffee table in the small lounge next to the nursery, Mary nodded to Sam McBride, young Corey Blake, Mrs. Darden—the chief ward clerk of the neonatal unit—and several house staff Mary was sure Sam had dragged along to the meeting. Mary watched Sam as he joked with the pediatric interns he was supervising. Corey sat alone at the edge of the group.

Corey Blake was the midwifery student who had delivered Baby Hernandez in the ambulance on the way from Comstock County Hospital. She spoke Spanish fluently. Blake had pulled a minor miracle in just getting the baby to the unit. A Furman graduate, she had earned her RN and then spent time as a nurse in the Southwest with a missionary group. Her parents lived in Atlanta, and she had returned to Emory to enter the two-year midwifery program that was now receiving state funding. Mary knew Corey had originally intended to return to New Mexico, but her field supervisor at Memorial was encouraging her to stay. In a private personnel review with her supervisor, Mary remembered her saying that there were certainly enough poor, pregnant women in the surrounding counties to keep Blake happy for all of her days. Everybody in the county seemed poor since the recession had hit and the textile mill in Comstock had closed.

When Mary had encouraged the hospital board to accept the midwife supervision program at Memorial, she wasn't adverse to the income or the promise of more if additional state funding came through. She also saw the logic of programs directed to the low-cost preventive medicine that the midwives were being trained to deliver. The 80 to 90 percent increase in survivability of low-birth-weight babies was because of improvement in medical care, not because of prevention of low-birth-weight babies.

Mary recalled a major Institute of Medicine study. Low-birth-weight babies (2,500 grams or less) were forty times more likely to die than normal weight babies and had increased risk of long-term handicaps. Inadequate prenatal care appeared to be directly linked to low birth weight. Corey's program focused on this kind of care, especially for poor, nonwhite women. Studies indicated there were as many as two thousand indigent, high-risk, pregnant women in the six counties surrounding Memorial. Mary saw the long-term logic of putting state funds here. But she wasn't sure yet that midwives were the answer.

Mary knew that, in spite of her skill, Corey Blake was having a hard time being accepted by the medical staff. Mary recalled a conversation she had overheard between two interns about "those damn midwives." It wasn't that they disliked Corey, but all she preached was "feeding the poor" and "vitamins." And in spite of her license, she would never be able to handle any "real emergencies."

Mary shifted her attention to Sam McBride as he called the group together. In Mary's estimation, Sam was a fine doctor. An Emory graduate, he had taken his pediatric training in Pennsylvania before returning to the state university as a fellow in neonatology. He had been hired by Memorial fifteen years ago to head the neonatology staff. Late one night over coffee Sam had shared with Mary some "war stories" of his first years at the hospital. Those were the heydays in the development of neonatal care. New techniques were coming out every day, survival rates of the mid-weight babies were excellent, and the neonatologists were a fun, swashbuckling group. No one complained that the annual meetings were held at Aspen; they were all good skiers. Mary knew that underneath that jovial exterior Sam had not only skill but a driving passion for saving the babies.

Sam opened the meeting with a frank discussion of the Hernandez baby's current and future problems. The infant, barely twenty-five weeks, weighed only 500 grams, less than one pound. He had developed a refractory hypoglycemia and respiratory distress syndrome (RDS) necessitating a respirator. Then, as the baby's RDS got better, he went into heart failure. Sam suspected intraventricular hemorrhaging due to a combination of prematurity and possibly lack of closure of the ductus arteriosis. He was considering calling in a cardiac surgeon. Sam added that even five years ago most kids this small didn't live long enough to be troubled with hemorrhaging.

As of this morning, the baby's hypoglycemia and jaundice were under control and the RDS was getting better. But the boy was not weaning well from the respirator. In addition, Sam was convinced that because the baby had required long-term supplemental oxygen, retinopathy (blindness) was a strong possibility. He also noted that 30 percent of the babies with intraventricular hemorrhaging had residual neurological impairment, and many developed cerebral palsy. The baby's nutrition was poor, and the only weight he seemed to be gaining was water weight. Hyperalimentation (providing nutrients intravenously) is plagued with complications, but it seemed the only reasonable route to get the child through this nutritional crisis. Sam wished the baby's mother had eaten better.

During this long discourse, Mary Flemming had become increasingly upset. She struggled to keep her voice under control. "Dr. McBride, do you have any idea what this gift from the county is costing us, not only in terms of dollars but in staff time and energy? We've got to consider the broad picture. Many more cases like this one, and you ultimately threaten the very survival of the hospital. Is there any possibility you can transfer him back to Comstock County Hospital?"

Sam McBride did not respond to Mary's question. Instead, he turned to Corey and asked her to tell the staff what she knew about Anita Hernandez. Corey glanced quickly at both Mary and Sam McBride. Her initial hesitancy soon turned to confidence as she began to share her observations. Ms. Hernandez should have gone home long ago, wherever home would be for her now, but she had not done well following her delivery. Although

Anita told Corey that she was twenty-two, she looked more like sixteen and was very frail and underweight. She also smoked constantly, a habit that Corey said was obviously not going to change.

Corey continued: "As you all know, following delivery Anita developed a pelvic infection; it was pretty rough for a few days until we brought the sepsis under control. But this did give me a chance to talk to Anita about her life. She was born down around Harlingen, Texas, and has been making the trek north and east following the sun. She ended up here weeding peanuts and processing peaches. This was her second pregnancy. Her first baby, a girl, lives with her grandmother just south of Harlingen. The baby is very pretty in the picture, a chubby three year old with gorgeous eyes. Quite a contrast to Anita right now."

Corey paused a minute and then added that there was one thing that particularly bothered her. Anita didn't go down to the nursery to see her son very often, and she hadn't named him yet. Corey paused again briefly and then continued: "I guess I need to say too that I don't know where she'll go when she leaves the hospital. She won't be strong enough to work for several weeks. There's a good possibility this baby will be physically handicapped as long as he lives. This will be a tremendous burden for Anita." Corey's voice became stronger. "I know you all realize that in our surrounding counties there are hundreds of women in worse shape than Anita. I spend most of my days in the county clinics and in the shacks where our rural poor people live. Between the mill closings and the crop failures, there are people out there starving to death."

Before Mary or other members of the staff could respond, a nurse hurried into the lounge to call Dr. McBride. In the nursery, the cardiac-arrest alert sounded shrill in contrast to the monotonous beeps of the other monitors. There was a flurry of surgical green as the nurses went to work on Baby Boy Hernandez.

The staff meeting was postponed until further notice. Mary Flemming walked slowly back to her office.

Commentary

Baby Boy Hernandez

From Mary Flemming's perspective this case poses two questions. The first is what kind of care Baby Boy Hernandez should receive. The second is how to make the neonatal unit financially secure. In Flemming's mind these two questions are closely connected. Both questions in turn provoke other questions. Who should decide the fate of this child and others like him? On what criteria should the decision be based? Should the financial security of the neonatal unit, and perhaps the hospital, be secured by limiting access to the unit to those who can pay? These questions raise an issue that Flemming does not consider but that underlies all the others: Is the overall health care delivery system, of which this neonatal unit forms a small part, just and equitable?

SCRIPTURAL AND THEOLOGICAL RESOURCES

Scripture can be a powerful source of Christian norms relevant to this case. Though it does not directly address issues in medical technology, scripture has a great deal to say about the value of life and the place of death in life. For scripture, life is more than existence alone. When Deuteronomy 30:19 says "choose life," it explains the choice of life over death as a choice for goodness, for loving God, for keeping God's laws, for community, for prosperity, and for achieving fullness of life. Physical life is not the ultimate value. Stories in the Hebrew scriptures make clear that individual life, while valuable, can be sacrificed in the interest of the quality of life of the community; war and capital punishment are taken for granted in the stories of the patriarchs, the Exodus, and in the Mosaic Law. Within Israel the Mosaic Law was to ensure that the life of the poor and powerless was respected by the rich and powerful. This included provisions such as one that stated that the poor be allowed to glean the edges of the fields of the rich (Lv 19:9–10) and another that declared that the cloak of the poor man not be taken overnight as security for loans (Dt 24:10–13). David's killing of Uriah in order to hide his adultery with Bathsheba was a scandal not merely because he shed blood, but because he abused the power entrusted in him by Yahweh by killing another in his charge (2 Sm 11—12).

Many of Israel's laws prohibited idolatry. One such command was that the Israelites not sacrifice children (Dt 18:10) as their pagan neighbors did in the dedication of their public buildings in order to appease the gods who threatened earthquake, winds, and lightning. If we interpret this prohibition literally, as merely forbidding the killing of children on altars to pagan gods, we fail to understand scripture as relevant to our lives. The purpose of the prohibition was to remind us that social institutions are not to be secured by the sacrifice of innocent life. Rather, for the Law, the purpose of social institutions was to safeguard the life of persons and community.

According to the gospels, Jesus, too, understood life in broader terms than mere individual existence, or he would never deliberately and repeatedly have risked his own death in order to carry out his mission of announcing the reign of God (Mk 9:30–32; Lk 9:43–45; Mt 17:22–23; 20:17–19). Furthermore, he clearly calls his apostles in the name of fullness of life to risk death (Lk 21:12–18; Mt 10:34–39; Mk 13:9–13). Though each of us is also called to discipleship, we can only make the decision to risk ourselves. Thus, while life is not for the follower of Jesus the ultimate value, Jesus gives no support for deciding to end the life of another person in the name of a higher value. The decision that one should die in the interests of the many was that of Caiaphas, the high priest responsible for the death of Jesus (Jn 18:14).

Though the gospels detail Jesus' many warnings of the judgment to come for groups who exploit or mislead the poor and weak (such as the scribes, the Pharisees, and the moneychangers in the Temple), he himself refused to judge and condemn individuals. He not only refused to condemn the adulterous woman, but he intervened to stop the crowd from stoning her as the Law prescribed (Jn 8:11). He refrained from condemning his own betrayer (Jn 13:18–30), and he promised salvation to the thief crucified beside him (Lk 23:43). If Jesus was not willing to condemn the guilty, can it be legitimate to condemn the innocent?

The theological traditions of Christianity reflect scriptural traditions that raise up the value of life and the need to protect the life and welfare of the weak. From early times Christianity condemned infanticide. Furthermore, in the development of just-war teachings, the church placed both women and children in the protected category of noncombatants who were to have total immunity from war. The theological and moral teachings most directly relevant to this case are twentieth-century teachings in medical ethics. Among Roman Catholics the 1952 distinction made by Pope Pius XII between ordinary and extraordinary means of preserving life gave what seemed to be helpful criteria to the debate about euthanasia. Pius XII maintained that there are extraordinary measures of preserving life that are not morally required. For many in medical ethics even outside of Catholicism there followed two decades when this was the standard often used: ordinary means of preserving life, such as food, water, oxygen, and common medications, could not be denied to the sick and/or dying, but extraordinary measures, such as mechanical respirators, food tubes, radiation, and surgery, or experimental techniques in general, were not required.

This teaching was easily applied at both ends of the treatment spectrum. On the one hand, it supported standard medical practice, which insisted that the poor, the retarded, and the otherwise defenseless had moral rights to ordinary medical care that could not be denied. On the other hand, for seriously ill patients who wanted to be allowed to die without painful or intrusive interventions that could only possibly or minimally extend their lives, the teaching made clear to what extent families and medical personnel could accommodate their wishes. The teaching was understood as objective and concentrated on means of preserving life rather than on complicated subjective judgments of quality and length of life.

But there were problems with this teaching. One that became obvious in succeeding decades is that advances in medical science tremendously alter what medical personnel understand as ordinary and extraordinary measures of preserving life. What was extraordinary a decade ago is standard today. At any given time, it may be difficult to judge whether a particular treatment is ordinary or not. Innumerable surgeries and mechanical techniques that used to be experimental are now routine.

Some analysts of our health-care system point out that another problem with the ordinary/extraordinary teaching is that it functions to justify the provision of a higher quality of health care to the rich than to the poor. Everyone is to have access to ordinary measures of preserving life, but within a capitalist society, the voluntary nature of extraordinary measures serves to make them dependent upon the ability to pay. This is certainly the case with Baby Boy Hernandez. The infant unit is understood to provide extraordinary measures of care, far above the standard care of other hospitals. The child whose right to the care is questioned is the one who cannot pay.

Recognition of these problems with the ordinary/extraordinary teaching has led to an unwillingness on the part of the medical profession in the last twenty years to decide treatment on the basis of means alone. Instead, there has been a shift toward joining the means issue with an evaluation of the possible benefits weighed against the counter-indications for treatments. Sometimes this consequential evaluation is done on medical grounds alone. More recently, medical ethics has moved toward incorporating more perspectives in this evaluation, as we see by the varied personnel involved in the conference described in the case. Chancy or experimental treatments are more likely to be morally required when they offer the possibility of restoring full life and health with minimum pain and risk.

RIGHT TO DECIDE

Also of great interest in the theological/moral literature on preserving threatened life is the question of who makes the decision. Cases where patients are not competent to choose for themselves—in this case, a baby—are the most difficult. In cases involving infants, treatment is usually decided by the parents or close relatives in conjunction with the medical staff. In this case Anita Hernandez, the mother and natural guardian, may be either uninterested in or incapable of representing the best interests of the child. The decision may have been shifted to the hospital team by default. This is a difficult position for medical personnel, for the presumption in their training is that they deal with a competent patient or relative whom they can expect to represent the psychological, relational, and personal values of the patient, while the medical staff represents the medical interests of the patient. Only relatively recently has it been recognized that medical personnel also inevitably represent their own interests and the interests of the institution as well as the medical interests of the patient. These interests can sometimes conflict.

In this case Corey Blake, a member of the hospital staff, is the spokesperson for the relational situation of the child. As she presents the situation, the mother does not seem interested in the child and is hard pressed to care for herself. The child will probably have serious long-term medical problems. It would be easy to be swayed by the fact that the person who presents this grim analysis is the member of the staff who has dedicated herself to medical care for the poor and who was earliest involved with the mother and child. There is the temptation to see Corey as the natural advocate of the child. If even she cannot make a good case for continuing care, then who could? But Corey also represents a midwife program, a primary-care health program appended to a major institution devoted to emergency medical intervention. From the perspective of primary health care, priority funding should be aimed at ensuring that all have basic nutrition, vitamins, vaccinations, sanitation, and health monitoring, so that the need for emergency intervention is greatly reduced. In this case Corey's program is now funded largely by the university and the state, with hope for additional state funding. Midwifery is understood by the staff as unequal in the real work of emergency intervention and more or less peripherally valuable. Corey, more than anyone else, may feel threatened by the financial burden this baby poses, since hers may be one of the programs most vulnerable to state financial cuts.

Even if Corey were to become an advocate for the child, there are other factors undermining such advocacy. By reason of both her sex and her professional credentials, Corey is not accepted as an equal by some of the other members of the professional staff. Even if she were strongly to advocate prolonging the life of the child, her relationship with other medical personnel suggests that she might not be taken seriously.

Is there an advocate for this child? And if there is, on what criteria should advocacy be based? On an absolute right to life, whatever the social and medical conditions? On an equal right to the quality of care given children who can pay? Or only on a strictly medical evaluation that this child has a good chance to live a normal life?

SOCIAL ANALYSIS

If we apply social analysis to this case, an issue that immediately emerges is the question of whether to allow this child to die would not have arisen if the parents were able to pay for his care. Within a health-care system designed, as ours is, around centers that specialize in emergency intervention, treatment is both therapeutic and experimental. That is, the treatment of newborns is designed not only to save this particular child but to develop thereby new techniques that save future newborns. Specialized units such as this one have greater success than ordinary hospitals precisely because they can call on greater experience in experimenting with technique. Such experimental systems, however, have no internal brake. They are inherently inflationary; the number of possible interventions increases exponentially over time, and it becomes difficult to discover medical reasons not to expand treatment constantly. The only brakes are financial, so treatment expands until there is no more money to support its maintenance or expansion. Preservation of such units is often understood to be essential because of their proven success in saving babies, so financial limits often press administrators to see the problem in terms of limiting access. Since the threat is financial, the most obvious criterion for limiting access is ability to pay.

Critics maintain that such a system ensures that public monies support centers from which the disadvantaged end up being excluded, thus perpetuating their disadvantaged status. Our health-care system, because it is organized around such specialized intervention centers, tends to neglect basic health care and to support high levels of care for only part of the population. This is why we have the ironic situation of being the nation that represents the apex of sophisticated techniques for saving newborns and at the same time has one of the highest infant-mortality rates in the developed world. If the purpose of our system were to save as many lives as possible and to ensure the health of the greatest number, the available funds would be spent on relatively inexpensive diagnosis and treatment of the most common health problems rather than on high-technology interventions for the few.

When we understand that present medical personnel are trained and employed in the high-tech system, which also supports employment in high-tech equipment industries and the construction and insurance industries, we can see a large interest group supporting the present system. In this case the medical conferences held in resorts across the country and the close relationships among hospitals, physicians, and pharmaceutical companies illustrate this point. Those elements that are best rewarded by the present system—doctors, administrators, and pharmaceutical executives—are those who are best organized to wield political power and are recognized by media and government as the experts in the field of medicine. But support for the present system is not merely a matter of self-interest on the part of those employed within it.

The present system is also one geared to produce astounding breakthroughs in medical science. The quest for new knowledge and techniques that will save lives is a major attraction of the present system for researchers and investors, as Mary Flemming makes clear in speaking of Sam McBride, the head of the neonatal unit. Such people are willing to work long hours, expend great energy, and dedicate themselves to their work. The work is exciting, fast evolving, and the gratification that comes from saving frail, underweight babies is both immense and immediate. The system is set up to support this scientific quest, which has far outstripped the ability of the system to distribute the products of the quest to the entire population.

REACHING A DECISION

What seems to be happening in this case is that the question of how to treat the Hernandez baby is being confused with the question of how to balance the neonatal unit's budget. This seems to be a mistake. What kind of treatment the Hernandez baby should receive should not be determined on the basis of the financial health of the neonatal unit. Treatment should be decided using the same criteria that are used for all the other infants in the neonatal unit. The criteria applied to all the infants will certainly be influenced by the financial resources of the neonatal unit. This seems necessary and appropriate.

Furthermore, the resources available to the neonatal unit should not represent the sum of the funds available for maternal and infant care. The basic needs of some should not be neglected in favor of the extraordinary needs of others. This is not a matter of equalizing spending for all infants; the most threatened have a primary claim on our care and resources. But among those infants who are threatened, spending should be allocated so as to save the largest possible number in the fullest manner possible.

It is not possible to equalize completely medical care for the poor and the non-poor, just as it is impossible to equalize education or housing for the poor and the non-poor, for none of these services exists in a vacuum; all are interrelated. Even if the neonatal unit is able to keep this child alive in the short term, because he is so underweight and underdeveloped for his age, his long-term recovery will depend upon the level of food and housing, not to mention health monitoring, that his mother can provide. A major issue for Christian ethics is whether in such situations we apply the norm of equity to the means or to the end. Do we give the same care to the poor and the non-poor, or do we give to the poor whatever is necessary to allow them future equity with the non-poor? If the Hernandez baby continues to receive extraordinary care, should he be released at the weight at which middle-class babies are released, or should he be allowed an extra margin due to the fact that his food and housing and overall care will likely be less than theirs after his release? If we insist on the same degree of care for the same medical condition regardless of class, then in marginal cases the extraordinary care will have been wasted on the poor child, for the resources to sustain long-term recovery are lacking. And yet, while we attempt to reform the very structures of our nation in the direction of greater justice, we must also work to see that existing structures do not exacerbate or reinforce existing discrimination and injustice by excluding the poor from basic opportunities such as life-saving medical care.

ADDITIONAL RESOURCES

Dyck, Arthur J. *Life's Worth*. Grand Rapids, MI: Eerdmans, 2002.

Goreyca, Jefferey T., et al. *The Extremely Immature Newborn: The Dilemma of the Microbaby*. Okemos, MI: ProNational, 2005.

Humes, Edward. *Baby ER*. New York: Simon and Schuster, 2000.

Keown, John, ed. *Euthanasia Examined*. Cambridge, UK: Cambridge Univ. Press, 1995.

Kilner, John. *Life on the Line*. Grand Rapids, MI: Eerdmans, 1995.

———. *Who Lives, Who Dies? Ethical Criteria in Patient Selection*. New Haven, CT: Yale Univ. Press, 1990.

Lammers, Stephen, and Allen Verhey. *On Moral Medicine: Theological Perspectives in Medical Ethics*. 2nd ed. Grand Rapids, MI: Eerdmans, 1998. See especially Chapter 15, "Care of Neonates."

Shannon, Thomas, ed. *Bioethics*. 3rd ed. Mahwah, NJ: Paulist Press, 1987.

Vohr, Betty, MD, and Marilee Allen, MD. "Extreme Prematurity: The Continuing Dilemma." *The New England Journal of Medicine* 252, no. 1 (January 6, 2005).

Wyatt, John, "Neonatal Ethics." London: Christian Medical Fellowship, File 27, 2004.

Case

A Family Decision about AIDS

Joyce Kyomuhendo surprised herself with her determination to stand by her daughter, Mangalita. Joyce knew that this was not an easy decision, and that many in their rural Ugandan village would be opposed. Even more troubling to Joyce was that she had seldom challenged the decisions of her husband, John, in their thirty-five years of marriage. But she must try once again to convince him to take their eldest daughter back into their home.

Both Joyce and John had agreed to take the decision to Reverend Esau, their parish priest and a trusted family friend. Joyce hoped that Reverend Esau, a man of compassion who had attended an AIDS Awareness event with a few members of his congregation, would support her on this matter.

Mangalita had been rejected by her husband after ten years of marriage because she was barren. Two years later, when she became pregnant, she tested HIV-positive. Soon after she delivered a healthy baby, she learned that she had tuberculosis. She had nowhere to go and begged to return to her parents' home.

John and Joyce Kyomuhendo lived in Sheema County in Ankole, a poor, rural area of western Uganda. Joyce remembered with a smile when Mangalita was born—a tiny, beautiful child. Mangalita was the third child in the family. The family lived on a four-acre plot in a one-bedroom house with a tin roof. Like most people in this rural area, the Kyomuhendo family survived on the food they could grow on its piece of land. Any cash for extras such as clothing, sugar, and oil came from what they could sell in the village market. Joyce knew that there was never enough food to eat, and

This case was prepared by The Rev. Dr. Tom Tuma, Church of Uganda, and Alice Frazer Evans. Copyright © The Case Study Institute. Published in the *Journal for Case Teaching* 11 (2004). Revised for US readers. Used by permission. The names of all persons and institutions have been disguised to protect the privacy of those involved.

when it came to sleeping at night, the children had a sleeping mat in the sitting room with either a piece of cloth or a torn blanket to cover them.

In spite of this poverty, John and Joyce wanted their children to go to school and receive at least some elementary education with modern skills of writing and reading. Mangalita, like her two older brothers, was enrolled in primary school three kilometers from their home. The fees for school uniforms and books stretched the family's meager resources to the limit. Joyce recalled her pride in seeing the three of them together with several other village children walking happily to school and back every day.

Unfortunately, Mangalita was a slow learner and had to repeat the first two classes. When it became clear that she would have to repeat the third class as well, she lost interest in attending school. She was sixteen, and at that age many girls in the village were already married and carrying their first child. Mangalita, already in love with Felix, who was ten years older, decided, with Felix's advice, to drop out of school and marry him. They planned to live in a village thirty kilometers away where Felix owned a small house. John and Joyce did not oppose Mangalita's decision to drop out of school. It came as a relief to them. The burden of school fees had been growing as their three youngest children had also begun attending school.

Although Mangalita had gone into marriage with high hopes and expectations, her hopes began to fade as she failed to become pregnant. In most Ugandan villages a woman's worth is determined by her capacity to conceive and bear children. With no children, Mangalita had become a common topic for conversation in the village. Joyce, who occasionally received desperate messages from Mangalita, knew that her daughter felt isolated and miserable. Mangalita endured the situation for ten years. Felix, who had initially shown understanding and support, bowed to pressure from his relatives and decided to marry another woman. He brought home two more wives in the same month.

The new arrivals joined forces against Mangalita and treated her so badly that she was forced to leave her home. Mangalita wrote to her mother that this was the only way to keep her sanity. She walked out of Felix's home with virtually nothing—neither child nor property. The only things Joyce was sure her daughter had were a broken heart and a very unsure future.

Mangalita needed work, but she had no skills to sell. She had not stayed long enough in school to learn English. She had heard of women who earned a living by selling themselves, but she did not want to do that, at least not as a first option. She felt very fortunate to find a job as a matron in a boys' primary boarding school.

Joyce kept in touch with her daughter and learned that Mangalita loved the job. Although she had no children of her own, God had given her hundreds to care for. Joyce felt that Mangalita's original joyful self was beginning to resurface. Because this was her first job, Mangalita had never earned

dissent from the pastor's decision, his "taking sides" with one parent may drive a wedge between those who support the position of the other parent. Assuming responsibility for the decision would also limit the pastor's role in involving the congregation and the community in the resolution.

An alternative is for Reverend Esau to mediate the conflict, supporting Joyce and John and encouraging them to listen to one another genuinely and to come to a mutual agreement. If this is possible, they will be more likely not to blame the other but to take joint responsibility for a decision about the most loving way to care for their daughter and grandchild. The pastor must then seek support from members of the congregation for the Kyomuhendo family, including Mangalita. Reverend Esau's response should be based on ethical principles of justice as well as practicality. By using his authority to mediate rather than dictate, he offers a model of pastoral care for a congregation and community dealing with issues of AIDS as well as a model of respect for all voices and needs of those involved in family and social conflict, especially women and others who are marginalized.

Joyce and John Kyomuhendo

Joyce and John are struggling with questions of personal priorities that are far from theoretical for poor families in Uganda and around the world. Theirs is not necessarily a cruel choice about receiving or expelling a daughter and granddaughter; it is a decision about the welfare of the whole family. Often persons with AIDS, especially in poor communities, drain limited family resources and bring the separation and isolation that John fears. His two dependent daughters may not find suitors due to the stigma of AIDS, and perhaps most threatening, the family could well be shunned by the community. In most traditional cultures one's identity is tied to the community. Being cut off from the village endangers livelihood, emotional support, and even the future of one's children. These are deeply held cultural patterns that are even more difficult to change than building acceptance of modern medical findings about the cause of disease. An Anglican priest of the Church of Uganda, Gideon Byamugisha, contrasted AIDS with other diseases and conditions that lead to serious suffering and death: "It is not the condition itself that hurts the most, but the stigma and the possibility of rejection and discrimination that HIV-positive people have to deal with."

COMMUNITY

Community is a highly valued concept in Uganda, as it is in Christian theology. How a community encounters an individual, family, or clan can be either life-giving or life-crushing, redemptive or destructive. Uganda's history helps reveal why its deeply rooted ethos of community brings both life and death.

Uganda was described by Winston Churchill as the "Pearl of Africa" because of its lush agriculture, scenic beauty, and rich culture. This East African country borders Kenya and the northern shores of Lake Victoria, the source of the Nile River and one of the largest fish reservoirs in the world. Ancient indigenous kingdoms from the fourteenth century included the Ankole, Baganda, and Busoga people who thrived with artistic, learned cultures and little penetration from the outside world until the nineteenth-century. Invasions of Arab ivory and slave traders and European explorers led to a colonization process characteristic of most of Africa. The 1890 Treaty of Berlin sliced up much of Africa into colonial empires, disregarding an-cient traditional and cultural boundaries. Great Britain claimed Uganda and appointed colonial administrators who maintained power through unequal relationships with different tribal kingdoms. More than half a cen-tury of competition for favor and influence hardened tribal loyalty and seeded the intertribal conflicts that were to rip Uganda apart following independence in 1962.

Milton Obote, the first president, was deposed by a coup that brought in Idi Amin Dada, initiating an eight-year reign of terror. Amin's rule cost the lives of 300,000 Ugandans, most of whom were from opposing tribal groups. Christian leaders who were outspoken critics of Amin's policies were executed. Amin was also responsible for expelling a 70,000-strong Indian professional community, the collapse of the economy, and the slaugh-ter of the country's prolific wildlife. Amin lost an ill-conceived war with Tanzania, which led to a series of corrupt, incompetent, often tribally bi-ased rulers. The proliferation of weapons and a national climate infused · with fear and distrust drew small communities together for mutual sup-port and survival. Many Ugandans have said that only their faith in God and small communities of family and trusted neighbors caring for one an-other enabled them to live through these desperate years with any hope for the future.

The National Resistance Army led by Yoweri Museveni finally consoli-dated power in 1986. His pragmatic administration focused on the recov-ery of the economy, anti-corruption, and decentralized government pro-grams. By the mid 1990s, however, as Uganda was rising to become the most influential nation in the Horn of Africa, Museveni faced another mas-sive challenge. Uganda was identified as having proportionally the high-est level of AIDS infection of any country in the world. The first case of AIDS was identified in Uganda in 1982. The epidemic spread quickly, and by the end of 1992 more than 18 percent of the population was either in-fected with the virus or had AIDS.

This history of community conflict sets the background for the greatest reversal of AIDS known in the world to date. A narrow understanding of community in the form of tribalism, linked to colonial oppression, was the catalyst for destruction. Community in the sense of a generic family of human beings whose bonds were strengthened by Christian commitments to compassion and hope for the future brought healing and restoration.

A strong church-led initiative emerged to address the crisis of AIDS. Advocates such as Rev. Dr. Tom Tuma of the Church of Uganda argued for a multi-sector approach that called for the involvement of the entire society. This approach challenged government, religious, civic, educational, and professional leaders to develop concrete programs to provide education, care, and rehabilitation at local, district, and national levels. This response was in stark contrast to the denial and judgmental attitude that unfortunately still inform the ethos in many AIDS-plagued nations. Early in his government Museveni established an AIDS Control Program that was consolidated in 1992 as the Uganda AIDS Commission. Bishop Miseri Kauma, whose commitment was motivated by the AIDS-related death of his own son, was appointed chairman. The commission reported directly to President Museveni.

High political commitment at every level and openness about HIV/AIDS are now seen as principal factors in the declining rate of infection and AIDS. Religious and political leaders broke cultural taboos by openly discussing sexuality and how the virus is transmitted. They challenged cultural myths, such as AIDS is a homosexual disease, with the reality that in Africa, AIDS is primarily transmitted by heterosexual couples. Sexual patterns of an entire nation began to change through culturally relevant education by trusted local leaders such as schoolteachers, clergy, and traditional midwives; unprecedented support from international development partners, beginning with religious communities; and a variety of programs by all sectors of government and civil society coordinated by the Uganda AIDS Commission. The ABCs of the anti-AIDS campaign were posted in almost every public building in the country:

Abstinence, Be faithful, and use Condoms

A second factor in Uganda's effective resistance to AIDS is the powerful attribute of community, particularly the willingness to accept and care for others as members of one's own immediate family. In South Africa this attribute is known as *ubuntu*, which loosely means "I am because you are." My humanness is not lodged in my individuality but in my community. This powerful bond of community is reinforced by a similar Christian commitment that has been nurtured in Uganda's majority Christian community. In his letter to the Romans, Paul reminds them to "welcome one another, therefore, just as Christ has welcomed you, for the glory of God" (Rom 15:7). Christians believe that through Christ's life and work they have been welcomed, redeemed, or healed. Christians are then called to offer healing to others, especially those who have physical or spiritual needs. That a believer receives the undeserved love of God becomes the basis for welcoming or standing with a neighbor in need. The church as the body of Christ is mandated to be Christ's presence in compassion for, acceptance of, and service to those who suffer and are ill. Reverend Esau would do well to draw on this resource in seeking support for Mangalita. The Muslim communities in Uganda have similar strong commitments to works of mercy and healing.

Nowhere is this reality of community acceptance and support more clearly demonstrated in Uganda than in the care of AIDS orphans. In the mid-1990s Rakai, a district on Lake Victoria, was ground zero of the AIDS epidemic. One in every three children was an orphan, and in some villages 80 percent of the children were orphans. This community's response is even more amazing in light of the collapse of the farming and fishing infrastructure with the death of most of the working adults and the crumbling emotional and psychological foundations of the society. The Ugandan government policy was not to institutionalize orphans. The traditional Ugandan coping system took over. Young boys and girls of nine and ten years old assumed responsibility for their younger siblings and for one another. Grandparents took in as many children as their homes could hold. This miracle of a caring, healing, restoring community occurred not only in Rakai but in many other villages in Uganda. It did not happen everywhere, of course, and the care of orphans is still an open question in this case study. Many knowledgeable observers, however, believe profoundly that community triumphs over tragedy.

Uganda's ethic of caring community—shaped by traditional values, historical events, and religious faith—offers Reverend Esau a solid base to build a support community for Mangalita and her child. Coupled with education about AIDS and strong personal leadership, he has powerful tools at hand to counter the fear-based rejection of those who are "different" or perceived to threaten the survival of the community. This approach would also help alleviate John's deep fear of his family being rejected by the congregation and the village. Educational materials from his denomination and the Uganda AIDS Commission will add credibility to Reverend Esau's efforts to counter the often deadly rumors that spread quickly in fearful communities: "You will get AIDS if you look at a sick person or eat crops they have grown," "Condoms are a plot to keep us from having children," and "Having sex with a virgin will cure AIDS."

ROLE OF WOMEN

Like contemporary societies, traditional societies have strengths and weaknesses. The role of women in traditional societies is crucial both in terms of vulnerability and healing. Mangalita and her mother characterize both perspectives.

African scholars such as Dr. Brigalia Bam suggest that in many historical African societies men and women had distinctive roles that were equal
in status. However, with the arrival of Islam and Christianity, interpretations of scripture introduced a dominant role for men and a subservient
role for women. This differentiation was exacerbated by industrialization,
which drew many rural men into urban centers to earn money, leaving
their wives on the land not only to raise and educate the children but also
to assume full responsibility for tilling the soil and growing and harvesting
the crops. Men frequently established a second family in the urban center,
leaving even less support for the rural family.

The traditional value of women as childbearers was based on the importance of children for sustaining traditions, honoring the dead, providing
necessary labor for subsistence living, caring for elderly parents, and as
symbols of fertility and prosperity. However, in a society demanding multiple roles for women, tying their value to the role of childbearer contributes to the vulnerability and inferior status of women, like Mangalita, who
are deemed unable to bear children. Entrenched role identity for women *or*
men endangers their human dignity and limits the potential of their unique
gifts and possibly their most effective roles in society.

A narrow role interpretation conflicts with one of the foundational interpretations of Christian theology: "There is no longer Jew or Greek, there
is no longer slave or free, there is no longer male or female; for all of you
are one in Christ Jesus" (Gal 3:28). This passage undergirds the understanding that Christians should make no distinction in status between persons
regardless of ethnic origin, social role, or gender. However, many religious
traditions, including groups within the Christian faith, highlight selected
passages of scripture that imply the superiority of men over women in a
number of categories.

The subservient role ascribed to women becomes a major problem when
women are subjected to injustice. After ten years of marriage Mangalita
has no right to housing or property when she leaves the marriage with
Felix. Women in many societies are treated functionally as property with
few or no individual rights. A great danger in the AIDS epidemic is that
women who are economically dependent often have no choice about sexual
intercourse if it is demanded by a spouse or other partner. At the same
time, many societies hold men and women to different standards of fidelity. One result is that a growing number of women who are faithful have
been infected with HIV by their male partners. Those religious bodies that
insist on the conjugal rights of husbands and reject the use of condoms
increase the vulnerability of women. At an international AIDS conference a
young Ugandan male made a moving presentation on Uganda's successful attack on AIDS, citing the importance of the ABC program. He emphasized the first principle of abstinence as the most critical step. He was challenged by a woman Ugandan delegate who reminded him that most African

women, particularly the thousands of very young women selected for marriage by older, sexually experienced men, have no real choice about abstinence. The requirement to submit to a husband or male partner can be a death threat.

Although many developing nations have laws to protect women's rights, these are often not enforced as strictly as traditional norms. Gender-biased social and legal inequities around the world result in a great disadvantage for women in getting a job, owning land, and even accessing health services. These factors leave women and girls vulnerable and economically dependent on men. For some women and girls, selling sex is seen as a matter of survival, an option Mangalita considered when she was desperate. Among fifteen to twenty year olds, women make up 67 percent of all HIV/AIDS infections in the developing world. Thus it is not just the role of women but also the *rights* of women that become a major community concern in the struggle to survive the tidal wave of AIDS.

Although women are especially vulnerable, they also have a powerful redemptive role in most developing nations, including Uganda. In the Ugandan approach to the control and prevention of AIDS, women's actions and voices most frequently promoted community as transformative caring. Women continued their role as the principal caregivers in religious, family, and civil society as they became the principal caregivers for persons with AIDS (PWAs). In Uganda women have been the sustaining force behind the multifaceted anti-AIDS program. Women are also the primary guides and staff members of long-term programs such as The Aids Support Organization (TASO), a local NGO that provides free counseling services to people living with AIDS, offers them hope, and teaches them to live positively. TASO has given men and women the courage to live with and conquer AIDS by involving PWAs as speakers. Persons who are living positive, full lives with the infection are also powerful educators, especially in remote rural areas like Sheema County where myths about AIDS are still strongly held. People listen more carefully when a PWA challenges traditional views of sexuality and speaks openly of transmission of the virus through sexual activity.

THEOLOGICAL ISSUES

Joyce and John Kyomuhendo are deeply divided about the cause of disease, which raises theological issues about AIDS. They have different perceptions of the role of unseen powers in the lives of living persons. The Rev. Dr. Tom Tuma, co-author of the case and former professor of church history at Makerere University, Kampala, Uganda, explores the impact of traditional beliefs on the spread of AIDS.

Dr. Tuma explains that Mangalita's father, John, believes that his daughter's illness could have been caused by angry spirits. In traditional

African society, disease or illness is caused by either witchcraft or angry spirits. In the 1960s a phrase, *the living dead*, was coined by African scholars to describe the ongoing relationship between the living and their dead relatives. Even if they are physically gone, dead relatives remain in spiritual form, interacting with living relatives. One way the departed communicate with the living is either by possessing a person and speaking through that person or by causing a person to fall sick. The spirit or spirits select a person, normally a relative, and the one who is picked may not have done anything wrong. The sickness cannot be cured by either European or African medicine. However, once the spirit's reason for the illness is identified through a spirit medium, necessary action will be taken to appease that spirit and the sick person will begin to recover.

Many African children grow up with the understanding that disease and death are caused by witchcraft or aggrieved spirits, and it is virtually impossible to supplant this with a notion of germs or viruses. In spite of the many years of exposure to other world views, this mentality prevails in the minds of Africans in regions such as Sheema County.

In 1982, when the AIDS virus found a home in Uganda, the vast majority of people were not aware of viruses and could not see viruses as agents of death. The Rev. Dr. Tuma believes that this, more than anything else, helped the deadly virus to spread within the country without any serious challenge for several years.

John Kyomuhendo has added a Judeo-Christian interpretation of scripture to this traditional understanding of sickness. In his youth he was taught that a person is punished by sickness as a direct result of his or her actions or the actions of an ancestor.[3] Mosaic Law taught that persons with leprosy, for example, were to be banished from their community. People were required to follow strict rules of bathing and sacrificing lambs as "guilt offerings" for their sinfulness (Lv 14:19). This theological understanding provides a rationale for many Christians who "blame the victim" and reject those who have AIDS because they are believed to be responsible for their sickness. AIDS is interpreted by some Christians as God's punishment for the sinfulness of immorality and having many sexual partners.

Joyce's response is founded in a different understanding of unseen powers. She has come to believe that illnesses such as AIDS are neither signs of God's punishment nor possession by spirits. She has learned about the power of unseen viruses, which can be transmitted physically, regardless of the "sinfulness" of the recipient. Mangalita was faithful to her husband, yet she was given AIDS. For Joyce, her deep love for her daughter calls her to reject social customs and follow Jesus' model of not placing blame but accepting and caring for those who are cast out. As a sign of God's love of all people, Jesus spoke to, touched, and healed lepers, who were deeply feared and reviled. He modeled loving and accepting those most in need and called his followers to do the same. Jesus repeatedly challenged his followers to move from judgment to compassion.

Reverend Esau, in a mediating pastoral role, may help John and Joyce talk about their fears as they explore the implications of allowing Mangalita to return to their home. These are not only fears of being isolated from the community, but also fears based on views of ancestral spirits and a judgmental God. In relating to John's perceptions and those of the wider community, Reverend Esau may want to raise an understanding of natural events as part of God's creation, contrasting this with a vengeful God who uses disasters to punish people for evil deeds. There are times when the meaning given to a disaster can be much more damaging than the initial event. Christians find comfort and motivation in seeing God's loving power in people's response to a tragedy rather than in its cause.

As Reverend Esau reminds his congregation of its strong community tradition of caring for one another in times of crisis and the importance of helping Mangalita raise her child in a stable and loving environment, he may want to remind his congregation also of the early church, among whose members "everything they owned was held in common . . . [and] there was not a needy person among them" (Acts 4:32, 34). An understanding of his members' traditional beliefs also gives him unique insight into their fears as he seeks to interpret Jesus' model of caring and acceptance of all people.

It is clear that not only in Sheema County but around Africa and around the world there is both an opportunity and a need for theological education related to AIDS. This may come through the pastoral role of the parish priest, pastor, rabbi, or imam. The church and other religious institutions need to conduct or co-sponsor workshops that not only address critical issues such as AIDS control and prevention but also give people a place to share their fears and talk about their image of God and God's role in healing and restoration. As they challenge their communities to resist judgment and imitate Christ's example of loving care in their response to people living with AIDS and HIV infection, clergy and lay leaders will gain insight and support as they share their concerns with one another and use resources about AIDS from church bodies, ecumenical councils, and interfaith advisory groups.

A GLOBAL RESPONSE

The Uganda case study offers readers a snapshot of a specific family, church, and community dealing with AIDS. However, the case is situated in a global context. The setting of rural Uganda shapes distinctive social and cultural patterns, but the feelings of fear, rejection, and responsibility, the issues of exclusion, and the impact of theological understandings of God's role in human affairs are universal. In the same way, the small country of Uganda offers a global model for responding to the AIDS crisis even though the country still faces significant challenges, as the case study indicates. Although Uganda had the highest acknowledged level of HIV infection in the most AIDS-ridden continent in the world in the mid-1990s, it is now one of the few countries in the world to have reduced significantly the level of new infections and to bring hope and returning wholeness to a population that feared "slim" would destroy their society. World leaders from North America, Asia, Europe, Latin America, and other African countries make pilgrimages to Uganda to praise and, more important, to learn from this redemptive process.

It is now clear that, like a great tsunami, the waves of the AIDS epidemic have reached every shore. In June 2001, in declaring his commitment to addressing HIV/AIDS, United Nations Secretary General Kofi Annan declared, "For there to be any hope of success in the fight against HIV/AIDS, the world must join together in a great global alliance." Subsequently, staff of the newly formed Joint United Nations Programme on HIV/AIDS, UNAIDS, gathered physicians, researchers, advocates, caregivers, and victims in an international conference to study programs and approaches such as Uganda's in order to develop a comprehensive, systemic approach to the epidemic.

In seeking to understand why poor, agrarian nations seem to be most affected, their study showed hunger and poverty to be central to the spread of AIDS. When farmers fall ill, the harvest declines or fails, and the result is less available food. Time and energy are diverted to address the illness. People's nutrition deteriorates. Those who are undernourished and HIV-positive are more susceptible to other infections. The farmer is forced to revert to subsistence farming and abandon cash crops, which means less food for the family and for the nation. AIDS threatens food security for the present and the future. Dr. Peter Piot, the director of UNAIDS, captures the foundation for this case: "The famine in Southern Africa brings the world face-to-face with the deep and devastating impact of AIDS. What we are seeing in a number of countries of sub-Saharan Africa is an HIV epidemic that is overwhelming the coping resources of entire communities."[4]

In the search for contributing factors and potential solutions to the global spread of AIDS, UNAIDS has identified a number of critical categories:

1. *The status and rights of women* were highlighted earlier in this commentary. Women have 67 percent of all HIV/AIDS infections in the developing world. UNAIDS calls for the empowerment of women as essential to any effective AIDS strategy.
2. *Poverty and debt* underlie the hunger issue. It is difficult for many people in the West to imagine that 95 percent of Africans infected with HIV/AIDS live in abject poverty, surviving on less than one dollar a day. The debt structure of international lending agencies toward impoverished African nations has forced many of them to sacrifice health and education budgets to pay their international debt. One solution lies in the forgiveness or major restructuring of debt to direct income from national resources for internal use. In Malawi debt release

of $28 million allowed the purchase of critical drugs and the estab-
lishment of locally staffed health clinics. Debt relief can free resources
to seek meaningful solutions to the AIDS crisis

3. *Wars and refugees* spread AIDS. Through visits to sex workers, 90 percent of whom are believed to have AIDS, soldiers become carriers of
HIV/AIDS. The virus is spread as soldiers use rape as a weapon or
return home to their families. Violent civil conflicts and the subsequent flood of refugees add to poverty and spread the disease, which
is six times more likely to be contracted in a refugee camp. An obvious solution is not only better education of military forces, but also
more foundational efforts in systemic peacebuilding to avoid, contain, or transform civil wars. Peacebuilding contributes to the control
of AIDS.

4. *Stigma and denial* are critical systemic issues for both individuals and
nations. Refusal to acknowledge the reality and magnitude of the problem has led to stigmatization of individuals and communities. Denial
and inaction deepen the crisis and make governments and religious
institutions responsible for the humiliation and death of hundreds of
thousands of people. In contrast to the model of Uganda, most governments have been slow to acknowledge accountability. In their denial governments and religious bodies fail to address issues of sexuality or engage honestly and realistically with sex education and HIV
prevention.

   Some African churches are courageously challenging this trend.
Banners over the front entrance of many South African Methodist
churches announce: *This church has AIDS.* The subtext proclaims, "If
one member suffers, all suffer together" (1 Cor 12:26). Posters inside
these houses of worship describe HIV/AIDS and ways to prevent
infection. This kind of bold action depends on religious leaders who
are willing to break the silence and speak out about AIDS; provide
culturally appropriate education; and demand confidential and voluntary HIV testing, comprehensive health care accessible to all, and
affordable life-extending antiretroviral medication.

5. *Social and cultural factors* are complex and vary from one community
to another. They include unsafe sex practices, insecure blood supplies,
unclean needle use, and polygamous relations. As Ugandans learned,
however, an underlying factor in the solution is providing "safe
spaces" for people to discuss and explore answers to questions that
were previously taboo. The task is to provide reliable information and
forums for exchange at every level, and to build trust and understanding rather than to cast judgment. This often requires change in ethos
for governments, civic organizations, and religious communities.
Church leaders may need to reconsider theological views on sexuality and AIDS. In an interview with Mangalita following the writing
of her case, she stated: "AIDS in Uganda will be greatly reduced if

people change some of their traditional values and world views about disease and death. Governments are not as good at this kind of thing as churches. There must be more determined efforts to fight AIDS by the religious bodies. Religion changes people, and they acquire new values; they end their old ways as they acquire new ones."

6. *Access to treatment* evidences the great divide between the so-called developing and developed worlds in the battle against AIDS. Increasing numbers of people in poor countries know that life-prolonging drugs are available to some and not others; they find it inconceivable that their governments, employers, or religious institutions cannot make these medicines available on a broader scale. Most perceive that responsibility lies in greed and/or bureaucratic incompetence in dealing with the cost of drugs or restrictive trade laws, which are often given as reasons for the exclusion of the poor. When one compares the amount the home countries of the drug manufacturers spend on national security and weapons of mass destruction versus health, education, and welfare, including foreign humanitarian aid, those national priorities become clear.[5] The lack of affordable drugs is a matter of priority, not cost.

In developing countries between six and nine million people need antiretroviral medication; less than 5 percent have access due to poverty or restrictive trade laws. Some 2.5 million HIV-positive women give birth every year in the developing world; only 5 percent of them have access to drugs that could prevent transmission of HIV from mother to child. The cost is $2 per child to decrease the transmission of HIV by 50 percent. Some nations like India, Brazil, and Cuba are finding alternative methods for getting these medications to poor people. However, they are being prosecuted by Western pharmaceutical companies that raise issues of patent infringement. The national bodies involved are challenged to move from litigation to analysis and discussion of global needs and priorities. Perhaps the resolution lies in a combination of direct contributions and more generous discounts by drug manufacturers, subsidies by wealthy nations for both drugs and additional research that will benefit the poorest nations, and additional funding for health programs in these receiving nations.

CONCLUSION

Hope for the future is also a systemic factor in addressing the dilemma of AIDS. Archbishop Desmond Tutu declared, "If the Churches can't offer hope, they should just close their doors!"[6] Not many religious institutions seem to be taking this option very seriously. Yet there is abundant hope even in the midst of the flood waters of AIDS. The Ugandan model of a strong coalition of government, interfaith religious bodies, businesses, nongovernment organizations, and international development agencies shows that this kind of cooperation reaps results. International coalitions such as UNAIDS provide systemic approaches and a global network of mutual support. Hope comes in small acts of kindness—a hug, a prayer, a song, a gift of presence and time, as well as in larger acts of mercy through a support program, an internship, a vocational decision, an act of advocacy, or a check. The Ecumenical Response to HIV/AIDS developed in Nairobi in 2004 by African church leaders proclaimed: "It is time to speak the truth. It is time to act only out of love. It is time to overcome fatigue and denial. And it is time to hope."

The massive wave of AIDS demands our ethical analysis and our response. Christian and other religious bodies have shown both creative leadership and dismal failure in understanding and action. Case studies such as this provide the opportunity to "live into" a global crisis through the experience of a small Uganda village. The case and this commentary call on readers to respond by accompanying those who are caught up in a global tsunami. Desmond Tutu captures the spirit of this commentary when he speaks about children with AIDS and AIDS orphan: "These are the faces of children and families living in the world of AIDS. Their spirit, their determination, and their resilience inspire all of us to join the fight. We are one world, and these children are our children. Their destiny is our destiny. Each of us can make a difference. Each of us can help save lives."[7]

NOTES

1. *Together* magazine [World Vision International, Pasadena, California] (July-September 1995).
2. AIDS is not a direct cause of death. The virus destroys T-cells, which are part of the body's immune system that fights infection. A person infected with the virus (HIV-positive) has AIDS when sufficient numbers of T-cells are destroyed so that the body's immune system can no longer resist "opportunistic diseases" such as tuberculosis, pneumonia, liver disease, or viral hepatitis. These diseases become the direct cause of death.
3. Leviticus 26:14–39 and other texts in the Hebrew and Christian scriptures.
4. "UNAIDS Report on the Global HIV/AIDS Pandemic" (2002) (The Joint United Nations Programme on HIV/AIDS). Available online at the UNAIDS website.
5. In 2004 the United States' proposed budget for the Pentagon was $400 billion. The total budget for international humanitarian aid was $10 billion.
6. Stated in a private conversation with the author in July 2003.
7. Desmond Tutu, quoted in "Faces of HIV and AIDS," Program Committee on Education for Mission (National Council of Churches) website.

ADDITIONAL RESOURCES

Barnett, T., and A. Whiteside. *AIDS in the Twenty-First Century: Disease and Globalization.* New York: Palgrave Macmillan, 2002.
"Global AIDS: Facing the Crisis." In *Facts Have Faces.* Elkhart, IN: Church World Service, n.d.
Keenan, James F., SJ, et al., eds. *Catholic Ethicists on HIV/AIDS Prevention.* New York: Continuum International Publishing Group, 2000.
Messer, Donald E. *Breaking the Conspiracy of Silence: Christian Churches and the Global Aids Crisis.* Minneapolis: Fortress Press, 2004.

PART VII

SEXUALITY

Case

Getting Away from It All

"I wish you would have died in that fire and not my father!" The apartment door slammed as Alicia stormed out. Helen Edwards grimaced as another piece of plaster fell in the narrow hallway. She walked to the front window and peered out to see Alicia emerge from the stairwell and run across the littered cement courtyard to the next housing block where her friend Mae lived. Would it do any good to drag her fourteen-year-old daughter back to the Mid-Town Teen Clinic?

Rock music blared from Alicia's portable radio. As Helen went to turn it off, she looked at the clock and hurried to get her handbag. She could not stop now to find Alicia or she would be late for work again. Helen did not cry very often. It was not her way. But she was as close to tears as she had been in a long time.

She tried to imagine what Alicia was feeling, to remember what it was like to be so young. Helen's hands felt cold as she maneuvered her old car through the heavy morning traffic. Helen felt as though she had never been young. Her eldest, Joe, had been born when she was fifteen. Then Sam came along a year later. When Alicia was born, Helen swore she would never let her become a teenage mother and fall into the same trap she had gotten herself into. Daniel Moore, Alicia's father, had had some problems, but he had been a good man. They had struggled to raise their three children, but then their life together had ended when Daniel died in a fire at the factory where he worked.

Six months after Daniel died, Helen married Jim Edwards. She remembered the arguments with Jim about a baby. Helen had said there was no way they could afford another child. Jim was employed temporarily with odd jobs. Hers was the only steady salary. Jim was insistent and eventually won out. Jackie, their baby, was now nearly a year old and looked just like Jim.

It had not worked out too badly. Jackie was a good baby, and everybody loved her, especially Jim. Helen clenched the wheel when she remembered that Jim had spent nearly a week's salary on baby clothes that Jackie outgrew in less than a month.

Helen had worked for the Andersons for about six years. Although she started as a domestic, she increasingly took over the care of their four children. Mrs. Anderson had said that Helen should think about going to the vocational school to get her child-care certificate. She could even start her own center. But there were too many nights she stayed late at the Andersons, sometimes overnight. Helen remembered feeling proud that Alicia, even at ten, could put together a supper for her brothers.

The Andersons had given Helen a month's leave to have Jackie and welcomed her back afterward. Some days she could even bring Jackie to work. Usually she left the baby with Mrs. Morris, an older neighbor in their apartment block. Alicia was supposed to pick her up after school. That was happening less and less.

Helen's mind went back over the past few months trying to piece together the changes she saw in Alicia. Even though Jim had been with them for nearly two years, Alicia still did not get along with him. Close friends did not help much when they kept commenting on how much Alicia looked like her father. Then, when Jim was drunk, sometimes on weekends, he would shout at Alicia. Alicia would stay away from the apartment for hours at a time. Helen learned she was running around with a much older group of teens in the project. Some of them were dropouts. Several had police records. Helen's oldest boy told her it was a rough crowd. A lot of them were into drugs.

Helen became determined to move her family out of the project. She spent hours reading newspaper ads, looking for anything they could afford. Because Mrs. Anderson did not make her fool with social security, Helen's take-home pay, including overtime, was sometimes over $1,160 a month. They needed at least three bedrooms, and most rents started at $840 a month. Helen had found a place she thought they could afford, but the manager refused to show it to her when he found out she had four children.

Several weeks later, in September, Helen learned that Alicia, then thirteen, had a boyfriend who was seventeen. Not long after he gave Alicia two tapes and a bracelet, Helen made an appointment for Alicia at the Mid-Town Teen Clinic. Helen had already tried to talk to her about not getting pregnant. She was still a little girl. For her own sake as well as that of a child she might have, she needed to wait until she was older. Helen hoped Alicia would listen to someone at the clinic.

When Alicia came out of the interview with Ms. Wilson, she showed Helen a six-month supply of birth-control pills and promised her mother she would take them. Alicia made an appointment to come back again in six months. Helen continued to search for a new place to live. Less than three months after the visit to the teen clinic, Alicia told her mother she thought she was pregnant. Helen talked to Mrs. Anderson the next afternoon. Mrs. Anderson made arrangements for Alicia to see her own gynecologist. Helen would have to pay $100 for the visit. Helen took the day off to take Alicia to the doctor's office. She sat and waited for over an hour in the lounge while Alicia saw the nurses and then the doctor. Alicia was very quiet when she came out. She cried on the way home. She told her mother the doctor had been very straight about the options, and that if the tests were positive, she had to decide what to do. She said that she wanted to talk to her boyfriend first.

The doctor's office called Helen at the Anderson's the next day. The blood test was negative. They were sure Alicia was not pregnant. That night Alicia said she would go back to the clinic. She had thrown the pills away when she thought she was pregnant. Helen took another afternoon off to drive Alicia back to the teen clinic. Alicia promised again she would be careful.

Over the next two months Alicia drew further and further away from the family. She began spending every afternoon with her friend Mae. Helen learned from her oldest boy that Mae was eighteen and had dropped out of school when she had a baby. She lived with her mother and got $235 a month from welfare.

Helen had not worried too much about her boys. Joe and Sam seemed to manage all right in high school. They worked odd jobs when they could. Helen remembered seeing on television that unemployment for teens in the city was over 75 percent. But just keeping Alicia in school was a problem. Her truancy had gotten so bad that Helen had taken to driving Alicia to school to make sure she got there. Then pressure at work made this impossible. If Helen could not make it to the Andersons by 8:30, they would have to get someone else.

Things at home seemed to get worse. It was a bitterly cold winter, and the heat bills were high. By the end of January Helen hardly had enough money to buy groceries. The phone company had come and taken out the phones again. Jim still had not found anything steady. He was going on weekend binges more often. One night after he hit Helen and swore at Alicia, Helen decided that Alicia needed to go to live with her cousin in Atlanta. Alicia was back home in three weeks. Her aunt refused to keep her. Helen never found out what happened.

Jim left the first week in March. A week later Alicia's school counselor called Helen at the Andersons. Alicia was being suspended for fighting with another girl in school. Helen told the Andersons she needed to quit work and stay at home with her daughter. She made arrangements for a good friend at church to work temporarily for the Andersons.

Two weeks later Helen went back to work for the Andersons. She had hoped staying at home with Alicia would help, but Helen found Alicia almost impossible to handle. Several days she did not come home at all. Helen remembered one night she was so mad at Alicia that she told her she would turn her over to the juvenile court. When the period of suspension was over, there were days when Alicia left school soon after she got there. The school counselor told Helen she had a caseload of over four hundred children. She did not know what to suggest for Alicia. Had Helen tried taking her to the Mid-Town Teen Clinic?

For the month Helen had been back at the Andersons, Alicia seemed a bit more responsible and was coming more regularly to pick up Jackie from Mrs. Morris. Helen knew that Alicia had another boyfriend, but she refused to talk about him.

Then this morning, when she was taking off the bed sheets to do laundry, Helen found Alicia's unused container of birth-control pills under her mattress. Helen shooed the boys off to school early and told Alicia to stay. "What do you think you are up to? Why aren't you taking these things? I know your cycle. You still have time to start this month. Has this new boyfriend of yours put ideas into your head? There's no way I'll believe that boy is using any protection." Helen tried to keep her voice under control but knew she was shouting at Alicia.

Alicia glared back at her mother. "My boyfriend gave me that blouse you wouldn't buy me for my birthday. He treats me like a woman. He thinks it would be cool to have a baby. You can't make me take those things. I'm old enough to make my own decisions. Besides, my boyfriend doesn't want me to take them. You're always picking on me. I wish you had died in that fire. . . . "

As Helen pulled her car into the Andersons' long driveway, she saw Mrs. Anderson waiting with the two year old. She smiled as Helen got out of the car. "Helen, I have a wonderful surprise. This next week when the children's private school has spring break, Mr. Anderson and I plan to take the family to St. Simon's Island. We learned yesterday we can have one of the larger houses, and there would be just enough room for you and Jackie. I've heard you say you have never been on a trip and that you have never seen the ocean. With so much for them to do, the children should be easy for you to watch on the beach. And Mr. Anderson and I would be around most evenings. Helen, you really look tired and need to get away from it all. Why not come along with us?"

Commentary

Getting Away from It All

It is important to note at the outset that the case does not state the ethnic background of the Edwards. As more then 50 percent of the population of most urban housing projects are black or Hispanic, it would be understandable if one assumes the Edwards are members of an ethnic minority. However, using statistics as an entry point for this case may be a trap into stereotypical responses that could obscure deeper issues. In order to understand better the ethical decisions that Helen and Alicia face, one should enter the case through their personal perspectives and the subculture of the urban housing project in which they live. In this case conditions of poverty are far more relevant than issues of race.

CHARACTERS: THE PERSONAL DILEMMA

Alicia

"Getting away from it all" may be a temptation for Alicia as well as Helen and many other characters in the case. Alicia is experiencing pressure from several directions. She is faced with the persistent love of a mother trying to protect her at a stage in life when independence is particularly important. She also cares for a baby sister and has responsibility for meal preparation for two brothers, duties that began when she was only ten. These tasks are made more burdensome because the baby, Jackie, is the favorite of Alicia's stepfather, while Alicia is rejected. When Jim is drunk, he alternately ignores and yells at her. Alicia may have had no time or way to grieve after the death of her own father.

Alicia is probably also experiencing physical withdrawal of affection by her mother. Traditionally, when children reach adolescence and parents become aware of their sexuality, there is an unconscious withdrawal of parental touch. Though Alicia hears her mother express concern, she experiences her as demanding, and because of Helen's work schedule in a distant suburb, as absent.

If this is a typical low-income urban area, then school provides more pressure. Alicia's mother wants performance in an urban school system that probably is predominately segregated and has high dropout rates and overburdened teachers. Alicia knows the score and so does Helen: there are no jobs, even if one finishes school; the big money is in drugs.

Alicia knows from experience how hard it is to get advice and help. She recalls how embarrassing it was to have her mother take her to the teen clinic. The counselors were so busy they could only spend a few minutes with her, and nobody is that quick with good advice. Then, when Alicia was both scared and happy she might be pregnant, she had to go to Mrs. Anderson's doctor. Alicia may resent the Andersons as the cause of her mother's absence and react with anger to their privileges and access to a private physician in contrast to the public clinic. It would not be surprising if Alicia finds neither dignity nor meaning at home or in school.

Through her sexuality Alicia finds the intimacy, affection, and attention she craves, as well as a possible means of getting away from the trapped feeling of the housing project. The normal hormonal changes in her body and increasing sexual energy offer a viable outlet for her frustration. Her boyfriend wants a baby, and Alicia wants to please the only person in her life who makes her feel special. Alicia knows her mother was pregnant at fifteen. She suggests that she and her boyfriend could make it on TANF (Temporary Assistance for Needy Families).[1] Then she could be free and on her own. Alicia's stated desires are in contrast with the perspective of many of her peers. While some teens want to get pregnant, an increasing number of poor teenage girls use contraceptives to prevent pregnancy and consider long-term relationships neither realistic nor an option. In many poor urban communities there are three women for every marriageable man.

We can only imagine what Alicia's genuine needs and desires are. She is aware that some of the women who have been in the project for two or three generations, like Mae's mother, aren't all that happy. Husbands who last more than two years are in short supply. Alicia must wonder whether she has any real choice or any real hope.

Alicia is a remarkable young woman. She has homemaking and survival skills at age fourteen that would surpass most of her peers in the affluent suburbs. Refusing to be dominated by her mother or her aunt, she appears determined to make her own decisions and create some kind of a meaningful future.

Helen

As the mother of a teenage daughter on the verge of perpetuating the cycle of children bearing children, Helen recalls swearing at Alicia's birth that this would not happen to her daughter. She may feel terrible guilt that she is unable to control the situation. Helen is offered a way, at least temporarily, of getting away from it all. Would a trip to the ocean that she had so longed to see be the break she needs? She knows the Andersons gain the most by her going. They seem to be good people, even if paternalistic and probably uninformed about life in the projects. Helen tries not to think about the power they have to shape her situation. Helen must be angry and lonely; Daniel, her first husband, is dead, and Jim now is gone. But if she goes away at this critical time, is this surrender to a system that will swallow up her daughter as well? They will both be victims when that boy disappears and leaves her with a daughter and a grandchild to care for.

Helen also may wonder whether it really makes any difference if she goes or stays. Although the unfolding story seems already out of her hands, she still feels responsible. Helen may dream of the child-care certificate and the independence it promises. However, the price is high in precious time, money, and energy—with the likelihood of disappointment at the end.

Helen Edwards is a woman of loving instincts with an extraordinary capacity to care for others while still sustaining her own family. She is resourceful in securing medical options for Alicia, finding vocational possibilities for herself, and seeking housing alternatives for the family. Helen is a woman of determination and commitment.

Jim Edwards

For many middle-class readers Jim may be the most difficult of the characters to understand. Many males in poor urban areas are killed or disabled through gang or neighborhood clashes and police confrontations. Others are in prison or institutionalized for drug or alcohol abuse. A disproportional number of those in prison or addicts are children of teen mothers. Poor urban men are also caught in a system in which inner-city unemployment can be ten times higher than unemployment in surrounding suburban communities. Unemployed men are viewed by the dominant society as redundant or disposable. There must be some place to show your manhood, and fathering children is an honored tradition. Alcohol and drugs are a means of getting away from it all that few would condone, but certainly most who are knowledgeable would also understand.

Jim has the right to seek a loving relationship, including the pleasure of a baby in his house. However, if he is unable to find work, Jim's very presence in the household reduces the social welfare benefits the family is eligible to receive. He may be taking, in his judgment, a responsible, caring, and painful decision by distancing himself from the family. Whether his getting away is a sign of abandonment or concern may be a question of perspective.

The Andersons

Helen's employers are clearly middle class or upper-middle class, whether they are white, black, or Hispanic. As concerned employers, they have granted maternity leave, offered medical assistance, and encouraged Helen's vocational advancement. Yet Helen's schedule of evenings and overnights does not suggest the job is designed with the needs of a parent-employee in mind. Although it is illegal, they have agreed with Helen's decision not to withhold social-security payments from her salary, which also eliminates payment of a matching employer contribution. While Helen states she needs the extra cash now, this decision will not be to her benefit in the long run. The case gives no details about Helen's employee benefits, such as guaranteed medical care or paid vacation time. However, benefits beyond social-security payments are rare for domestic help and child-care providers, despite the value of these services if measured by their impact on the quality of an employer's family life. The Andersons appear genuinely concerned about Helen and her family in terms of immediate personal problems. They have provided understanding, some work flexibility, and special resources such as access to their family physician.

The case raises a number of personal and moral questions, however, for non-poor readers. How can the welfare of their children be compared to the welfare of Helen's children? Does their access to wealth, at least compared to the Edwards, provide rights of time and attention not equally owed to Alicia, Jackie, and their brothers? To what degree are wealthy employers responsible for the structural injustices that burden families such as the Edwards? The gap between poverty and privilege widens when social injustice is reduced to a private concern for a single individual.

Questions of structural justice are more complex than the personal issues. What responsibility do the Andersons, or any member of a privileged segment of society, have for the inadequate housing, education, employment, and medical facilities for the poor? Where are the limits of responsibility for the welfare of employees, who are also children of God, with special needs for their families? A critical moral issue in this case may be what the famous twelfth-century rabbi Maimonides called the eighth and most meritorious step of charity: "to anticipate charity by preventing poverty."

THE SITUATION: A NATIONAL TRAGEDY

A double-edged national tragedy that this case reveals is the growing level of poverty concentrated among children and youth and the higher levels of teenage pregnancy that are both a consequence of and a contributor to that poverty. The United States is progressively being divided into two nations. The communities are as distinct as the separation of the rich and the poor worlds at the global level. The gap runs along lines of economics, gender, and race.

For the citizens of one of the wealthiest nations in the world the statistics on poverty should be profoundly disturbing. According to the Luxembourg Study, while child poverty has remained the same in most industrialized countries during the past thirty years, child poverty has increased significantly in the United States. In the United States one child in four is born into poverty, and one child in five lives through adolescence in poverty. Poverty hits children and young mothers hardest. One of the most disturbing indices of poverty in the United States according to the Population Reference Bureau's 2004 World Population Data Sheet is a higher infant-mortality rate than in thirty-seven other nations in the world. The United States takes pride in world-class medical care. However, the dramatic decline in the number of those who have access to this world-class care or to health insurance for basic care is a national tragedy that challenges our self-perception as a humane, just, and progressive people. Sixteen percent of the US population is without health insurance.

Teenage pregnancy is linked to poverty. Although US reports document that national teenage pregnancy by young women from ages fifteen to nineteen declined by an average of 28 percent between 1990 and 2000, the United States still has the highest adolescent birthrate of any industrialized nation. Various expert analysts attribute the decline to anxiety about sexually transmitted diseases, awareness of and more effective contraceptives, and changes in sexual behavior. However, the overall statistics vary widely by states, with an increase rather than a decline in rural poor and major urban areas.

Over 850,000 teens become pregnant each year. A high percentage of teenage parents' own mothers conceived in their teens, as did Helen Edwards. The disproportionate number of these who are poor, single, black, or Hispanic exposes the deep roots of class, gender, and race in our culture. The greatest challenge for those who are extremely poor is often not stronger ethical norms but survival. The dominant Christian norm for sexual relations within marriage presupposes a loving relationship. Yet the realities of poverty threaten the fulfillment of sustained, loving relationships between sexual partners. The ethical crisis in this case is not simply Helen's parental dilemma about more supervision or Alicia's decision about childbearing. It is, in many ways, a class-action case that challenges the morality of a society that perpetuates the dehumanizing conditions in which some people live and fails to address the complex causes of poverty and teenage pregnancy. Ed Ayala, a Hispanic pastor and community activist, frames the challenge for Christians: "Christian faith is an invitation to have life in abundance. Teen pregnancy prevents our youth from being fully alive, trapped in early complications of adult life and limited in wholeness. Dreams are shattered and turned into nightmares. The commitment for religious communities to be involved should not be optional."

A SYSTEMATIC AND PERSONAL APPROACH

Having the basic necessities of life, human dignity, and a sense of security seem to be essential for sustaining loving relationships. Perhaps all the members of the human community must own some responsibility when the support systems for basic needs do not exist or cease to function. In exploring the problems of the ethics of societal structures as well as personal relationships, we should consider which conditions and policies promote and sustain the love of God and neighbor. Three categories emerge for consideration: education, economics, and freedom and responsibility.

Education

An analysis by the Alan Guttmacher Institute of federal policies adopted between 2000 and 2004 raises serious concerns about recent legislation involving sexual and reproductive health for young people.[2] Much of the report concerned education, citing increased federal funding for abstinence education with a parallel decrease in funding for family-planning clinics. The report also noted that the government is proposing severe cuts in Medicare, which currently provides health care and family planning for one in three low-income women of reproductive age. In addition, the report cites serious misrepresentation of scientific evidence on the effectiveness of condoms by high-level social conservatives who promote abstinence in place of the use of condoms.

In late 2004 the US Department of Health and Human Services released its 2002 National Survey of Family Growth. Findings related to teens show that while younger teens (fifteen to seventeen) were more likely to postpone sexual activity and teens of all ages were more likely to use contraceptives, older teens indicated that they had received no formal instruction in school and had no conversations about birth control with their parents before they were eighteen. Because of lack of consistency and correct usage, the failure rate of contraceptives is disproportionally high among teens. Other factors affecting teen pregnancy are strong peer pressure to become sexually active and, in many US cultures, an increased acceptance of having children out of wedlock. With changing social norms, inadequate education, and decreased availability of family-planning services, there are strong indications that teenage pregnancy will increase in coming years in the poorest areas of the country.

Major studies reveal that many Americans are seriously misinformed about the nature and roots of the problem. Better information is especially important for those who are responsible for legislation, school policy, and the stated priorities of religious and private institutions. Public forums and seminars must draw on areas of agreement about the data and point to avenues of support and participation.

Myths and stereotypes about teenage pregnancy need to be challenged by comprehensive comparative studies. One of the Alan Guttmacher Institute's studies compared US statistics with those of six other countries with similar cultural and economic backgrounds, including England and Canada. The results indicate that the United States leads every developed nation in the number of teenage pregnancies, childbearing adolescents, and in abortion rates. While the number of teenage mothers is disproportionately high among poor black and Hispanic families, it is misleading to conclude that high US figures are simply a result of an ethnic population that lives in a degree of poverty unknown in most of Western Europe. The per capita rate of teenage pregnancy in the United States for white non-poor adolescents also exceeds that of other countries in the study.

Developing an approach to teenage pregnancy requires raising awareness of the high cost of failing to invest in solving the problem. The dislocation created by teenage pregnancy takes an incredible emotional, physical, and economic toll on the lives of teenagers, their families, and finally, on society as a whole. The pregnant teenager is "at risk" in terms of being dramatically less likely to complete high school and to secure or maintain a job. More than two-thirds of girls/women who have children before they are eighteen never earn a high-school diploma. These same young women are significantly more likely to abuse drugs and alcohol, to give birth to a child with physical and mental handicaps, to have children who become teenage parents, to live in poverty, and to attempt suicide. The direct costs to the society in terms of welfare, medicine, and human suffering are staggering.

A variety of sources identify causal factors of teenage pregnancy as (1) lack of available courses on family life; (2) lack of access to accurate birth-control information and resources; (3) the depiction of sex by the media; (4) peer pressure; and (5) social alienation caused by the breakdown of the family and the loss of support structures for a meaningful future.

In regard to sex education the Guttmacher Institute study draws an important overall conclusion. It is not that American culture is obsessed with sex, as might be concluded by a sampling of the media, especially television. Rather, the institute concludes that American culture as a whole is prudish and intolerant of premarital sexual activity. These attitudes stem in part from a fear of sexuality that causes many parents not only to be unable to deal openly with sexual activity but to withdraw physical affection from their adolescent children. The church is cited as a factor in this view of sex, which also results in a frequent polarization in discussions about mandatory or even voluntary "family life and sex education" classes, to say nothing about the establishment of school-based health clinics that offer contraceptive information. The debate is fueled by the belief that providing information about birth control undermines the message of abstinence and leads to earlier or more frequent sexual activity and thus higher pregnancy levels. This perspective has significantly affected federal poli-

cies regarding support of sex education, with a radical shift toward abstinence education and curtailment of funds for sex education. However, this
approach is not supported by most reliable research. One example is that
sex education has been compulsory in Sweden since the 1950s; that country has significantly lower levels of pregnancy and abortion than the United
States.

Other voices, which may agree with the importance of urging young
people to postpone having children, also call for a reality check. Almost
three-fifths of US teens are sexually active by the time they are eighteen. A
study by the Brookings Institution suggests that while many US schools
have some form of sex education, "these courses often are too short and
come too late to do much good . . . and the controversies surrounding them
have prevented public school teachers from providing the kind of guidance they might give their own children at home."[3] Several studies suggest
that a crucial step toward addressing teen pregnancy is to introduce mandatory family and life education courses from kindergarten to grade twelve
in as many public and private schools as possible. A clear conclusion regarding this debate is that education is needed not only for teenagers but
also for the adult Americans who ultimately determine public policy and
influence moral values.

School-based health clinics that are accessible and confidential could also
be an important factor in the solution. While some states have school-based
clinics supported by both pro-life and pro-choice groups with a common
interest in preventing teen pregnancy, other state programs are blocked by
religious bodies opposed to contraception and abortion on ethical grounds;
they challenge the use of public tax dollars to support facilities that may
dispense information contrary to their teachings. As in Alicia's case, many
clinics, even when available, are not near the schools, are often underfunded
and understaffed, and have parent boards that restrict the use of contraceptives or any advice about pregnancy termination. Given the current
polarized climate, enacting necessary legislation for courses and clinics will
be a public struggle.

One of the most hopeful developments for poor urban communities is
the formation of coalitions and comprehensive programs that involve young
children, teens, and adults. These public/private partnerships combine state
and federal resources of education, health, and social services with those of
residents, churches, corporations, foundations, and civic organizations. One
of the most successful coalitions, Breaking the Cycle, began in 1995 in Hartford, Connecticut, under the auspices of The Hartford Action Plan on Infant Health.[4] In 1994 Hartford, one of the ten poorest cities per capita in the
country, had the third highest teen pregnancy rate in the United States. By
2003, Breaking the Cycle had contributed to a steady decline in birth rates
for Hartford teens aged fifteen to nineteen, a greater decline than the national average. Its programs include "Let's Talk" (in English and Spanish
by and for parents), neighborhood businesses such as barber shops and

hair salons providing information materials, "Always on Saturday" programs in schools and public libraries, comprehensive school-based health education and services, and a school-based program on postponing sexual activity for fifth graders (ten and eleven years old) taught by high-school teens. This active coalition provides a model for other communities to examine and adapt to their own special circumstances.

Economics

The breakdown of family life in all classes and races, but especially in poor ethnic communities, has been linked to economic pressures and the inability to control or even participate in the shaping of one's future in a meaningful way. These pressures are in part due to racism and the failure of the wider community to provide support in terms of *adequate* employment, housing, health, and other social services. Understanding the complex causal factors of family disintegration and the resulting loss of hope for a meaningful future for both teenagers and parents may be the most critical and also the most complex challenge presented by the case. Without a sense of worth and dignity it is difficult for an individual to use the resources made available in schools, clinics, churches, and community organizations.

The Census Bureau predicts that more than 60 percent of the children born in the United States will live for some time with only one biological parent, usually the mother. Ninety-six percent of all children whose families receive federal and state support are from homes with a single head of household, and 85 percent of single-parent families are headed by mothers. In the debate about the most effective ways to address the devastating effects of poverty on women and children, conservative analysts insist that public support encourages teenage girls to become single parents and raise their children on their own. However, studies that compare international economic support for out-of-wedlock children indicate that US welfare benefits are less generous than those in countries with proportionately much lower numbers of unmarried mothers.

Counterproposals to breaking the cycle of poverty and single-parent homes include encouraging long-term involvement of the father through subsidized employment or other support systems to help build a sustainable family. A study of welfare reform and teen pregnancy by the Brookings Institution suggests that to help change the cycle of child poverty and children having children, young unwed mothers need better education, subsidized health insurance, and child care.[5] Other studies propose more accessible family-planning facilities, support for parental leave, and greater income support for working poor families. This last proposal reflects the fact that during the past thirty years, the value of the US minimum wage has dropped 40 percent; a quarter of full-time employed workers live below the federal poverty line for a family of four.

It is revealing that surveys of mothers with dependent children taken prior to the enactment of the AFDC program, which was a part of the 1935 Social Security Act, showed that these mothers opposed the program. These women preferred programs of child care, health insurance, and job training to cope with their economic problems, not welfare payments. A proposal for welfare reform by The National Council of State Human Services Administrators entitled "One in Four" evokes the challenge of children in poverty. It calls for programs to enhance self-support and self-sufficiency for poor families through income security, education, and employment and thus returns to themes articulated by poor mothers in 1935. The report has a special section of recommendations for preventing adolescent pregnancy.

There is scant evidence that any nation has significantly addressed the problem of unwanted pregnancies without providing a degree of economic security and hope for a more meaningful life.

Families such as Mae's or Helen's have inadequate resources and virtually no hope that the cycle of poverty will be broken. Unless the systemic issues of poverty—unemployment, underpaid employment, scarcity of affordable housing, inadequate education, lack of day care, limited or no health insurance, and limited medical services—are dealt with, other strategies to reduce teenage pregnancy may reap minimal results.

Freedom and Responsibility

At the heart of the Christian tradition is a relational norm, the love of God and neighbor. The Christian is called first to love God "with all your heart, and with all your soul, and with all your strength, and with all your mind; and your neighbor as yourself" (Lk 10:27). Theologian H. Richard Niebuhr described the principal purpose of the community of faith called the church to be "the increase of the love of God and neighbor." He also suggested that the basic guideline for making an ethical choice is to ask, "What is the loving thing to do?" The biblical standard is a quality of relationship called love that nurtures both freedom and responsibility. This is the freedom for human beings to realize their full potential and for individuals and societies to care for one another. The Christian call to a loving relationship with God, neighbors, and even with enemies is the basis for the concept of justice.

The biblical mandate for justice makes it ethically necessary that Christians support systemic changes that ensure a basic standard of living for all. In this case study the Andersons and the Edwardses both have responsibilities in moving toward this goal. Power within the system rests more with the Andersons. They could respond with adequate salary and health-pension benefits for Helen as well as becoming advocates in their schools, church, and community on strategies for the prevention of teenage pregnancy. Helen is doing her best with an insufficient salary to get her family not only together but "out of the projects" and into decent housing. However, she and other parents in the project also have an obligation to demand and help develop child-care programs, safe housing, and a school-based health clinic. Though it will challenge family patterns, Helen's sons need to assume their share of child care and meal preparation. System modification for the sake of justice is a responsibility of all, though what and how much one can do is in part determined by one's resources.

The case does not introduce the faith background of the Edwards family. However, all major religious traditions affirm the sanctity of marriage. A Christian understanding of marriage is a loving, sustainable, and liberating relationship, not only between partners, but among those within the wider family structure. In agreeing and even seeking to have a child out of wedlock, Alicia is in line with increased acceptance of unwed mothers in various US cultures, including the entertainment industry. Alicia is demanding emancipation, but she has a responsibility to look beyond her own needs. With the strong possibility of not finishing high school, she must seriously consider the likelihood of not being able to provide a loving and sustainable home for her child.

This case also raises the pain and alienation that accompany broken relationships. Alicia and Helen need both a commitment and a way to mend their relationship. They need to be able to understand and come to terms with their differences. This calls for openness and an ability to hear each other's deepest needs and a commitment to change the destructive patterns they have established. Often this level of conflict needs a third person to be the listener and supporter in order to move into a process of reconciliation that could enable both of them to better realize their potential.

We must also consider the tragedy of broken relationships between the poorest people in our society and those who have the capacity to address their poverty. The New Testament reference to love of neighbor comes in the context of Jesus' story of the compassionate Samaritan's rescue of an unknown traveler who had been robbed and beaten (Lk 10:30–37). Being neighbor to others means reaching out to the most marginal people in very concrete ways. The Samaritan's actions are in stark contrast to the actions of the two religious leaders who "passed by on the other side of the road," choosing not to see or respond to the traveler. The case and this passage challenge those who are able to respond to do so with energy and commitment. How do those of us respond who have the capacity to press for increasing the minimum wage to a living wage and to seek other concrete ways to address systemic issues of poverty, inadequate health care, and inferior education?

Freedom and the ability to participate in decisions and structures that shape our own lives and the lives of others are what distinguish us as human beings. The freedom provided by empowerment and self-determination is as important to the issue of teenage pregnancy as education and economics. The concept of being liberated from the attitudes or structures that limit one's human potential is central to this volume. Alicia needs the experience of being loved and affirmed for who she is as a person with a choice about the sexual and parental obligations she wants to assume and at what stage of her life. These choices are determined to a degree by what Alicia, her family, and her peers believe are real options for the future. Those caught in a life of poverty are seriously limited in the options available to them. Without some trust that the cycle of poverty and dependency can be broken, there is little motivation to risk new ways of being or relating.

Though the economic issues are more immediate in the urban projects and in areas of rural poverty, concerns for meaningfulness and hope are alive and pressing in every part of American culture. The symptoms of drug abuse, self-endangering sexual activity, community-alienating behavior, and increasing teenage suicide point to deep problems of identity and motivation. Non-poor adolescents from suburbia drift into drugs and loveless sexual experimentation because, they claim, life is boring and unfulfilling. The pressing problems in this case are pregnancy and parenting. But a critical question is whether or not individuals can become free enough from the present to live out the possibilities of loving and just relationships.

Addressing poverty and teen pregnancy with realism and empowerment of those most directly affected can liberate people to live to their fullest potential. More dedication, imagination, and collaboration need to be devoted to "getting with it" rather than "getting away from it all."

NOTES

1. Temporary Assistance for Needy Families (TANF), administered by the US Department of Health and Human Services, was created by the Welfare Reform Law of 1996. TANF replaced two programs commonly known as welfare: Aid to Families with Dependent Children (AFDC) and the Job Opportunities and Basic Skills Training (JOBS). TANF provides federal funds to states to develop and implement their own welfare programs for needy families.

2. Rebecca Wind, "Top Ten Ways Sexual and Reproductive Health Suffered in 2004," Alan Guttmacher Institute Report (New York, December 20, 2004).

3. Isabel V. Sawhill, "Welfare Reform and Reducing Teen Pregnancy," *The Public Interest* [The Brookings Institution] (Winter 2000).

4. Jack Cullin, "Breaking the Cycle," Hartford Action Plan on Infant Health, The Parisky Group (2003).

5. Sawhill, "Welfare Reform and Reducing Teen Pregnancy."

ADDITIONAL RESOURCES

Darroch, Jacqueline E., and Susheela Singh. "Why Is Teenage Pregnancy Declining?: The Roles of Abstinence, Sexual Activity, and Contraceptive Use." Alan Guttmacher Institute Occasional Report, 2002.

Miller, Barbara. *Teenage Pregnancy and Poverty: The Economic Realities*. New York: Roosen Publishing Group, 1999. This book is designed for teenage readers.

Moffitt, Robert A. "The Effect of the Welfare System on Non-marital Childbearing," cited in *Report to Congress on Out-of–Wedlock Childbearing*. Publication PHS95–1257. Hyattsville, MD: Department of Health and Human Services, Center for Disease Control, 1995.

The National Campaign to Prevent Teen Pregnancy, 1776 Massachusetts Ave., NW, Suite 200, Washington, DC 20036.

Rainwater, Lee, and Timothy M. Smeeding. *Poor Kids in a Rich Country: America's Children in Comparative Perspective*. New York: Russell Sage Foundation, 2003.

"U.S. Teenage Pregnancy Statistics: Overall Trends, Trends by Race and Ethnicity, and State by State Information." Alan Guttmacher Institute. Updated February 19, 2004.

Case

More Light

Don Chandler read again the resolution presented by the social-involvement committee: "Shepherd Presbyterian Church will not exclude any active member from election or ordination to office on the basis of race, class, gender, marital status, or sexual orientation." He examined the faces of the other members of the church session (governing body) and heard the pastor, Elaine Campbell, saying, "You understand that passing this resolution will declare us to be a 'More Light' congregation, and that is the intent of the motion. Is there any discussion?"

Don thought back to where it all began. Shepherd Presbyterian was a small church of 130 mostly young, well-educated members, with a fair record of social ministry in Tucson. Two years earlier the congregation had elected Morris Wilson, who made no secret of his homosexuality, to an unexpired term on the nine-member session. It had been a contested election. Morris had been nominated from the floor, the election had been postponed, and the session and pastor had led the congregation in six weeks of prayer and study on the issue of homosexuality and ordination. A 1978 decision of the denomination's General Assembly (national governing body) offered "definitive guidance" that "self-affirmed, practicing homosexual persons" should not be ordained. A subsequent amendment to the national church's constitution added language that said church officers must "live either in fidelity within the covenant of marriage between a man and a woman, or chastity in singleness." That complicated the matter, but when it came to a vote at Shepherd Presbyterian, Morris was elected by a two-to-one margin. The pastor ordained and installed him on the session. Shepherd's session informed the presbytery (the regional governing body) of its action, and there had been no adverse response.

The debate on Morris's election had been intense, but things seemed to settle down after his ordination. Don remembered how uncomfortable he had felt with the whole subject, opposed at first even to discussing it. But after working with Morris for two years, things had changed. Morris had become a real Christian brother and a partner in the session's ministry. Don still felt uncomfortable about Morris's sexuality, but in talking with the pastor and others he had decided God did not want him to ground his actions in fear and prejudice.

During the second year of Morris's term a few gay and lesbian people started to come to Shepherd Church, their numbers eventually reaching nine or ten. Three of them went through the class for new members and joined the church. Don had been concerned but later discovered when talking with them that several did not know Morris at all. He remembered one comment in particular: "We heard that this was a safe place to worship God."

It seemed to Don that the pastor felt a particular calling to care for the homosexuals attending Shepherd. He remembered a few sermons in which Elaine mentioned gays and lesbians specifically as people who needed to be welcomed into the family of faith. The session began to discuss the possibility of declaring Shepherd a "More Light" congregation. In collecting information and ideas, they wrote to all the "More Light" churches in the denomination, receiving answers from most. Two representatives from the session of a Colorado church paid them a personal visit.

Don learned that "More Light" congregations were those that had in some way voted to include homosexuals as members eligible for election and ordination as church leaders, thereby ignoring the denomination's guidance and possibly placing the congregation in open defiance of the amended constitution. The Permanent Judicial Commission of the denomination had long since ruled that the assembly's guidance was binding and that "More Light" decisions were unconstitutional. In several places around the country, presbyteries had taken disciplinary action against congregations defying the ban. Those rulings heightened the discomfort and confusion on the part of the Shepherd session. Don learned that the ruling had been a particularly hurtful decision to the gays and lesbians in the congregation. One person in particular, Jake Owens, had been threatened by the ruling. Jake was an intelligent young architect who had come to the point that he would openly share his hurt and loneliness with members of the congregation. Now he shared his fears with Don. Jake had felt attacked and wounded by churches in the past, and to Don he seemed vulnerable. A friendship had developed. Don felt paternal toward Jake. Some of Jake's pain had touched Don. He recalled Jake saying to him, "I'd hope to become a full member of this church, but I've been here before. I'm afraid Pastor Campbell has led me out on the dance floor only to leave me there. How much control does the denomination have over our congregation?"

Then the lid blew off. Several people suddenly left the church. The pastor began to look weary, and over lunch one day she shared with Don that she had been making calls every night. The focus was the gay issue. "I know what the people opposed to the gay and lesbian members want," Elaine said, "but I want them to love one another and make room."

Don also had received several phone calls from upset church members in recent weeks. Don was an official with the Red Cross and had credibility in the community and frequent contact with members of the church. He was a long-time member of Shepherd Presbyterian and was serving his fourth year on the session. People in the congregation, as well as other members of the session, seemed to give weight to his opinion and often sought him out to talk.

Peter Chapson had called him. "What's going to be next? The church is attacking everything I believe in. First, we can't call God 'Father' anymore. Then I found out that Elaine is working with illegal aliens. Now we're getting this gay business forced on us constantly. When they get up and use those words—gay and lesbian—they're describing sexual acts right in the worship service. How much am I supposed to put up with?"

Patty Becker had called to say she was concerned about her children. "This is not good modeling. The Bible calls homosexuality a sin. I have young children, and I don't want to teach them that it isn't. Look how unhappy those people are. We used to be a family-oriented church. But there's very little emphasis on children or family relationships anymore. Whatever happened to the Ten Commandments? Isn't anything right or wrong anymore? Have we reached the point where anything you want to do is acceptable?"

Jane Weller told Don how upset she was because her husband was leaving the church. "I don't mind if the gay folks are there," she said. "We've always said we were an inclusive and pluralistic church. I don't want us to turn away anyone who loves Jesus. It's okay if they're there, if only they wouldn't be so vocal. When they become so visible, when you put labels on people like gay and lesbian, all it does is separate us into categories. If we hadn't made such an issue of it, we wouldn't have a problem, and John wouldn't be leaving the church."

Don considered the phone calls as the session turned to the "More Light" resolution. Then he thought about Jake Owens, at home and anxious over the outcome of tonight's meeting. The discussion began in earnest. Morris Wilson sat, restrained and calm as usual.

Alberto Tarver, with occasional nervous glances at Morris, attacked the resolution at once. "We can't condone or accept homosexual activity in any way without flying in the face of biblical anthropology. The model in Genesis for full humanness is partnership—male and female. In the New Testament the church is the bride of Christ—same model. Paul classifies homosexuality with idolatry. Will we condone idolatry just to be nice?"

"You know what bothers me?" Lynn Carrasco jumped in. "Everyone keeps talking about this like there is a civil rights issue here. But ordination isn't a right; it's a responsibility. It's how the church chooses leadership, and leadership has always been a select few. 'Many are called, but few are chosen.'"

"Why take a position?" said Alice Royal. "Maybe there's another way. I can't agree with Alberto, but we've got a good thing going. Why mess it up by taking a formal vote and making public proclamations? This resolution won't affect our local ministry, and it will only split our congregation. We've reached out to the gay community and fully included gay members in our church life. The congregation will come around eventually. Meanwhile, we can always take 'no action' on this resolution."

Joan Wall, one of the session's newer members, spoke. "I might favor this," she said, "But first I would need to know how the gays in our congregation feel themselves. May I ask Morris a question? Is this resolution important to the gays? Will they understand it as a sign of care and support, or will it further set them apart and single them out? If we don't pass it, how hurt will they be? Will we lose them?"

Morris sat forward in his chair. "Everyone's different, of course. Yes, it would be affirming, a sign of solidarity. And passing this motion would serve to keep the sexuality issue from coming up every time there is an election. But I doubt anyone would leave if we fail to pass the resolution. Most gays and lesbians are accustomed to rejection and oppression and tend to accept them. I would say most of us would be quite disappointed but not surprised."

"We ought to do the right thing," said Dennis Bench, "whatever the cost. I'm uncomfortable when the denomination asks us to exclude from ordained office one, and only one, group of people. It makes them second-class church members. And the apostle said a lot of different things. In his best moment he said, 'If you belong to Christ, then you are Abraham's offspring, heirs according to the promise' (Gal 3:29). Jesus called all kinds of different people to his side and empowered them to serve. If there is any idolatry here it is thinking sexuality is so all-fired important it could make you unfit for ordination. We've said we are a pluralistic church and the body of Christ. Who is outside God's call? Whom shall we exclude from full participation in Christ's body?"

"We don't have that choice," Millie Stewart replied. "The General Assembly acted, and our highest court ruled on it. We're still a Presbyterian congregation. We are part of a connectional church. If you disagree with a law, you work to change it. You don't break it. You can always petition the General Assembly to reverse itself. It's the only thing you can do."

Don felt Elaine Campbell's eyes fall on him. "You've been unusually quiet tonight, Don. Where do you think we should go on this?"

Commentary

More Light

The issue before Don and Shepherd Presbyterian Church involves choices on three distinct matters. Deciding how to respond to the More Light resolution will require prior decisions about biblically and theologically based moral assessments of homosexuality, about the purpose and shape of Christian ministry, and about the binding character of denominational guidelines. Before taking up each of those issues, it may be helpful first to explore briefly some new information on and perspectives toward homosexuality.

NEW LIGHT

Today most Christian denominations are divided over the issue of homosexuality, largely because the unequivocal condemnation of homosexuality that once characterized Christian traditions has been challenged by recent scientific research, by different interpretations of scripture, by increased openness on the part of homosexuals, and by the resulting increase in knowledge and experience of homosexuals by heterosexuals. Though the sciences have not by any means answered all the questions about homosexuality, there is a great deal of new light.

One conclusion of the research is that there is an important distinction between homosexual orientation and homosexual activity. Homosexual orientation refers to a predominate sexual attraction to persons of the same sex. Homosexual orientation for most homosexuals seems to be set at a very early age. It does not seem to be voluntary, often presenting itself to the individual as a fait accompli. This research has led many Christians and Christian denominations to conclude that if homosexual orientation is not chosen, it is not sinful. Homosexual activity is sexual activity with a person of the same sex. To act sexually on the basis of homosexual orientation is a choice, just as to act sexually on the basis of heterosexual orientation is a choice. The Presbyterian Church (USA) does not exclude persons of homosexual orientation from ordination, only those who are self-affirming and practicing homosexual persons.

There is a great deal of research data, some of it contradictory, on the mental health of sexually active homosexuals and the adequacy of relationships among them. In 1973 the American Psychiatric Association removed homosexuality from the category of mental disorders. The tentative conclusion of most researchers in the last two decades has been that, while social attitudes make it more difficult for an individual to accept a homosexual orientation than a heterosexual one, homosexuals who have fully accepted their orientation match adjusted heterosexuals in mental health and stability. One explanation for the earlier classification of homosexuality as a mental disorder is that social attitudes kept gays and lesbians in the closet, thus ensuring that data on homosexuality would be based almost exclusively on those who required psychiatric help—those who were dysfunctional.

There is no one clear cause for homosexuality. Some researchers believe there may be a genetic predisposition to homosexuality, a disposition that may be triggered by fetal or infancy experiences. Others assume that unknown environmental factors during early childhood cause homosexuality. Research on the childhoods of homosexuals and heterosexuals reveals no particular phenomenon as especially consequential for either homosexual or heterosexual development. While male homosexuals sometimes show a slightly higher rate of absent fathers, there is some debate about how significant this is, given that it is not the norm. Homosexuals do not differ from heterosexuals in the frequency of heterosexual dating during high school, though they enjoy it less. Despite widespread assumptions to the contrary, homosexuals are less likely than heterosexuals to have been seduced by older or more experienced partners in their initial sexual encounters.

Most therapists agree that exclusive homosexuality is extremely difficult, if not impossible, to change to fully functional heterosexuality, though bisexuals and persons of heterosexual orientation who turned to homosexual encounters due to sexual problems in heterosexual relationships can more often be brought to function fully as heterosexuals.

There is a great deal of variety in homosexual lifestyles. About half of lesbians and one quarter of gays are involved in a primary relationship. About 11 percent of lesbians and 16 percent of gays seem little interested in either sexual activity or committed relationships. In between these extremes there are many patterns as well as significant differences between lesbians and gays. Lesbians, for example, are far more likely than gays to have few partners (the majority have fewer than ten over a lifetime) and to be involved in exclusive relationships.

BIBLICAL AND THEOLOGICAL ASSESSMENTS
OF HOMOSEXUALITY

In general, the attitude of the Bible toward homosexuality is negative. Though it records no teaching of Jesus on homosexuality, the Bible does refer to homosexuality both directly and indirectly. The Mosaic Law (Lv

18:22; 20:13) and Saint Paul (Rom 1:26–28; 1 Cor 6:9–10; 1 Tm 1:9–10) condemn homosexual practices. The Bible story most often cited in regard to homosexuality is the story of Sodom and Gomorrah in Genesis 19 and Judges 19:16–30. This story is not a good source because of its indirectness. It is not clear that the immorality for which God punishes the cities is homosexuality. The event that precipitates the destruction is not homosexual intercourse per se, but the attempt to homosexually gang-rape strangers who should have been protected by hospitality. Rape in US prisons is likewise predominantly an act of dominance and shame, not of homosexuality.

The biblical story of David and Jonathan is often cited as one in which homosexuality is approved. Certainly the story suggests a level of intimacy and romance between two men that in our society might suggest a homosexual relationship. But homosexuality is not explicit in the story.

Many biblical scholars insist that condemnation of homosexuality by biblical writers should be understood within the context of those writers' times. Biblical writers did not recognize the existence of homosexual orientation and thus assumed the perpetrators of homosexuality acted out of a heterosexual orientation. Condemnation of homosexuality in Mosaic Law probably was based on viewing it in terms of its common practice in pagan temple ritual, and Saint Paul's condemnation may have referred to the Greek practice of pederasty, the sexual exploitation of young boys by older men. Since none of the biblical references gives any rationale for its stance on homosexuality, the biblical evidence alone is definitive only for those who view the Bible as a compilation of absolute divine laws.

Those who would not see biblical condemnations of homosexuality as determinative for Christian churches insist that they are not dismissing the Bible. They point out that clear biblical imperatives, such as stoning adulterers and the determination that celibacy is a heresy, relate to historical contexts and are no longer applicable. They note that their acceptance of homosexual persons merely responds to what they regard as stronger biblical imperatives, especially the command to love one's neighbor and to do justice. Jesus' own ministry, they maintain, focused special concern on marginalized groups, on persons despised and excluded for aspects of their lives beyond their control.

Further, those who insist homosexuality is not sinful argue that the essence of sin is that it offends God. But this does not mean that the designation of what is sinful and what is not is, or could be, arbitrary on God's part. That which offends God does so because it runs counter to God's intentions for creation and because it destroys or impedes the formation of peaceful, loving, and just relationships within human community. When we forget this and presume that designations of sin depend totally on the judgments of religious authorities who "represent" God, ignoring the need to test designations of sin by examining their consequences, we allow the concept of sin to be used to exploit.

This was the situation Jesus objected to in his own religious milieu. Priests, scribes, Pharisees, and almost all Jews understood sin as failure to obey the Mosaic Law. The common people were understood as sinners due to their ignorance of the Law. The Pharisees in particular blamed the poor masses for Israel's status as a conquered, occupied nation; this situation was understood as God's punishment for the people's failure to obey the many and varied prescriptions of the Law.

Jesus strongly objected and called into question this understanding of sin that characterized his age. He refused to treat those designated as sinners with the prescribed avoidance and disdain. He presented God as loving Father rather than legalistic judge and lifted concern for persons above concern for Law. When he said he had come not for the righteous but for sinners, he was referring to those whom the religious authorities regarded as sinners, those for whom the Law offered no hope. Jesus did not prejudicially regard all these persons as unredeemable sinners, as did the purveyors of the Law; his chief message to these despised masses was that they should have hope in the saving action of the Father who loved them. The sinful deeds, even of prostitutes and tax collectors, who were considered the worst of the public sinners, were not his focus. For Jesus, the real mark of righteousness was concern for the poorest, weakest, and most despised, and the keynote of sin was turning one's back on those persons and, ultimately, on God. This is what the parable of the Good Samaritan (Lk 10:29–37) is all about: the good person may be a heretical sinner (a Samaritan), and the priest who obeys every part of the ritual Law and worships in the Temple may be damned.

Viewed from within this framework it seems unreasonable to condemn homosexuality simply on the grounds that "it is sin." Christians have an obligation to evaluate homosexuality and ask whether and how it separates us from loving, just relationships with God and neighbor. It is not enough to say that this is a sin because Saint Paul says so in 1 Corinthians 6:9–10 and 1 Timothy 1:9–10. We must question whether homosexuals per se belong in a list of sinners with idolaters, adulterers, drunkards, slanderers, swindlers, and thieves. Certainly some forms of homosexuality belong in such a list—those that include coercion, the molestation of children, or the use of others as objects—as do some forms of heterosexuality. We must probe deeper than this. When we fail to probe the concrete reality of a behavior but decide it is sinful because we are told so by an authority we respect, we take the risk of imitating those who condemn the poor as sinners for their ignorance, the risk of wrongfully judging others as sinners.

Theological, as opposed to biblical, treatment of homosexuality has traditionally included two major objections to the practice. The first of the tradition's major objections to homosexuality is that it is not procreative. For those who view procreative possibility as a normative aspect of sexual activity, sometimes even as the only factor that legitimates sexual pleasure, homosexuality lacks moral validity. Within the Roman Catholic Church interpretations of natural law based on the causal relation between sexual intercourse and procreation have produced a rejection of any use of sexual faculties that is not open to the possibility of procreation within heterosexual marriage. This argument carries much less force among Protestants because they reject the interpretation of natural law on which the argument rests. Protestants do not understand procreation as a normative purpose of sexuality, as demonstrated by the acceptance of artificial contraception by Protestant churches.

Further, as to the criterion of procreation, we can question whether it is really a definitive and consistent grounds for condemnation of homosexuality. Those who raise this question point out that Christian tradition has never denied marriage to the sterile or to women past menopause. Thus it does not demand procreation as a criterion for all sexual acts. Nor does the Presbyterian Church (USA), or many other Christian churches forbid the use of contraceptives. For those churches, then, sexual activity can be licit for heterosexuals, even when it does not intend or cannot result in procreation. Working from these bases one can go on to argue that homosexuality should not be condemned on the grounds that it is not open to procreation. A variation on this position is that procreation should be normative only for heterosexuals, those for whom procreation is possible. For those with exclusively homosexual orientation, procreation would not be normative.

The second traditional theological reason for prohibiting homosexuality is the assumption that gender complementarity is an essential part of creation. The assumption that men and women were made essentially different and intended for each other so that together they become one whole has been prevalent in our history. Today it is much more difficult to make this case than in the past because in recent years it has been demonstrated that the vast majority of traits and gender roles that once were assumed to be based on gender are in fact learned rather than inherent. There are very few traits and no roles that seem to be inherent in greater numbers of one gender than the other, and those few traits are exclusive to neither sex. Therefore, it would seem that in terms of traits and roles wholeness is not predicated upon complementary relations with a person of the opposite sex. We can raise other questions about the notions that the interplay of complementary traits and behaviors is necessary for wholeness and that we gain access to that complementarity only in relations with persons of the opposite gender. Some simple but key questions in this regard are: Aren't persons of the same sex often more different from us in personality structure and behavior than members of the other sex? Does not such wholeness, then, come from our relations with persons of both genders? In short, if traits and roles are not specific to either gender exclusively, then where lies the "natural" complementarity? These and other questions and counterpositions are frequently raised by those who challenge the positions on homosexuality that have been traditionally held in the church. As further research is done into homosexuality and into the positions of theology and scripture on the matter, the debate is enriched and enters new levels.

In summary, we can say that the morality of homosexuality is not easy to assess in clear-cut and simple terms. For many, it seems reasonable to assume that homosexuals should be bound by the same moral criteria for sexual activity by which heterosexuals are bound. Many others take a stance similar to that expressed in an October 1986 Vatican letter to the US bishops entitled "On the Pastoral Care of Homosexual Persons," which affirmed the existing ban on homosexual sexual activity and insisted that while homosexual orientation is not sinful per se, it is a disorder because it precedes and often leads to homosexual behavior. The letter urges bishops to discourage organizations of homosexuals on the grounds that, for persons with homosexual orientation, such organizations constitute situations of temptation, called "near occasions of sin."

Clearly, at this time much of the difficulty of assessing homosexuality swirls around the distinctions between homosexual orientation and activity. Until we can separate what is essential to homosexuality from the dysfunctional aspects that attach to it because of social rejection and stigmatization, it will be difficult to judge. Such a separation can occur only where there are no social sanctions against homosexuality.

CHRISTIAN MINISTRY

The three options presented to the session at Shepherd Presbyterian—to accept the proposal, reject it, or take no action—seem to represent different conceptions of what Christian ministry means. Comments of members about concern for family life and the development of sexual orientation in their children indicate that these people see ministers and elected church lay leaders as role models, persons who represent to the community the shape of authentic Christian life. It is true that ministers and lay leaders of all sexual orientations do serve as role models, yet both sociologically and theologically there are limits to this modeling. Religious leaders are not the only models children have of leaders, of respected men and women, or even of religious men and women. In addition, most children will be exposed to more than one minister and will therefore not need to choose any one person as a model. Theologically, no single person or group can ever represent the fullness of Jesus Christ. We have only a sketch of three years in the life of the historical Jesus; our imitating Jesus in new times and circumstances will produce myriad models.

Those strongly opposed to the More Light resolution protest that homosexuals are a threat to family life, and we can assume that that protest is largely based on the belief that homosexuals are dangerous models that subvert normative family structure and the orientation of children. However, we know today that modeling is not a cause of homosexuality. Children raised by homosexuals are no more likely to become homosexual than those raised by heterosexuals. The real issue is not modeling but our definition of the normative family. Most pleas to protect family life today refer to the endangered two-parent nuclear family in which the father works and the wife keeps house. However, this type of family accounts for less than 20 percent of the families in the United States. Thus the norm is a decided minority, and we can expect that in the future the vast majority of families will continue to diverge from the traditional norm regarding families.

Should the church retain this norm that implies that most North American families are somehow defective? Where did the norm originate? The Christian church was originally structured as a family precisely to substitute for the natural family, since the majority of the early members were estranged from their families by the fact of their Christianity. The early church was founded on those who were outside the predominating model of family. It is ironic that today some Christians propose that those who are marginalized from the predominating model of family should be excluded from the church in order to protect nuclear families.

This leads to a final issue regarding Christian ministry, one already raised above. It is simply this: homosexuals are marginalized, and a major feature of Jesus' project was solidarity with the marginalized. Thus it is important to consider what kind of church we are modeling when we work to exclude the marginalized from full membership or ministry.

DENOMINATIONAL GUIDELINES

Beyond these issues that revolve around the models and roles of ministry and the purpose of ministry itself, the function of denominational guidelines in ministry is in question. Alice Royal's "no action" proposal seems to presume that the purpose of ministry is to unify persons in an inclusive community and avoid conflicts that could disrupt that community. She argues that Morris's election despite the General Assembly's guidance to the contrary proved that Shepherd was inclusive, and that passing the More Light resolution would only create unnecessary dissension.

Those against the More Light resolution appear to invoke a vision of ministry that is based on witness to Christian law. The guidance of the General Assembly is understood by this group to set clear limits on local congregations' ministry. In addition, many of those opposed understand scripture as a legal source and read its references to homosexuality as final. The role of the local congregation is to abide by the judgment of scripture and the governing body. Ministry in the local congregation then takes the shape of witnessing to these judgments.

Supporters of the More Light resolution insist there is a Christian obligation to demonstrate inclusiveness of gays and lesbians because they have been despised and excluded in church and community. This group seems to understand ministry in terms of personal and communal outreach to the marginalized.

It is probable that there are other motives animating some members of these groups, motives that are questionable from an ethical perspective. Individuals who oppose the resolution may be acting out of homophobia, an unreasoning fear and hatred of homosexuality. Homophobia is common in our society and often prevents rational approaches to this issue. On the other hand, those supporting the resolution may be denying that sexuality is a moral concern; they may understand it as private, a matter of individual preference. Neither of these perspectives is acceptable. The first is prejudice; the second fails to understand that all aspects of our lives have moral dimensions and are subject to the gospel.

The "no action" supporters may be seeking to avoid conflict at any cost out of an understanding of unity based on conflict avoidance. But there is no love without a willingness to risk conflict. Real unity arises from resolving conflicts, not from avoiding them after they are present. We have obligations both to reach out in love to those outside the community and to protect the common life of the community. There is often a real tension between these two obligations, a tension that does not resolve itself without conflict.

One way to think about the issue of who should minister is to try to reach an original position regarding what rules should be binding. If we all sat down to construct the rules for a society and were ignorant of what roles we would play in that society, we might see other sides of the issue. For example, if we did not know whether we would be male or female, straight or gay, white or black, president or migrant worker, we might be forced to stretch our imaginations when seeking to structure a just society. If we suddenly discovered a homosexual orientation in ourselves, would it change our stance?

Another way to approach the issue of who should minister would be to look to crisis situations. What would happen if a devastating tragedy hit the community at Shepherd Church? What if a number of the teenage children of the speakers at the session were killed or seriously injured together in an accident or in some other type of tragedy? The next weeks and months would be filled with desperate needs for comforting the grieving and supplying emotional, material, and spiritual help to the families who had suffered the tragedy. The community would need to grapple with its faith in the light of this suffering of the innocent. If Morris were to demonstrate his ministerial gifts and his fellow gays their Christian neighborliness in such a time, would that affect the situation? Would the crisis shed any light on the purpose and meaning of Christian ministry?

Finally, one of the problems with the guidelines from the General Assembly is that they only bar from election and ordination self-affirmed and practicing homosexuals. Covert homosexuals can still be elected and ordained, though research shows that these are the homosexuals most likely to have adjustment problems and relational dysfunctions. To the extent that such a guideline encourages homosexuals who desire service roles in the church to remain covert, it seems both to encourage dysfunction among homosexuals and to perpetuate homophobia through ignorance about homosexuals. The guideline penalizes homosexuals for honesty.

ORDINATION

In most Christian denominations those who hold office are installed by means of a special rite. This rite is generally known as ordination. In the Presbyterian Church (USA) individuals are ordained to three offices: minister of the word and sacrament, elder, and deacon. For ministers of the word and sacrament, ordination comes at the end of a process that includes character and leadership assessment, seminary education, written examinations, and approval by a committee of the presbytery (the association of local Presbyterian churches made up of equal numbers of ministers and elders) and the presbytery as a whole. As part of the ordination rite, ministers must promise to "further the peace, unity, and purity of the church." In the case, Elaine is a minister of the word and sacrament.

The session or ruling board of Shepherd Presbyterian Church is made up of elders. The congregation chooses elders on the basis of good character and leadership potential. Elders must have knowledge of doctrine, the government of the church, and church discipline.

The constitutional prohibition against ordaining sexually active homosexuals is enforced unevenly by presbyteries and congregations. Shepherd Presbyterian Church has already ordained Morris West as an elder without much reaction from the presbytery.

Other denominations have different processes leading to ordination. The Roman Catholic Church, unlike Protestant churches, considers ordination to be a sacrament. Some churches openly ordain gays and lesbians, for example, the United Church of Christ. Conservative Protestant denominations prohibit ordination.

ENCOURAGING GROWTH

In regard to the morality of homosexuality, both Catholic and Protestant churches are torn by divisions both among theologians and between church teaching and beliefs of vocal members. Adopting the Catholic rejection of all sexual pleasure and activity outside those heterosexual marriages open to procreation would mandate that no Christian church could ordain anyone who identified himself or herself as an active homosexual. The decision would then be to reject the More Light resolution.

However, for those who accept either artificial contraception or sexual activity outside of marriage and who believe that complementarity can occur outside of heterosexual relations, it is entirely possible to reach some sort of provisional acceptance of forms of homosexuality that meet moral criteria for responsible sexual relationships, given the inconclusive nature of biblical and theological reflection on homosexuality and the lack of definitively negative social science data. Whether the best method of moving in this direction is to pass the More Light resolution or to take the "no action" option while planning informational programs for Shepherd is open to debate. No action alone, without some clear attempt to create support for inclusion of homosexuals who desire to minister, seems too simple a way out. It could be understood as the choice for unity over justice and hard-won community.

Given the debate stirred up over ordaining self-affirming and practicing homosexuals at Shepherd Presbyterian and in our society and churches in general, it is clear that the issue will continue to divide Christians. In recent years the issue of ordination has been joined on the front burner of church conflict by the issue of marriage.

GAY AND LESBIAN MARRIAGE

The issue of gay and lesbian marriage is similar to the ordination question because advocates and opponents use the same biblical and theological arguments to justify their positions and usually reach the same opposing conclusions on both questions.

The two issues overlap because opponents of gay and lesbian ordination and marriage generally insist that sexual activity be confined to marriage. Some of these opponents also insist that marriage is a holy union between one man and one woman. Still others, arguing natural law, insist on gender complementarity in marriage. Obviously gays and lesbians seeking ordination or marriage do not qualify under one or more of these criteria.

The two issues differ because ordination and marriage are different institutions, each with distinctive theological foundations. They differ also because ordination is a matter for churches to decide, while marriage involves both church and state decisions. Churches set the rules for pastors performing marriages under ecclesiastical auspices, while state governments guide secular officials who perform civil marriages. Finally, they differ in the amount of preparation they require. Most churches require candidates for ordination to satisfy a number of requirements before they are qualified, for example, education and character assessment. While those who contemplate marriage are advised to assess their own readiness and go through pre-marriage counseling, the only requirements are those imposed by the officiating officer, who may easily be circumvented by seeking out another official more willing to perform the wedding.

ADDITIONAL RESOURCES

Alexander, Marilyn Bennett, and James Preston. *We Were Baptized Too: Claiming God's Grace for Lesbians and Gays*. Louisville, KY: Westminster Press, 1996.

Brash, Alan A. *Facing Our Differences: The Churches and Their Gay and Lesbian Members*. Geneva: World Council of Churches Publications, 1995.

Boswell, John. *Christianity, Social Tolerance, and Homosexuality*. Chicago: Univ. of Chicago Press, 1980.

Brawley, Robert L. *Biblical Ethics and Homosexuality: Listening to Scripture*. Louisville, KY: Westminster Press, 1996.

Evangelical Lutheran Church in America. *Journey Together Faithfully: The Church and Homosexuality, Study Guide Part One*. Chicago: Evangelical Church in America, 2003.

Gagnon, Robert A. J. *The Bible and Homosexual Practice: Texts and Hermeneutics*. Nashville, TN: Abingdon Press, 2001.

Genovesi, Vincent J. *In Pursuit of Love: Catholic Morality and Human Sexuality*. Wilmington, DE: Michael Glazier, 1987.

Hultgren, Arland J., and Walter F. Taylor. *Background Essay on Biblical Texts for Journey Together Faithfully Part Two: The Church and Sexuality*. Chicago: Evangelical Church in America, 2003.

McNeill, John J. *Taking a Chance on God: Liberating Theology for Gays, Lesbians, and Their Lovers, Friends, and Families*. Boston: Beacon, 1988.

Nelson, James B. *Embodiment: An Approach to Sexuality and Christian Theology*. Minneapolis: Augsburg,1978.

———. *Between Two Gardens: Reflections on Sexuality and Religious Experience*. New York: Pilgrim, 1983.

———. *The Intimate Connection: Male Sexuality, Male Spirituality*. Philadelphia: Westminster, 1988.

Siker, Jefferey S., ed. *Homosexuality in the Church: Both Sides of the Debate*. Louisville, KY: Westminster John Knox Press, 1994.

Smith, Ralph F. *Heterosexism: An Ethical Challenge*. Albany, NY: SUNY Press, 1992.

Wink, Walter. *Homosexuality and Christian Faith: Questions of Conscience for the Church*. Minneapolis: Fortress Press, 1999.

PART VIII

LIFE AND DEATH

Case

A Matter of Life or Death

The antiseptic smell of clinics and hospitals had always made Sue Ann Thomas feel sick to her stomach. As she waited alone in the cold reception room, her mind flashed back to two weeks ago when she had told Danny she thought she was pregnant. He wasn't so much angry as he was confused and kind of dazed. They talked about what she could do.

Sue Ann was eighteen, a freshman at South Central Community College, and she was afraid to tell her parents about the baby. Danny had also finished high school last year and had a job in a garage in South Chicago. She felt that Danny had been honest about how he felt. "You are really important to me, Sue Ann, but I don't think either of us is ready to get married right now. I guess we have to figure out what to do." They decided that by pooling their savings they could get together the $300 for an abortion.

Sue Ann remembered the name of Dr. Engles. Her mother had gone to him a couple of times. Making an appointment under another name, Sue Ann told him she that she wanted an abortion. Dr. Engles talked to her after her examination when the pregnancy tests proved positive. He told her about what he thought was the best health clinic in Chicago for pregnancy termination. While Sue Ann was still there, he called the clinic for a counseling date and a surgery date the next day, wrote out the papers for her to take in, and asked her to make an appointment with the nurse to see him three weeks after the abortion to make sure everything was all right. As Sue Ann walked out of the office, she thought that Wednesday—one week away—would never come soon enough.

The next week of waiting had been hell. Sue Ann was only seven weeks along, but she was sure she would begin to show. When Wednesday came, Sue Ann told her mother she was going over to a girlfriend's house for

This case was prepared by Alice Frazer Evans. Copyright © The Case Method Institute. The names of all persons and institutions have been changed to protect the privacy of those involved.

supper so she would be home late. When Danny came by early that morning in his old Ford to take her to class on his way to work, Sue Ann was sure her parents would never know.

Both her mother and her father had been bugging her for a couple of weeks now. She had been able to hide her nausea, but her mother said she didn't look well. Sue Ann knew they were worried about her. She also felt their pressure and their pride. She was the first member of the family who had ever attended college. Sue Ann thought that having a younger brother and sister who really looked up to her didn't help either. She knew her dad got pretty good wages working for a construction company, but her mom had started working part-time to help pay for her books and school fees.

Danny and Sue Ann didn't say much on their way into the city. Danny was already going to be late for work, so he let her out at the clinic door and said he'd pick her up after he got off work about 5:30. She had seemed so confident, so sure of herself last week, and even this morning, but as she handed the papers to the receptionist and paid the clinic cashier, she was aware of how cold and clammy her hands felt. She jumped when the nurse called her into a small office to take her blood pressure and temperature.

Dr. Engles had told Sue Ann what would happen during those two days. Today was for a checkup and counseling. She was healthy and still in her first trimester, so the clinic doctor would do something called a "vacuum aspiration" tomorrow. This would take about fifteen minutes. Then she would have to wait at least an hour before she could leave.

Sue Ann was taken into a large room with five other women, all older, for a group counseling session with a social worker. Two of the women looked as if they were in their fifties. She had known that at some time during the day before the abortion there would be a group counseling session. She remembered a couple of weeks ago telling her closest friend, Sharon, that she was pregnant. Sharon had blurted out that she could never have an abortion, that it was wrong and that she would feel too guilty. Sue Ann realized that Danny was the only other person she had told about the baby. She was already afraid of having to talk with these women about it. Sue Ann chose a corner chair and stared out the window as she waited. It had begun to snow.

For the first time Sue Ann let herself think about Paul Reynolds. She hadn't dated anyone else during her last two years of high school. Paul was older, he went into the army, and they wrote to each other nearly every day. They planned to be married as soon as Sue Ann finished high school. But last summer the army found that Paul had a heart defect. He came home on an extended leave, and he died in June. Sue Ann still couldn't really believe it. She had cried for weeks. Her friends and her mother said that she needed to move on and that she had to think about her own life. They all said that beginning college in September would be the best thing for her.

Sue Ann had known Danny since grade school and started dating him not long after her classes began in the fall. He was good company but nothing like Paul. She and Danny had a good time together; he made her laugh. When Danny said he loved her, Sue Ann thought that having sex with him would help her forget Paul, but it didn't. Paul had been a Roman Catholic. They had talked about sex a long time before they went to bed together. This was after they had decided to get married. Paul said that this meant having sex was okay with the church, but she wasn't sure he was right. She remembered reading that the Catholic church was against premarital sex and also said abortion was murder. Sue Ann didn't want to think about what Paul would have said about the baby.

Getting an abortion had seemed the only thing to do. It was all so easy. Sue Ann began to tremble. She wondered if the baby was a boy or a girl.

The social worker came in and introduced herself. The women began to talk, to tell their ages, and to give their reasons for choosing to have an abortion. A girl in her twenties, who introduced herself as Mary, laughed uneasily and asked if anyone had ever backed out this far along. Connie Davies, the social worker, responded very seriously. "Yes, over the past six months of this particular program there have been three women who chose at the last minute not to terminate their pregnancies. Two of them decided to give their babies up for adoption. That's one of the reasons I'm here to talk with you, to make sure you are clear about what you are doing."

Sue Ann dug her nails into her palms and began to feel the tears well up in her eyes. She had come this far. What could she do if she backed out? Sue Ann was the only one who had not spoken. Connie Davies turned to her and waited.

Commentary

A Matter of Life or Death

Sue Ann Thomas, with her friend Danny, faces an agonizing decision: whether to terminate with medical assistance an unwanted pregnancy in its early stages. With her decision Sue Ann enters the arena of fierce public debates over the definition of human life, the meaning of motherhood, the issue of who should control the abortion decision, and the role of sacrifice in Christian life. If all this were not enough, she must also work through how she will relate to her parents.

In facing this decision Sue Ann needs to consider the facts about abortion in her society; the resources of scripture and Christian tradition regarding abortion, definitions of human life, and parenting roles; and the choices and roles open to her and other women in contemporary society.

FACTS ABOUT ABORTION IN THE UNITED STATES

Sue Ann's option to elect to have a legal abortion is provided in the United States under the landmark 1973 Supreme Court decision *Roe v. Wade*, which ruled that in the early stages of pregnancy prior to the viability of the fetus, the decision to have an abortion must be left to a woman and her doctor. Only after viability may the state prohibit abortion, and then not when the woman's life is in danger. This ruling threw out the laws of most states enacted in the second half of the nineteenth century prohibiting abortion unless a physician could claim compelling medical indications.

According to the Alan Guttmacher Institute, slightly over 1.3 million legal abortions are performed in the United States each year. This number has declined from a peak of 1.6 million in 1990. Approximately one in four pregnancies ends in legal abortion, with over 90 percent of these being in the first trimester. Another 15 percent end in spontaneous abortion (miscarriage).

Of women who get abortions about 80 percent are unmarried and 20 percent are teenagers. Of the 750,000-850,000 or so teens who get pregnant each year, 200,000, about 30 percent, get abortions. The rate is much higher for teens from affluent families than it is for those from poor families, and among all women, the rate is higher for blacks than for whites. Of the 56 percent of teens who give birth, an overwhelming number (more than 95 percent) keep their children.

Abortions are relatively safe for the woman involved. Only one woman in 140 experiences complications. The maternal death rate due to abortion-related causes is 1.6 per 100,000. The figure for live births is 14 per 100,000. Women seek abortions for many reasons. Contraceptive failure was not mentioned in this case, although women frequently cite it when seeking abortions.

In the United States, opinion polls indicate substantial acceptance of abortion in cases of rape, incest, danger to the mother's life and mental health, and a deformed fetus. Most polls indicate majority approval of the *Roe v. Wade* decision, although a few polls indicate a fairly even split. Disapproval of abortion is greatest when it is viewed as a form of family planning. Studies also indicate that for most women the decision to abort is an agonizing one that is often followed by feelings of guilt and sometimes regret.

SCRIPTURE AND TRADITION

As one surveys Christian traditions, scripture, and the contemporary views and roles of women, five central issues rise to the fore. These are the goodness of life, natural law, self-sacrifice, freedom, and the well-being of women. In the rest of this commentary these issues will come up again in varying combinations and will be viewed from various perspectives. Students and instructors may find it helpful to keep these central issues in mind as a way of focusing dialogue and thought as they reflect upon the case.

Historically, abortion has not been a major issue in Christian traditions. For centuries it was unsafe, children were considered an economic benefit, and underpopulation, not overpopulation, was the problem. The Bible itself has nothing directly to say about the morality of abortion. Although the Bible does not legislate about abortion, the Old Testament does indirectly provide some insight. Within the Mosaic Law, fetal life was held to have value. Anyone who caused the loss of fetal life was held guilty and subject to sanctions. But the loss of fetal life was not of equal weight with the death of the already born. Responsibility for loss of fetal life was not considered murder but a lesser crime for which payment in coin was to be made in restitution. It is perhaps most accurate to say that the Mosaic Law regarded fetal life as potential human life and therefore of value. The New Testament does not directly deal with abortion or the value of fetal life.

The Christian theological tradition has been rather consistently against abortion since the early church. Some describe this as continuity within the tradition, but others make two points that undermine the value of the tradition's consistency. It may be useful at this point briefly to discuss those two points, for that discussion will help bring the key issues in the debate into focus.

The first point is that although abortion has been denounced within the theological tradition of the church, until relatively recently the term was understood to describe the deliberate termination of pregnancy after the infusion of the soul (ensoulment), which was generally held to occur anywhere from six weeks to four months after conception. Thomas Aquinas, the Scholastic thinker whose philosophy and theology were made normative for the Catholic church in 1878, adopted Aristotle's teaching and held that God infused the soul into the fetus at forty days after conception for males and eighty days after conception for females. In fact, popular folk practice for over a thousand years in Christian Europe, until after the Reformation, was to regard quickening (first fetal movement) as the definitive evidence of ensoulment, which was understood to be the cause of animation. Quickening usually occurs about the beginning of the fifth month. Until that time midwives regularly practiced various methods of terminating pregnancy, most of them dangerous.

Tradition carries great weight in theological and moral thought, especially when it has been consistent. This is appropriate because of the recognition that the Holy Spirit not only enlightens the present generation but has also enlightened past Christian communities who passed this tradition on. But if all Christian communities condemned abortion but permitted termination of pregnancy for some time after conception, does this really constitute a consistent tradition for banning all termination of pregnancy?

A second issue raised concerning the critical views of the Christian tradition on abortion is the fact that at least some of the tradition's opposition to abortion rested upon false understandings about the nature of conception and the natures of men and women. Many of these beliefs are no longer accepted by Christians. In the past there was widespread agreement in the theological tradition that the primary purpose of marriage was procreation; that the only purpose of sexuality was procreation; that women as a sex had been created by God solely for motherhood (although they could renounce sexuality through religious vows of celibacy); and that a woman's sole contribution to the process of procreation was acceptance in her body of the self-contained seed of her husband, which it was her role to shelter and nourish. Christian churches have modified or abandoned all these beliefs.

Today Roman Catholics and almost all Protestant churches agree that procreation is but one purpose of marriage and that the covenant of love between the spouses is equally or more important. There is similar agreement that sexuality is not an evil or near evil tolerated for the sake of children, and that sexual pleasure is itself legitimate and valuable for its role in bonding spouses to each other in love. All Christian churches accept the findings of biological science regarding the equal genetic contribution of parents in conception. All Christian churches recognize the equality of women, at least in theory, although there are tremendous divisions among and within denominations over whether women's nature is ordained for motherhood or is open to other roles that women might choose.

Those who support the ban on abortion are quick to point out that raising the above issues within a centuries-old tradition is not sufficient reason to reverse the ban. The heart of the issue is the preservation of human life. This is why much of the discussion within and outside the churches is about when in the process of gestation fetal life becomes human and should be protected by the law and about how much to emphasize the life of the fetus in relation to the life of the mother and others affected by a birth.

Finally, regarding the tradition as a whole, there is the matter of conscience. All churches, including the Catholic church, which takes a definite and rigorous stance on abortion, have longstanding teaching regarding the moral necessity of developing and following individual conscience. There are very complex relations among one's individual conscience, the teachings of one's church, and the values of the society in which one lives, but all churches agree that the conscience is a linchpin of the process of making important decisions.

This would mean that Sue Ann should not make her decision based on the fact that the majority believes that abortion can be moral, or that those who approve abortion tend to be more educated and middle class. Nor should she make her decision based solely on the teachings of a religious tradition or authority. She must consult all sources and judge for herself. Religious traditions can furnish arguments that Sue Ann will find ultimately convincing. Sociological data about the opposing sides in the abortion debate can illuminate the reasons individuals are more influenced by some reasons than others. But it is never legitimate to shortcut the formation of personal conscience and blindly accept the conclusions of others. *MB*

GROUNDINGS OF CATHOLIC AND PROTESTANT POSITIONS

In the ethical treatment of abortion in Christianity today great division appears at a number of levels. As was touched upon above, a primary division occurs over the definition and value given to fetal life.

The Roman Catholic Church has defined all fetal life as full human life, while most Protestant churches are unwilling to define any specific point at which the fetus is fully human. Pope Pius IX in 1869 stipulated excommunication for abortion and fixed conception as the moment when the fetus, in technical terms at this stage a *zygote*, becomes a person, and, religiously speaking, ensoulment occurs. In so doing he closed the door on the hitherto prevailing views that distinguished between an animate and an inanimate fetus; fixed the moment of ensoulment at quickening; and by implication, permitted abortion before quickening. Protestants in the United

States, influenced like Catholics by more than a century of opposition to abortion by physicians attempting to take over the birthing process from "unscientific" and "untrained" female midwives, generally followed suit with the pope. From the 1870s to the 1960s the matter was settled and debate virtually closed.

Today the Catholic church's strong opposition to the practice of abortion as well as to allowing women the legal option of abortion is based primarily on two moral principles. The first is that according to the natural-law tradition, God's will is embedded in the patterns of creation and can be apprehended by the human mind. According to the Catholic interpretation of this tradition, a rational investigation of sexuality reveals that its innate purpose is twofold: procreation and mutual love. Therefore every sexual act must be open to the possibility of conception and should express love. Anything that interferes with either thwarts God's intent. This perspective has been the backbone of Roman Catholic proscription of both abortion and artificial contraception. It is for this reason that abortion is understood as a sexual sin as well as a form of murder.

The second moral principle used by the Catholic church in its rejection of abortion is one that absolutely forbids the direct taking of innocent life. This is not a prohibition against all taking of life. Not all life is innocent. It is not forbidden for the state to take the life of the guilty in capital punishment, or for soldiers to kill other soldiers who are presumed to be trying to kill them, or for anyone to kill in defense of self or others under attack. Further, under this principle it is possible that one would not be held responsible for killing an innocent, if that killing is indirect. For example, indirect abortions can be permitted under this principle. If a pregnant woman has a cancerous uterus, a hysterectomy to remove the cancerous uterus is permitted if the delay until delivery poses a threat to her life. The purpose of the hysterectomy is to remove the diseased body part that threatens the woman's life. The loss of the life of the fetus is indirect and not intended, for the hysterectomy would have been performed had she been pregnant or not.

Most Protestants are not convinced by these Catholic arguments because they do not share Catholic biological interpretations of natural law or Catholic assumptions about full human life existing from conception. While virtually all Protestants accept the ban on direct taking of innocent life, many deny that fetal life is fully human and therefore protected by the ban. Nor have Protestants relied on natural law as a moral grounding. Historically, Protestant churches have understood the Fall to have corrupted human reason to such an extent that humans are without any natural capacity to comprehend God's will. They are instead dependent on God's grace for understanding.

Today natural law is receiving more Protestant attention than in the past largely because of its role in civil morality. But the biologically based model of natural law used by the Catholic church is rejected in favor of models that draw upon other human capacities as well. For example, one might find that numerous actions and goals—preservation of human life by avoiding overpopulation or the use of abortion when family income is minimal or a mother's health is in danger—rest on equally compelling interpretations of natural law, based on the belief that God gives human beings the desire to preserve the species with dignity.

A further problem with natural law for Sue Ann is the finiteness of human rationality. God's will can be intentionally or unintentionally misread and is always discovered through the eyes of a specific culture. What in one culture or historical period seems natural or clear does not in others. There is no way to decide what is natural for all short of imposing authority.

CONTEMPORARY ATTITUDES
TOWARD WOMEN AND MOTHERHOOD

Other religious arguments that favor or condemn abortion depend heavily upon the two issues discussed above: whether the fetus is a fully human life, and whether God's will can be determined through investigation of biological processes. How these two issues are interpreted not only shapes much of the basis for the way in which abortion is viewed but also affects our view of motherhood and the role of women in our society. As stated above, in Christianity much debate around the issue of abortion focuses upon nuances and inconsistencies in the Christian tradition's position on the nature of fetal life. Those positions and debates have been spelled out in the previous sections because they form part of the backdrop of and resources for Sue Ann's and Danny's decision. Without losing sight of those issues, this section will shift the focus to the varying conceptions of women and motherhood that are powerful aspects of Sue Ann's context as she strives to reach a decision about her pregnancy. A cornerstone in the debate about motherhood and women's roles is the norm of well-being, with its attendant norms of self-sacrifice and self-development, freedom, and justice and equality. The emphasis in this section is upon the perspective that stresses freedom, justice, self-development, and equality for women. The reason for emphasizing this perspective is that it has been a catalyst for the current debates about abortion.

Well-being

At the heart of the clash over abortion and what constitutes the well-being of women are two quite different views of motherhood and the role of women in society. Sue Ann is caught between these views, and her struggle runs much deeper than the decision of whether or not to abort. It involves how she understands herself as a woman and mother. There is, of course, a great variety of views on women's roles and what constitutes their well-being. Without doing too much injustice to these views and for the sake of clarity and discussion, these many views will be arranged under two opposing headings, the *traditional view* and what we will label a *late modern view.*

①   The traditional view stresses that a woman's well-being is fulfilled through her service to her children and husband. Such service is what truly frees. This traditional view is held by many of the most ardent opponents of legalized abortion. In part rooted in the natural-law position discussed above, this view holds that there are intrinsic differences between men and women, differences that lead to dissimilar roles. Men work in paid jobs and provide for women, whose primary role is childbearing and child-rearing. Male leadership, exercised in a benevolent way, is considered normal and right. Freedom for women to work outside the home or to control the birth of children may even be a threat because it appears to upset the natural pattern and downgrade traditional roles. Thus at one end of the spectrum of what constitutes women's well-being is the position which stresses self-sacrifice and service to children and husband.

②   Opposed to the above position is a view that women's well-being is fostered through equality with men and through the freedom to make choices about a host of issues—from careers to motherhood to the structure of relationships between men and women. Those who advocate this position hold that the context of women's lives today is radically different from the context in which the traditional view of women's roles developed. They point out that, for instance, dramatic changes are now occurring in the relation between men and women, changes partially indicated by the great increase of women in the work force. In 1970, 43 percent of all women age sixteen or over were in the work force. By 1980 that figure had increased to over 50 percent, in 1990 to 57.5 percent, and in 2000 to over 60 percent. This is not a mere change in numbers. This shift reflects a new concept of women as free and equal partners in society capable of doing what men do and having the right to pursue nontraditional roles.

This new understanding of women, dominant among those who advocate women having a choice about abortion, sees men and women as substantially equal. Traditional roles are seen as reflecting not the order of nature but the ideology of a male-dominated society. The combination of male domination and oppressive ideology inhibits the full development and well-being of women. Being a mother is important, and many will elect it, but it is not the only role for women. According to this view, women must have choices about service and sacrifice, two central Christian affirmations we would do well to explore in greater depth before moving on to the critical issues of choice and equality.

Self-sacrifice

Within the Christian tradition there are various views of self-sacrifice, all largely stemming from interpretations of the words and actions of Jesus. One powerful image that is frequently raised here is that of Jesus on the cross and the implied mandate to sacrifice self for others. In very broad terms, many who stress this interpretation of Jesus urge a woman such as Sue Ann to choose against having an abortion and opt to sacrifice for the fetus she carries. But here the discussion returns to the questions raised above: Is the fetus fully human? Does it constitute one of the "others" for whom Sue Ann is called to sacrifice?

There are also questions about the understanding of self-sacrifice. Counter to the more traditional position is one that stresses a different interpretation of Jesus' sacrifice on the cross. In this interpretation Jesus did not go to the cross for the sake of self-sacrifice but to bring others a full and new life in the realm he announced. Self-sacrifice was a means, not an end; the end is entrance into the realm of God. Thus what is normative is bringing others to this realm. Still, self-sacrifice, or, in less extreme terms, service to others, is often a good means to this end, so much so that in certain circumstances it is legitimately normative. The legitimacy of self-sacrifice depends on whether there is a self to sacrifice or to give in service freely. The self in its fullest realization is a gift given by God through Jesus Christ and received in mutual love and community. Under conditions of oppression or under the influence of repressive ideologies, the self in its fullest realization is often not possible and is replaced by false consciousness. In a sense, there is no self to give. It cannot therefore be commanded or exhorted from individuals. This is crucial. Calling for self-sacrifice from someone under such conditions, for example, a slave or an abused and passive woman, is not a call to new life but to further slavery and oppression because it does not produce but impedes the mutual love and community to which the realm of God calls us.

These crosscurrents over self-sacrifice are, or at least should be, affecting Sue Ann and the decision she faces. Sue Ann must carefully evaluate her personal situation. She must try to understand what kind of relationship she and the child would have and whether it ultimately could be one that supports the mutual growth of each. She must, in short, try to come to conclusions about the relative values of fetal life, her life and personal choices and development, and the life within the communities of which she is a part.

Freedom of Choice and Equality for Women

As has been discussed, the decision Sue Ann faces is in large measure left to her conscience. Hers is the freedom to exercise conscience, although the responsible use of conscience means consulting the wisdom available from the larger community, including her religious tradition, if any, and her society. Sue Ann must decide whether the use of her freedom to abort in this situation is a legitimate exercise of her power to control her own body or a misuse of her power to control her body by denying life to the fetus she carries.

Freedom is part of the biblically based understanding of justice that has evolved in Western thought. In the United States the legal system provides for individual freedom unless democratically determined laws are broken. The norm of freedom places the burden of proof on those who would restrict the control that Sue Ann and other women have over their bodies. Opponents of legalized abortion are convinced they have satisfied this burden. They argue that just as society rightly denies freedom to a murderer, so it should deny a woman the right to abort a fetus, which in their view has full rights as a person. Proponents of legalized abortion counter by denying full legal status to fetal life in the early stages of pregnancy and point to the injustice of the state or any other body compelling Sue Ann to bear a child. They argue that women should have the freedom to control conception in order to control their bodies and their lives. At issue is whether the power to control conception includes the right to abort a fetus, and whether this power to control fertility is essential to women's well-being.

Obviously, this notion of the right to control one's own body is a key element in the position that sees abortion as an option. Those who hold this position argue that in order for women to take control of their lives and to construct a meaningful life plan, they must have the capacity to break the link between sex and procreation. Otherwise their bodies, or whoever controls their bodies, will control them, and pregnancy will interrupt all possible plans except mothering. Statistically effective contraceptives and safe, affordable abortions make breaking the link possible for the first time in history. For many who support choice, the right to choose is more than just a symbol of the newfound freedom and equality of women. For those who hold this view, the freedom to choose is fundamental to all other justice claims of women. They argue that without the right to choose contraception and ultimately abortion—the last resort in contraception—women will be discriminated against. Employers, for example, may be reluctant to train women for or employ them in significant positions because those employers will anticipate that women will be in and out of the work force. There can be no equality in the work place when women and men function under the assumption that a woman's occupation will be subordinated to each and every pregnancy.

In essence, then, those who stand for women's choice argue that, for women, the capacity to choose is the capacity to gain equality, new identities, and new avenues for vocation. The very well-being of women is at stake, and society has a moral obligation to further this well-being.

Part of the well-being of women includes openness to the growth possibilities inherent in childrearing and homemaking. If women are to be free to choose how to pursue their lives, then obviously they must be free to choose childrearing and homemaking as focal points of their lives. It does no one good to draw the options as a choice between passive, dull housewives and active, responsible career women. There are many paths between these stereotypes.

SEX BEFORE MARRIAGE

Sue Ann and Danny by mutual consent engaged in sexual relations outside of marriage. Sue Ann also had sexual relations with Paul Reynolds. These relationships raise the ethical issue of premarital sex.

Christian reflection on the ethics of premarital sex is in a state of flux and has become part of the cultural wars that now rage over the family and sexual relations in general. On the one end of the spectrum are those who say the norm is clear and leads to only two moral outcomes: chastity outside of marriage and fidelity within marriage. This traditional view is still the official one in most churches, although adherence is hardly universal. Sexual relations outside of marriage are commonplace today, as they have been in other historical periods.

On the other end of the spectrum is the view that sex outside of marriage is appropriate for consenting adults. While not endorsed by many churches, this view is widespread both among Christians and in secular quarters as evidenced by the increasing number of couples living together and even raising families without marrying.

In between these two ends of the spectrum are a number of other perspectives. There is no consensus.

The more traditional perspective with its legal approach has certain attractions. Sexual relations are far more than physical intercourse that satisfies a strong instinct. They involve great emotion and go to the core of a person's being. They involve the giving and the receiving of the self that can lead to a deep sense of inner wholeness. They are one of God's greatest gifts, and it is not too much to say that humans may even experience God through them.

The same vehicle serves sin, however. Some do not love but seduce. They take advantage of a vulnerable other person in order to serve their own selfish purposes. Hurt and alienation follow, and this is one reason why Christian traditions have put up so many warning signs around sex. "Proceed with caution," they seem to say.

Even if seduction is not conscious, physical sex is easily mistaken for love. Momentary sexual attraction can give the illusion of deeper intimacy. Love is easily trivialized. Sexual relations should therefore be part of a deeply loving and committed relationship, and normally such relationships take time to mature.

Another critical reason for caution has to do with children. Marriage, or at least two-parent families, is still the best context for raising children.

Social scientists are in fundamental agreement that children of single-parent families face heightened risk. They drop out of school at a much higher rate. They have higher unemployment rates and are more likely to have a child before age twenty.

On the other side of the issue, many single parents do admirable jobs. Marriage is no guarantee of love or well-raised children. Marriage relationships are often unloving, some even involving spouse and child abuse. Loving relationships are found outside of marriage. The prohibition on sex outside of marriage is part of a patriarchal tradition that has been oppressive to women.

Today's more open sexual relations are also a breath of fresh air in the catacombs of prudity where sex is dirty and the inferior cousin of celibacy. They bring a measure of joy back to sex. For these and other reasons a rigid legalism is misplaced. But so is the contrasting perspective that offers no normative guidance, often trivializes sex, and is not nearly as "open" as it purports.

THE CHOICES

Sue Ann apparently has not reflected in any depth about her future role as a woman. She had planned to marry Paul Reynolds as soon as she finished high school. This suggests that she envisioned a more traditional role. After Paul's death and her graduation, however, she enrolled in a community college, the first in her family to do so. This suggests she may have other plans for her life that giving birth and mothering may interrupt, especially if she becomes a single mother.

Her options appear to be to give birth or to have an abortion. If she gives birth, she may keep the baby or allow someone else to adopt it. Adoption may be an attractive alternative, but she should be prepared for the bonding that develops between the mother and the unborn child that makes giving the baby away difficult.

The Mosaic view that regarded fetal life as potentially human and therefore of value, the norm of the goodness of life, and considerations of legitimate self-sacrifice would lead Sue Ann in the direction of preserving the fetus. The norm of freedom makes her morally responsible for the decision.

If abortion may be read as too "pro-self," then in contrast the decision to go to term and reject abortion may seem to her too "pro-birth." The norm of self-giving and self-sacrifice may be perceived as an alien demand forcing her to negate herself endlessly for childbearing and childrearing, unless she chooses the path of adoption.

Her choice between these options should be influenced by Danny's response. Danny seems to be dumbstruck by the pregnancy, and there is no indication what he intends to do. He is not pressing her to marry him at this time in their lives. Sue Ann does not say how she feels about marrying Danny but does not object to Danny's reading of the situation. Sue Ann is on the rebound from Paul Reynolds and probably had sex with Danny more in response to her grief than love for him. Danny says, "You are really important to me." This is a lukewarm statement of affection. He does, however, pay his share of the $300 for the abortion. This may be an indication he will provide further support, but the job he holds probably does not pay very well.

Should Sue Ann and Danny marry now that she is pregnant? Probably not at this time, but perhaps later. Marriages under these circumstances are at risk. There was a day when both church and social norms would have put more pressure on them to marry. These norms have weakened in recent years for a variety of reasons, including the high divorce rates of teens that marry without much love under pressure from family, church, and society. Perhaps the best advice is to proceed with caution.

Danny does have responsibilities to Sue Ann, however. If she decides to have the baby, he is responsible for providing support, as he is able. He should participate in the birth and the care of the child and act as a loving father. He should also care for Sue Ann by giving her emotional as well as financial support. Who knows, their love may grow into a mature, stable relationship where God is present.

Rather than facing alone an impossible choice between the potential life within her and her own needs, Sue Ann may be freed by considering her interdependence with other persons. She might ask how her decision would enhance not only her well-being, but also the well-being of her family and those in the wider community.

The place to start is probably with her own parents, whom she has not consulted. Her parents are concerned about her health, but Sue Ann is reluctant to tell them she is pregnant. Normally, young women in her situation are wise to seek their parents' help. Most parents are understanding, however disappointed they may be. Whether she is afraid of letting them down or being criticized by them, the case does not say. In some situations past abuse by parents may justify not telling them, but there is no indication of that here. Sue Ann's parents may also have different views about abortion than she does and could possibly put heavy pressure on her at a time when she is already under stress. Sue Ann certainly is not the first young woman to be reluctant to tell and seek help from her parents.

Whatever the decision, Sue Ann's seeming choice between guilt over a decision to abort and resentful surrender to having a child, even if only temporarily should she opt for adoption, must be faced. Perhaps both Danny and Sue Ann know the healing power of forgiveness that comes through faith in Jesus Christ. The task will be to unite head and heart so that this power can do its work.

ADDITIONAL RESOURCES

Baird, Robert M., and Stuart E. Rosenbaum, eds. *The Ethics of Abortion: Pro-life vs. Pro-choice*. 3rd ed. Amherst, NY: Prometheus Books, 2001.

Gilligan, Carol. *In a Different Voice: Psychological Theory and Women's Development*. Cambridge, MA: Harvard Univ. Press, 1982.

Harrison, Beverly Wildung. *Our Right to Choose*. Boston: Beacon Press, 1983.

Maguire, Daniel C., ed. *Sacred Rights: The Case for Contraception and Abortion in World Religions*. New York: Oxford Univ. Press, 2003.

Riddle, John. *Contraception and Abortion from the Ancient World to the Renaissance*. Cambridge, MA: Harvard Univ. Press, 1994.

Stallsworth, Paul, ed. *The Church and Abortion*. Nashville, TN: Thomas Nelson, 1998.

See also "Additional Resources," page 251 herein.

Case

A Good Death for Gleason?

Even a year later C.J. wondered if they had made the right decision. The death of his father, Gleason, had not been an easy one. C.J. reluctantly rehearsed in his mind the options the family had considered. Should they have pushed the physician harder on the appropriateness and availability of the lifesaving operation that was never offered to his father or the family? Had the physician's refusal to consider a lethal injection to end his father's life before the inevitable last few weeks of horrible deterioration and suffering really been humane? If the family members had been more courageous, would they have found someone to help Gleason out of his misery? Would more effective pain control have made a critical difference? Overshadowing everything in C.J.'s mind was a lingering uneasiness over the way the family had decided to discontinue aggressive treatment without explicitly involving his father in the decision.

C.J. resented having to rehash these wrenching choices, especially at the request of his pastor. Where had his pastor been when the family needed guidance to make the right decision in the first place? Reverend Julius Wilson had come to the hospital but kept his distance whenever critical choices had to be made. They seemed to make him uncomfortable. Reverend Wilson was generally regarded as a wonderful pastor, a judgment C.J. would have heartily affirmed over a year ago. But now C.J. was not so sure what to think.

The pastor's question when they had passed on the street that morning had really caught C.J. by surprise. Reverend Wilson had noted that tomorrow was the Fourth of July, exactly a year after the fateful meeting with C.J.'s family. He wondered how C.J. felt in hindsight about the decisions that had been made at the meeting. He asked C.J. to stop by his office to talk after the church worship service the next day. C.J. was not sure he

This case was prepared by John F. Kilner. Copyright © The Case Study Institute. The names of all persons and institutions have been disguised to protect the privacy of those involved.

wanted to do that. What would he say? His father's death had been quite an ordeal. But then, so had his father's life. Born to poor African American parents in the rural south, Gleason had headed north before completing high school. Working two low-paying jobs in the inner-city of Chicago had not been easy for Gleason, but C.J. had never recalled his father complaining. Gleason was proud he had been able to raise three children and that his wife, Cassie, never had to work full-time outside the home. Theirs was a blessed family in a neighborhood where two-parent families, not to mention employed fathers, were far from the norm. Blessed indeed, that is, until the illness.

Gleason had just turned sixty-five, amid kidding by friends and family alike that he was an old man now, when he began to feel the pains in his chest. He did not talk about them with the family, but C.J. could see that something was not right with his father. As the eldest of three children, C.J. felt a special sense of responsibility for his aging parents. He was reluctant, however, to press his father too aggressively when Gleason denied feeling poorly. It was not until later that C.J. learned from the family doctor how much pain his father had endured before collapsing at work and being rushed to the hospital.

Gleason had revived quickly, and some medication had been prescribed for a heart problem that Gleason had a hard time understanding. C.J. doubted in hindsight that his father had taken the medication. The disease gradually worsened. Gleason's lungs as well as his heart were soon seriously compromised. Upon hospitalization a second time, Gleason was found to have a form of pneumonia that proved resistant to treatment. Each time he was progressively weaker after the ventilator was removed, and each treatment was less effective than the previous one in combating the pneumonia. Gradually the disease did such damage that Gleason obviously was experiencing frequent chest pain. They moved him to the intensive-care unit. Even now, C.J. could clearly recall the sight of his father's deteriorating body.

Gleason was lethargic and often incoherent. He slept when the pain was not too great. C.J. was not sure if Gleason was even aware of his condition. Apparently his physician, Doctor Angela Perkins, did not think Gleason was competent to make decisions. Called in as a specialist on cardio-pulmonary disease, she seemed reluctant to talk to Gleason. She spoke primarily to the family, and C.J. wondered why. Did she think Gleason was incompetent, or was she afraid to tell Gleason something she thought he would not want to hear? Maybe she felt guilty about not being able to cure Gleason.

In light of Gleason's worsening condition and the family's evident concern, Doctor Perkins called a meeting to discuss continued treatment. C.J. could still picture the circular table as if it were yesterday. He sat wedged between Doctor Perkins and his mother, Cassie, with his brother, Jesse, and his sister, Roberta, on his mother's other side, and Reverend Wilson leaning back in his chair between C.J.'s sister and the doctor. The decision belonged to someone else, C.J. thought, and he felt awkward being thrust into the middle of the discussion.

Who was he to decide whether his father was to live or die? Did they think he was God or something? If somebody had to play the role, the pastor was clearly the man for the job. Or why did the doctor not just tell them what to do? After all, was that not her job? And why had his father not left them directions for what to do? C.J. felt totally unprepared to say anything. Certainly his education in the public school system had not equipped him for this day. Nor had over four decades at Ebenezer Baptist Church. Or perhaps that was going too far. He did have a curious sense of support as he inwardly cried out to God without knowing the words to use. "Leaning on the everlasting arms," they would have called it at Ebenezer. But that did not answer the questions at hand.

Doctor Perkins explained to the group her inability to arrest the progress of the heart and lung deterioration. When asked by Jesse if a heart or heart-lung transplant he had heard about on TV had been considered at any point in the course of the treatment, the doctor indicated that Gleason was not a good candidate "for a variety of medical, economic, and social reasons." What did the doctor mean by that? C.J. had wondered after the meeting. Everyone had been so fixated on what the doctor was going to recommend, he realized, that they had not wanted to interrupt her explanation. Now in hindsight the question seemed much clearer and more imposing: Had there, after all, been a way available to save his father's life? And what did she mean by social reasons? His father's race? age? value to society? Spared from addressing that issue by the family's passivity, the doctor went on to help the family members envision the suffering that both they and Gleason would experience during Gleason's final weeks. Reverend Wilson confirmed that what she was saying was accurate.

At this point two questions arose. Should Gleason be resuscitated if his heart stopped? Should he be placed on the ventilator again if his lungs deteriorated further? Explaining that these actions would extend Gleason's life a week or two at most, Doctor Perkins recommended "passive involvement," that is, no treatment except to provide comfort care should the need arise for emergency actions.

Cassie turned to Reverend Wilson to ask what she should do. While the pastor seemed to share the burden of her sorrow, he told her it was her decision to make. She then turned to her children. C.J. and Jesse suggested that the doctor knew best what to do. C.J. was shocked, though, by what his sister had to say. Roberta was so concerned by the suffering that lay ahead and by the mounting medical bills that she inquired about the possibility of physician-assisted suicide or even so-called active euthanasia, which she understood to mean painlessly inducing her father's death right away for his and the family's sake. While Doctor Perkins acknowledged that either could easily be accomplished, using an overdose of the right pills or intravenous potassium chloride, she refused to consider these options. So

Cassie, obviously upset, told Doctor Perkins to follow the course of passive involvement she had suggested.

At the same meeting, C.J. recalled, the doctor, family, and pastor had also considered whether to discuss the preferred course of passive involvement with Gleason himself. Gleason had consistently maintained his determination to overcome his illness. Cassie, in particular, felt that Gleason would maintain this attitude to the end for the family's as well as his own sake, but she added that Gleason would in fact appreciate the doctor deciding not to prolong the dying process. No one asked about Gleason's competence to decide. So it was determined not to discuss the matter with Gleason. The doctor proceeded to order that no emergency measures be taken to maintain Gleason's life and that only standard comfort care be provided.

The decision had made things easier for the family at first. No one wanted to face Gleason's impending death. Still, C.J. began to sense a distance between the family and his father during the days that followed. Had his father really known he was dying without being told? Would his dying days have been better if he and the family could have spoken together freely about his coming death and the end-of-life treatment decisions that needed to be made? Looking back a year later, C.J. felt less comfortable than he had at the time with the family's decision not to discuss the predicament with his father.

Shortly after this family meeting with the doctor and pastor, Gleason's condition began to deteriorate rapidly. Three days following the meeting, his heart stopped beating. No attempt was made to revive him. During Gleason's final days, C.J. and the rest of the family had been increasingly disturbed by the sight of him wasting away. Although he had received pain medication, the doctor's refusal to give him more than the "customary" dosage in times of particularly great pain frustrated Gleason and his family. While no steps had been taken to speed up Gleason's death, even C.J. had begun to wonder at the last if something should have been done to bring a quicker end to his father's suffering.

As he thought about speaking with Reverend Wilson the next day, C.J. realized he had more questions and uncertainty now than he had a year ago. He felt reluctant to admit such wavering over as important a matter as how his own father's death had been handled. He was worried about admitting to Reverend Wilson that he might have concurred in a wrong decision. But what about Reverend Wilson himself? Had he not concurred by his lack of suggesting any alternatives? Was it possible that a year ago Reverend Wilson had not thought these issues through any more than C.J. had? Had the pastor done any further thinking since then? Surely the Bible from which Reverend Wilson so regularly preached must have plenty to say about matters of life and death. C.J. began to wonder if a talk with Reverend Wilson tomorrow might not be so bad an idea after all.

Commentary

A Good Death for Gleason?

C.J.'s reflection on the process around the death of his father, Gleason, during the previous year includes a number of different questions. There are questions concerning whether the treatment option chosen was adequate; whether they should have at least tried to include Gleason in the decision-making about his treatment; what the doctor meant when she said that Gleason was not a good candidate for heart-lung transplantation for a variety of medical, economic, and social reasons; why Gleason was not sufficiently medicated against pain; and why Reverend Wilson had kept such a low profile during the ordeal but now wanted to talk about the decisions made a year ago. While it might initially seem that the central issue is whether or not the family was right in deciding for only standard comfort care rather than more aggressive measures to prolong life, the even more difficult issue is not what the family decided but the exclusion of Gleason from the decision-making. The family failed to prepare ahead for what to do in a situation of impending death when the competence of the patient might be in question.

RESPECT FOR LIFE

The biblical tradition tells us that life is a gift from God to be valued and respected. The Hebrew scriptures depict the value of life not in terms of enduring biological functions but in terms of participation within a human community. Accordingly, individuals who constituted a threat to the community were executed (murderers) or exiled (lepers) under Mosaic Law. In Genesis the punishment for the murder of Abel was exile for Cain. He was forced to wander the face of the earth, a punishment considered in Israel to be increased, not diminished, by God's vow that no one would kill him to end his exile. Individual physical life is not absolutely valuable; in the Hebrew scriptures the welfare of the human community comes first. Even so, those scriptures give no warrant for taking or shortening innocent life in the interest of community well-being.

The Christian scriptures contain no warrant for taking life at all, only for sacrificing one's life in the interests of others. The miracles that Jesus performed as signs of the coming realm of God functioned to restore community. The significance of the healing miracles was not merely the alleviation of physical ills but the restoration of the sick to the community. The lepers and the woman with the discharge were unclean and therefore excluded from community. Those possessed by demons, the paralytics—the chronically ill in general—were also excluded from participating in the life of the community until healed by Jesus.

Scripture does not tell us at what cost life should be maintained. Virtually all Christian theological traditions forbid Roberta's suggestion of a lethal injection for Gleason, although in some circles this prohibition is weakening as appeals are made to reduce suffering and even to allow physicians to assist suicide under certain circumstances. Roberta was concerned about the extension of suffering for the family as well as for Gleason and about the mounting medical bills. Many theologians would suggest that directly to kill a person in order to prevent high hospital bills or to save others from suffering an extended mourning process clearly violates not only the letter of "Thou shall not kill" but also the spirit. Roberta's suggestion for active involvement is not separated from the option for passive involvement by the consequences, for in both options Gleason dies. Nor is the real difference in the act itself, either an act of commission or an act of omission. While there may be some moral difference between denying a seriously ill person a readily available antibiotic and choking the person to death, most people would agree that both are serious sins against the life and dignity of the neighbor.

There seems to be a major difference, however, between injecting a dying person with poison and not putting him on a ventilator that could prolong his life for only a week or two. The primary difference is one of directness and indirectness. If the doctor had agreed to Roberta's suggestion, the direct cause of Gleason's death would have been poison. With passive involvement, Gleason dies of diseased heart and lungs—just as he would with a decision for more aggressive treatment.

Respect for life prohibits humans from using other human lives as means to ends. We cannot decide directly to end lives because they are in some ways a drain on the community, though amid scarce resources we may have to decide who gets adequate resources and who does not. While most religious traditions allow killing in self-defense, the threat must be an immediate threat to one's life in order to justify taking another's life. Gleason is no threat to anyone's life.

GOD AND DEATH

The authority to claim innocent lives directly has been understood in the Christian tradition as delegated by God to natural processes in creation. While it is common to hear Christians refer to death as God's prerogative, as if God decided on the moment and kind of death for each of us, Christian theological traditions are somewhat more nuanced and complex on this issue. In the Book of Job, God taunts Job for questioning God about Job's misfortunes:

> "Where were you when I laid the foundation of the
> earth?
> Tell me, if you have understanding.
> Who determined its measurements—surely you
> know! . . .
> Who shut in the sea with doors,
> when it burst forth from the womb?—
> when I made the clouds its garment
> and thick darkness its swaddling band,
> and prescribed bounds for it,
> and set bars and doors,
> and said, 'Thus far shall you come, and no farther,
> and here shall your proud waves be stayed?'"
> (Jb 38:4–5, 8–11)

God emphasizes here the distinction between creator and created. But it is one thing to assert that God has the *power* to control life and death. It is another to insist the God consciously and deliberately decides the moment and kind of death for each of us. To say this makes God the puppeteer controlling the strings of a drunken driver, a terrorist bomber, a sadistic kidnapper. A God who chooses to kill millions of innocents in events like the Holocaust is not the divine Father of whom Jesus said:

> "Ask, and it will be given you; search, and you will find; knock, and the door will be opened for you. For everyone who asks receives, and everyone who searches finds, and for everyone who knocks, the door will be opened. Is there anyone among you who, if your child asks for a fish, will give a snake instead of a fish? Or if the child asks for an egg, will give a scorpion? In you then, who are evil, know how to give good gifts to your children, how much more will the heavenly Father give the Holy Spirit to those who ask him!" (Lk 11:9–13)

God explained to Job that within the process of divine creation the world was set in motion. God is responsible for the pattern in creation. But creation, both human and nonhuman, is gifted with freedom and dynamism that reflect God's own nature. That freedom and dynamism in creation determine specific events in the world. God gives the example of the ostrich, who lays its egg out in the open where it may be crushed (Jb 39:13–18). When it is crushed, that is not God's decision, though it was God's gift of freedom to the ostrich that allowed the egg to be crushed.

God's presence in our world does not take the form of a puppeteer who controls the strings of events and occurrences. God's presence in our lives takes the form of the Holy Spirit, who supports and comforts, strengthens and energizes us to resist evil and tragedy. In the passage from Luke above, Jesus says God answers us by giving us the Spirit, not by reversing or saving specific persons from the natural tragedies of human existence.

Gleason's fatal condition is neither God's decision for Gleason nor an occasion for demanding a miraculous cure. The decision not to pursue prolongation of life aggressively for Gleason is morally acceptable, since there was no hope of prolonging life more than two weeks and he was in great pain. Such decisions are becoming more and more common, especially since increasing numbers of people, notably the elderly, leave explicit advance directions (living wills) not to put them on ventilators, revive them after heart attacks, or use other "heroic" measures of sustaining life unless there is hope of recovery.

Pope Pius XII first used the distinction between ordinary and extraordinary means of preserving life in such situations, stipulating that there is an obligation to supply ordinary means of preserving life but no obligation to supply extraordinary means. This distinction, which became widely accepted even outside Catholicism, assumes that there are some things that all patients have a right to, regardless of their chances for recovery. Ordinary care has been assumed to include food, water, oxygen, and adequate pain medication. It has not been considered to include any experimental treatments or drugs, any mechanical assistance, or any treatments that require undue sacrifice of the patient, the family, or society.

The rapid advance of technology in medical care, however, has undermined many of the original judgments as to what constitutes ordinary care. Surgery of any kind was originally considered extraordinary, as were antibiotics and all use of technology, including intravenous feeding, ventilators, and pacemakers. Today there is great debate in many societies as to whether artificially administered nutrition and hydration are ordinary or extraordinary for patients in a permanent vegetative state. In Gleason's case the only relevant question about his care is why his pain medication was consistently insufficient. It is accepted that though high levels of pain medication for dying patients often hasten death, freedom from pain is part of ordinary care whenever possible.

One of the relevant questions concerning the decision for standard comfort care is why Gleason remained in the hospital. This is not only a relevant question due to the scarce economic resources of the family, though that is certainly a concern, but it is also a social question. Gleason is sixty-five and therefore covered under Medicare. Medicare coverage, of course, is limited, and a prolonged hospital stay can still destroy the patient's savings. But because the major bill is paid not by the family but by society, the issue of why Gleason remained in the hospital is a social issue. Once the decision was made to abandon curative treatment in favor of comfort care,

Gleason had no need for a hospital. Hospitals are expensive, high-tech centers for medical intervention. The purpose of hospitals is cure, not comfort. In fact, hospitals are not restful places at all, as anyone trying to recover in a hospital knows.

Gleason should have either been sent home with proper medication for pain, or, if the control of pain required more medical oversight, to a hospice for the dying. Not only was he occupying a high-cost hospital bed he did not need, but keeping him in the hospital was against Gleason's own best interests.

WHO SHOULD RECEIVE SCARCE RESOURCES?

C.J. is right to note that someone should have asked the doctor to explain her statement that Gleason was not a good candidate for a heart-lung transplant; more information about that medical option would have dispelled any suspicion that Gleason might have been unfairly discriminated against on the basis of race or economic status. In fact, the two most relevant reasons for rejecting Gleason as a candidate for a transplant were almost certainly his age and medical status, both of which seem reasonable criteria. There is a tremendous shortage of organs for transplant in the United States. Heart-lung transplants are experimental and fairly rare, much more so than the more well-developed processes for transplanting kidneys and corneas. Persons over sixty-five are normally not eligible for organ donor programs. Their only hope of transplants comes from donations from close kin. While this is a rare but viable option in kidney transplants, because humans do have a spare kidney, the fact that humans have only one heart means that for Gleason to have a heart-lung transplant someone in his family would have to suffer a death that did not damage that person's heart and lungs.

The basic reason for the exclusion of those over sixty-five from organ donor programs is agreement that scarce donated organs should go to those who can obtain the most life from them. Persons who are already sixty-five or more are less likely to derive as much life from a transplant as younger persons, and older persons are more likely to have other damaged organs that will cut short their lives. This is almost certainly the case in Gleason's situation. The odds of a sixty-five-year-old man only two weeks from death being able to withstand the trauma of surgical transplantation of a heart and lung are very low.

GLEASON'S EXCLUSION

The decision of the family and the doctor, along with Reverend Wilson, to limit Gleason's care to that which would make him comfortable rather than that which would prolong his life was made without Gleason. Nor was Gleason informed of the decision after it was made. It may well be that the reason Gleason was kept in the hospital rather than sent home or to a hospice was that no one was willing to tell Gleason there was no longer hope of cure. A transfer would inevitably raise the issue.

The case points to the growing distance between Gleason and his family during the days that followed the decision. They knew that he was dying and that nothing would be attempted to hold off that death. They were forced to begin the mourning process as they grieved the death they saw looming. They inevitably reviewed their relationship with Gleason, blending the present reality of his emaciated and pain-racked body with images of the stronger, younger husband and father who unfailingly supported them through hard times. They were preparing for his death. But Gleason was not free to prepare for his death in the same way, because he was not told to give up hope of recovery. He was not told that his fight against his illness was doomed and would no longer be medically supported.

There are a number of reasons why the failure to tell Gleason of his situation is morally problematic. The first, of course, is that it was his life and his body. Who had the right to make decisions about his medical care for him? It is amazing that no one insisted that someone try to tell Gleason the fight was hopeless and obtain his consent to change the treatment plan. It is understandable that no one would want to be the carrier of such news. But the requirements of law as well as ethics require that the consent of competent patients must be obtained for any treatment. Next of kin can only take on responsibility for a patient's medical care when the patient has voluntarily abdicated it or is incompetent to exercise it. All persons have a right to control their own bodies. To this end doctors are obliged to obtain fully informed consent from the patient before examining, testing, or treating the body of a patient. It is clear in this instance that the doctor and the hospital significantly changed Gleason's medical treatment without obtaining his fully informed consent. This is a serious breach of professional ethics if, in fact, Gleason was competent. That the doctor and the hospital were in little danger of being sued by a dying man whose estate would be handled by the very relatives who collaborated in usurping his control over his medical care should not have affected, but probably did affect, the outcome here.

Having said this, Doctor Perkins apparently assumed or wanted to assume that Gleason was not competent because of his medical condition. The case says that Gleason was lethargic and often incoherent, and that C.J. was not sure if Gleason was aware of his condition. The family seems to follow Doctor Perkins's lead, although in hindsight C.J. does question her motives. The participants were not clear about what to assume. Gleason's state of mind was a big question mark. This state of affairs is not extraordinary in such situations, and someone needs to decide who is to decide.

Individuals and families may avoid such troubling decisions by careful planning. Advance written directives or health-care proxies that allow patients to designate someone to be their decision-maker if they lose the ability to make choices are useful. However useful, doctors have been known to turn to those designated in a health-care proxy or who have power of attorney to override advance written directions, even over the expressed desires of the patient, when in the doctor's considered medical opinion the patient is incompetent.

With advances in medical technology people who make life-and-death decisions will increasingly encounter ambiguity and consequent indecision. They should be prepared for it. The case of Gleason appears to be such a situation. In this case two things are clear. First, family members, including Gleason, failed to make contingency plans in advance. Second, Cassie, her children, the doctor, and the pastor did not even try to consult Gleason.

Cassie and her children owed Gleason respect for his right to control his own body. In this case we can see very clearly that denying Gleason the ability to control his own body—the medical treatment of his own body—denied him the ability to control his life. Most important, he was denied the freedom and impetus to prepare for his own death. Cassie seemed to think that she was sparing Gleason the pain of facing the inevitability of his death. She may well have been right to believe that discovering his helplessness would have been extremely difficult for Gleason, perhaps even more so than for many other persons who have more experience with and less anxiety around lack of control in their lives. But one must ask if anyone in the family considered that while Gleason no longer had a choice of whether to get well or die, he did have a choice as to how he would die.

The process of preparing for one's death is different for all of us. For some people it may focus on coming to grips with God and the role of God in one's life. For others it may center on coming to accept with peace the concept of personal death. For some it will entail taking leave of one's loved ones, or completing some major project, or cleaning up other loose ends in one's life. For some the immediate prospect of death causes a radical reorientation that has been incubating unseen, only to trigger such events as deathbed confessions and reconciliation of longstanding estrangements.

The traditional concept of a "good death" is largely unpopular in much of Western society, which is horrified by the prospect of consciously facing one's own death. Most people want quick, clean, sudden deaths, without any conscious knowledge of dying. Death is an enemy, as Dylan Thomas expressed so well for so many:

> Do not go gentle into that good night,
> Old age should burn and rage against the close of day;
> Rage, rage against the dying of the light.

There is a certain reasonableness to the desire to resist death and the knowledge of death. We have natural desires to maximize pleasure and to minimize the pain in our lives.

But there may also be a benefit to having time to prepare for death, time to move though the stages of dying, past denial and anger to acceptance and even peace. Had Gleason been included in the decision-making session about his treatment options, he and his family might have spent the last days communicating to one another their feelings about his life and impending death. They could have been an important source of consolation to one another in their grief, instead of feeling estranged by the secret between them. While Cassie might well have been right that resisting death was the option characteristic of Gleason, still the choice of whether to continue resistance or to pursue a peaceful death should have been Gleason's. Perhaps he would see courageously resisting death to the last breath as his best legacy. Since he was not allowed to make the choice, in some way Gleason's death is more tragic that it needed to be.

PASTORAL COUNSELING CONCERNS

Reverend Wilson's request that C.J. reflect on the events around his father's death and discuss them with him may be a very good thing. C.J. and his family may have to deal with similar issues as Cassie continues to age. One would hope that C.J.'s children, nieces, and nephews would learn from their own parents' involvement and be better prepared for, and perhaps somewhat more comfortable about, dealing with issues of death than their parents were. The issues raised in Gleason's death were not unique but have become the common experience of most families.

But Reverend Wilson may also have a personal agenda in his request to discuss Gleason's death with C.J. He may feel uncomfortable with his own role in the situation. According to the case, Reverend Wilson did not intervene during the family's meeting with the doctor, a fact that C.J. somewhat resented at the time. C.J. was uncomfortable making a decision about his father's treatment and resented the fact that the professionals—the doctor and the minister—did not make the decision. After all, the doctor was the expert in medicine, and the minister was the expert about morality. The question of treatment was a question of both medicine and morality, one which C.J. did not feel competent to decide.

Both Doctor Perkins and Reverend Wilson were right to refuse to make the decision. The doctor rightly refused to consider actively inducing Gleason's death. We should presume that Reverend Wilson would have spoken against such a step had the doctor not immediately refused. But the remaining treatment options were both well within the limits set by the Christian moral tradition. The choice between them was not Reverend Wilson's to make. The role of religious authorities is not to become the conscience for their members, but to help the members themselves develop well-formed consciences. Reflecting on moral decisions from hindsight is an important aspect of conscience development.

It is more difficult to explain why Reverend Wilson did not point out to the family and doctor the need to included Gleason in the decision-making. Perhaps he was intimidated by Cassie's assumption that she knew what Gleason would want. But one is forced to wonder how Reverend Wilson dealt with Gleason during those last days. How does one provide effective pastoral care for the dying without informing the dying person of his or her impending death? It may well be that it was Reverend Wilson's dissatisfaction with the quality of pastoral care he was able to give Gleason in those last days that alerted him to the need to rethink the decision made by the family.

ADDITIONAL RESOURCES

Callahan, Daniel. *What Kind of Life? The Limits of Medical Progress.* New York: Simon and Schuster, 1990.

Dyck, Arthur J. *Life's Worth.* Grand Rapids, MI: Eerdmans, 2002.

Guroian, Vigen. *Life's Living toward Dying.* Grand Rapids, MI: Eerdmans, 1996.

Keown, John, ed. *Euthanasia Examined.* Cambridge, UK: Cambridge Univ. Press, 1995

Kilner, John. *Life on the Line.* Grand Rapids, MI: Eerdmans, 1992.

———. *Who Lives? Who Dies? Ethical Criteria in Patient Selection.* New Haven, CT: Yale Univ. Press, 1990.

Kilner, John, et al., eds. *Dignity and Dying.* Grand Rapids, MI: Eerdmans, 1996.

Shannon, Thomas, ed. *Bioethics.* 3rd ed. Mahwah, NJ: Paulist Press, 1987.

Sherwin, Susan. *No Longer Patient: Feminist Ethics and Health Care.* Philadelphia: Temple Univ. Press, 1992.

Smith, Wesley J. *Culture of Death.* San Francisco: Encounter Books, 2000.

Steinfels, Peter, and Robert M. Veatch, eds. *Death Inside Out.* New York: Harper and Row, 1974.

Stewart, Gary P., et al., eds. *Basic Questions on End of Life Decisions.* Grand Rapids, MI: Kregel Publications, 1998.

Zucker, Arthur, Donald Borchert, and David Stewart, eds. *Medical Ethics: A Reader.* Englewood Cliffs, NJ: Prentice-Hall, 1992.

Appendix

Teaching Ethics by the Case Method

The authors' use of the case method to teach Christian ethics is conscious and deliberate. The method is problem posing and dialogical in contrast to traditional teaching approaches of the teacher/expert transferring information to the student/novice. Traditional methods, although well suited for some purposes, do not explicitly invite students to think for themselves, learn by discovery, and engage the teacher and other students.

The discipline of Christian ethics involves the transfer of information, of course. Students need, among other things, to know facts, theories, and contexts of situations. They need to be acquainted with Christian theology and ethical traditions. They need to understand how to apply Christian insights to the analysis of situations.

The discipline, at least in the minds of the authors, involves more, however. It finds its basis in faith, which, in Paul Tillich's understanding, includes reason, emotion, and will. The relationship of faith is a centered act of the whole person, something to be experienced, not just thought about. Information is only one part of its dynamic. The case approach encourages students to become part of the situation, willingly to suspend belief, to act as if they were one of the characters, and to make decisions that engage mind, will, and emotion.

In addition, one aim of teaching ethics is to enhance the limited freedom each person possesses to make choices. By freedom the authors mean *freedom from*, that is, freedom from ignorance, prejudice, paralysis of decision, oppressive ideology, and ultimately, sin. *Freedom from* opens the door to *freedom in* and *freedom for*. Freedom *in* is the freedom that comes through God and others and frees the self to be *for* others.

The authors think that a problem-posing, dialogical method is well suited to help people of faith learn to enhance the limited freedom they possess to make choices. Cases in this volume are not intended to give answers. Rather, they pose problems and encourage students to go through a relational process and experience their own freedom to decide. Cases taught in a dialogical style encourage this relational process. Whether in classes or discussion groups, the case approach allows students and teachers to learn from each other. Everyone participates in a process of discovery. The use of cases over time frees students to discover how to go about making ethical decisions so they are not stymied at the start by lack of direction and at the end by indecision. They become accustomed to making choices, even tough ones.

Finally, cases are useful in character formation. Students discussing cases unavoidably find themselves evaluating the characters, comparing themselves, and, one hopes, adjusting their own characters in accordance with the discoveries they make. They develop their own "habits of the heart" by putting themselves in the shoes of others.

The case approach opens doors to freedom, but it also opens other doors. First, it introduces students to contemporary ethical issues. The authors contend that thorough knowledge of issues is one of the first steps in a liberating education. Parenthetically, teachers may have to provide background in advance of case discussions using more traditional methods, especially in complex cases.

Second, cases are a way of entry into Christian traditions. At some point both teachers and students need to ask how the Bible, theology, and the church inform issues. The cases on life and death, for example, raise questions about abortion, euthanasia, the nature of God, the purposes of human life, and the meaning of death. The case "More Light" challenges traditional perspectives on sin. The cases on violence lead to an investigation of the church's historical stances. At the same time that students are addressing issues and making decisions, they are in a position to learn the content of Christian tradition and how to apply it.

Knowledge of traditions is liberating if it helps students detect selective and self-serving attempts to manipulate authority for the purpose of supporting conclusions arrived at on other grounds. Traditions provide alternative perspectives from which to understand and challenge cultural myopia. Traditions provide the wisdom of experience, lend authority, offer general guidance, set limits, and designate where the burden of proof lies—all helpful in finding ways through the maze of experience and conflicting opinion and on to appropriate moral choices.

Third, repeated use of case studies encourages students to economize in the way they approach ethical problems. That is to say, cases teach ethical method. The more cases are used and the more explicit methodological awareness is, the more indelible a pattern for making choices becomes. However little students retain of the content of a given issue or the theology that informs it, the authors are convinced they should leave a course in ethics knowing how to address ethical problems and how to avoid the confusion of too many options and conflicting guidelines.

The authors also believe that an essential component of any pattern of learning is drawing on the insights of others. Discovery of the limitations of individuals acting alone and of the liberation in learning to trust others in community is an important benefit of this dialogical approach. The case setting calls on participants to listen to one another, to challenge their own and others' perceptions, and to build on one another's insights and experiences.

Fourth and last, the case approach is an experience-based form of education. As one veteran case teacher put it: "Cases are experience at a fraction of the cost." The cases in this volume represent the experiences of others that students can make their own without going through all the turmoil. The cases encourage students to express and apply their own experience. Finally, the cases push students to practice resolving complex dilemmas such as parenting, personal responsibility, individual and community rights, and thus to add to their own experience.

CASES FOR GROUP DISCUSSION

As stated in the Introduction, there are numerous types of cases used in contemporary education. These range from a hypothetical problem, to a one-page critical incident or verbatim report of an actual event, to a four-hundred-page case history describing a situation. The type of case employed in this volume is modeled after those used by the Harvard Law and Business Schools and the Association for Case Teaching, that is, each case consists of selected information from an actual situation and raises specific issues or problems that require a response or decision on the part of one or more persons in the case. The problem should be substantive enough and so balanced in its approach that reasonable people would disagree about the most effective or appropriate response. As a pedagogical tool the case calls for a response not only from the case characters but also from those studying the case.

Although cases can be extremely useful for inducing reflection by an individual reader, they are specifically designed for group discussion. They might be used in classrooms, retreat settings, community gatherings, or with any group seeking to gain new perspectives.

As this is a distinctive educational approach, the authors feel it is important to offer suggestions for guiding a case discussion. To begin with, while it is possible to hand out copies of shorter cases—for example "Rigor and Responsibility"—and ask participants to read them immediately prior to discussion, the quality of discussion is heightened by careful advance reading. The case leader might suggest ahead of time that participants (1) read through the case at least twice; (2) identify the principal case characters; (3) develop a time line to indicate significant dates or events; (4) list the issues that surface; and (5) think through a number of creative alternatives to the dilemma posed.

The case leader functions primarily as organizer, catalyst, probe, and referee. Good case leaders know where they want to go with a case and what they want to teach. They highlight insights and assist in summarizing the learning from the discussion. As a facilitator, case leaders are responsible for clear goals and objectives for each discussion session and for guiding the quality and rhythm of the discussion. Many who have worked with cases suggest that the most crucial factor for a rewarding case experience is the leader's style. Openness, affirmation, and sensitivity to the group create the climate in which genuine dialogue can occur. Second in importance is that the case leader thoroughly master the case facts and develop a discussion plan or teaching note.

It is important to keep in mind that there is no single way to approach a case. The Introduction to this volume highlights the elements of making an ethical decision, and the commentaries offer authors' analyses of more specific issues. Case leaders might order the discussion of cases by proceeding from analysis to assessment to decision, suggesting that students not read the commentaries until after the initial case discussion. Alternatively, leaders might integrate the material in the commentaries and the discussion. Neither the Introduction nor the commentaries should constrain teachers or students from taking different entry points or addressing different topics or issues.

Whatever approach is taken should draw participants into dialogue, uncover what is needed to make an informed ethical decision, and push students to a critical consciousness and finally to a decision that will help them when they encounter similar situations in their own lives.

There are no right answers to the dilemmas presented in this volume. This means that the problems posed are open to a number of creative alternatives. This approach stands in contrast to a closed, problem-solving approach in which the right answer or solution, known only to the teacher, can be found in the back of the book. In contrast, the case approach calls for participants to become active subjects in the learning process, to consider various responses, and to analyze the norms that inform their decisions.

Experienced case leaders report that recording the essence of participants' contributions on newsprint or on a board gives order and direction to the discussion. A skilled instructor is able to help participants show relationships among contributions. The leader should be willing to probe respondents for additional clarification of points.

Honest conflict of opinion is often a characteristic of case discussions and can be quite constructive. The case leader may need to assume the role of referee and urge participants to listen to one another and to interpret the reasoning behind their conclusions. It is often helpful to put debating participants in direct dialogue by asking, for example, "Laura, given your earlier position, how would you respond to Mark's view?" The leader's role as mediator is also significant, especially as a discussion nears conclusion. It is helpful to encourage group members to build on one another's suggestions. One constructive process for closing a case discussion is to ask participants to share their insights from the discussion.

Case leaders employ two additional techniques. Leaders might focus and intensify discussion by calling participants to vote on a more controversial issue. For example, in a discussion of the case "More Light," one might ask, "If you were a member of the church governing board, would you vote for or against the motion to become a More Light church?" The dynamics of case teaching reveal that once persons have taken a stand, they frequently assume greater ownership of the decision and are eager to defend or interpret their choice. Voting provides an impetus for participants to offer the implicit reasons and assumptions that stand behind a given decision. It can also be a test of the group's response, especially if one or two outspoken participants have taken a strong stand on one particular side of an issue. If a vote is taken, it is important to give participants an opportunity to interpret the reasons behind their decision.

Another way to heighten existential involvement in a case is to ask participants to assume the roles of characters in the case for a brief, specified period of the discussion. When individuals are asked to assume roles before a group, they can either be asked ahead of time or invited on the spot from among those who have shown during the discussion that they identify with the characters and understand the issues. It is often most helpful for individuals in a role play to move into chairs visible to the entire group. Case leaders can guard the personal integrity of those who assume roles by giving them an opportunity to "de-role." This is easily done by asking them how they felt during the conversation and by asking them to return to their original seats. Then group members can be called on to share what they learned from the experience.

Notwithstanding the preceding suggestions for case teaching, the authors wish to acknowledge that a good case discussion is not ultimately dependent on a trained professional teacher or a learned group of participants. A gifted leader is one who listens well, encourages participants to do the same, and genuinely trusts the wisdom, insights, and personal experiences of the group. To benefit significantly from the cases a reader needs to be willing to wrestle honestly with the issues in the cases and to evaluate with an open mind the insights of the commentaries.

SAMPLE TEACHING NOTE

Most case teachers prepare in advance a teaching note with suggestions for the general direction of the discussion as well as clear, transitional questions to move from one topic to the next. The following note is intended as an illustration of how the first case in this volume, "Rigor and Responsibility," might be taught in a short session.

A. Read the case if not pre-assigned. (ten minutes)

B. Have the class sketch a biography of each character. (ten to fifteen minutes)

C. Identify the basic questions: How is a family to live in a poor and environmentally degraded world? Alternatively, should an affluent family follow the rigorous holy poverty of Jesus or another option, which might be called responsible consumption, stressing right use and good stewardship? (one to two minutes)

D. Identify alternative issues. (five minutes) This category could be eliminated if the basic question is the focus. Or one of the following issues could become the main issue:
   1. Stewarding an inheritance
   2. Living in an impoverished, malnourished, and environmentally degraded world
   3. Discovering the biblical and theological witness on justice, wealth, poverty, possessions, and consumptions
   4. Overworking in modern society
   5. Making a family decision
   6. Dealing with guilt
   7. Acting as an individual in a world dominated by mass consumption
   8. Distributing income and wealth
   9. Raising children

E. Ask each student to identify with one of the following: (ten minutes)
   1. Nancy or Clea
   2. Nathan
   3. Al
   4. The children

F. Adjourn to four separate groups. (twenty minutes)
   1. Discuss what is and what should be the normative position of the character selected. Point to:
      a. Biblical and theological views of justice, wealth, poverty, and consumption
      b. The two normative positions identified in the title of the case
      c. The norms of justice and sustainable sufficiency
                              OR
   2. Discuss the family relationships and how they should be worked through to arrive at a decision. Point to:
      a. The involvement of the Trapp family in a number of issues, the extent of its giving, and the crisis of the family in the United States

       b. Cultural attitudes in the local community
       c. Poverty, malnutrition, and environmental degradation in the world community
       d. Traditional patriarchal family patterns
OR

    3. Discuss the method question. How is a Christian family to decide?
       a. Point to the alternatives of using deontological, teleological, or areteological approaches
       b. Apply each to the case and note the differences
OR

    4. Discuss the character question. What are the characteristics of a person who responds well to the main problem? Point to:
       a. Basic character orientation, loyalties, and world views
       b. Character-building aspects of this situation

G. Conduct a role play, selecting one person from each group. Add David as an option. (ten to fifteen minutes)
    1. Role players discuss what the Trapps should do and how it relates to the main issue and to the alternative issues selected in "D" above

H. Debrief and generate discussion. (ten minutes)
    1. "De-role"
    2. Ask students to identify what they have learned
    3. Open a general class discussion of the main issue

If time allows, the case leader can provide background in lectures, readings, films, small study groups, and so on. The more background, the more open-ended the small group discussions can be.

CASES AND COURSE DESIGN

How might cases be used in a course in Christian ethics? For starters the authors recommend using the cases approach in conjunction with other teaching methods. Cases can be overworked, and the freshness they bring lost.

In terms of overall design the teacher might select one of the cases with high student interest and open with it the first day of class. Cases are good discussion starters, and early use can introduce students to the method, to the use of critical consciousness, and to the goal of liberating education.

Following this, several general sessions on ethics would be appropriate, including the elements of making an ethical decision discussed in the Introduction and how to use Christian sources to derive norms. Use of a case or two to illustrate specific aspects of the ethical discipline would also be appropriate.

The remainder of the course could be devoted to the specific issues in this volume. Using all of the cases in a single semester might be ill advised. Selectivity on the basis of student interest and teacher expertise would be more suitable.

The authors recommend that students write "briefs," that is, a three- to four-page analysis of a case. This process accomplishes several things. First, it brings writing into a course. Second, particularly if graded, briefs heighten interest by increasing the stakes. Discussion is more intense because preparation is more thorough. Third, briefs offer less vocal students another avenue of expression. Fourth, briefs are a vehicle for method, since method is implicit in any act of organization. Methodological awareness is more pronounced if the teacher requires a certain approach, or better, if the teacher insists that the students be cognizant of the approach they are taking. Finally, briefs may serve as the first draft of a term paper.

If briefs are used, students must be selective in what they cover. Three or four pages are not sufficient to analyze fully any case in this volume. In organizing their briefs students might follow the order of analysis, assessment, and decision outlined in the Introduction. Somewhere in the brief the "problem" should be clearly stated. The larger part of the brief should be devoted to ethical assessment, that is, to the derivation of norms, to the relating of norms to situations using one or more method, and to the relationships involved in the case. Briefs may be expository and present the various sides in a case, or they may be persuasive and argue one side in depth. While the commentaries in this volume avoid arguing for a particular side of an issue, the teacher may ask students to make a decision and justify it.

Lack of time makes selectivity a cardinal virtue in a workshop setting. The typical one-hour adult class is long enough for a good discussion of a single case, especially if it has been read prior to the session. Needless to say, the teacher should have a very clear idea of what he or she wants to accomplish and try to keep the class on task. An alert teacher, picking up on points in the discussion, can even insert background material through mini-lectures or asking students to elaborate. Small groups and role plays are especially helpful in stimulating discussion and breaking complex cases into manageable units.

LIMITATIONS OF THE CASE APPROACH

The case approach is not without limitations. First, case material must go through the personal filter of a writer. The situation is seen through the eyes of a single character with all the limitations of perspective. Seldom is enough information provided to satisfy participants. Crucial signals can be misread or misunderstood.

A second drawback is that the success of this form of education and presentation of material is dependent on the critical thinking and participation of students. This can be quite disconcerting, even threatening, for those who are accustomed to a process in which they are handed a complete analysis from the lectern. For most learners tutored in an educational system that fosters uncritical acceptance of the teacher's wisdom and authority, passive reception of information is the comfortable norm. This is, however, also the pattern of uncritical acceptance of the world as it is and contributes to a loss of vision. Case leaders need to develop a mode of open rather than closed questions to induce critical thinking and genuine dialogue.

Third, case discussion can consume more time and emotional energy than the direct communication of information. Intelligence is imperfectly correlated with the propensity to speak. Some participants are bent on dominating the discussion rather than learning from others. Tangents can carry the discussion into dead ends. These limitations call for good referee skills from the case leader.

Fourth, the forest can be lost for the trees, the macro for the micro, and the social for the individual by focusing on the particulars of a given situation to the exclusion of the context. For example, to reduce the discussion of abortion to a personal moral decision in the case "A Matter of Life or Death" is to lose sight of a critical social question about who should control the decision, the woman or the state. The cases, and in particular the commentaries, have been written to help avoid this problem, but it is well to keep it in mind. Teachers can easily do this by including these elements in their background material and case plans.

Finally, relative to other methods the case approach is limited in its capacity to convey large blocks of factual information. This drawback does not mean teachers need to revert automatically to lectures. There are alternatives to "depositing" information, and even the lecture style can be approached with a different spirit. Many case teachers, for example, use mini-lectures in case discussion to introduce relevant material when it is needed.

The case approach is no panacea and must be seen as only one of many effective educational instruments. The authors have attempted to respond to the limitations of the approach. They have not removed them. They trust, however, that the cases in this volume and the approach itself can lead to constructive, liberating engagements with what they think are critical contemporary issues. Their trust is based on many years of experience with the approach. They are convinced that the approach is not only a valuable and liberating pedagogical instrument, but also a way to build community in the classroom.

List of Authors and Contributors

AUTHORS

Alice Frazer Evans is director of writing and research at Plowshares Institute, Simsbury, Connecticut; senior fellow at the Centre for Conflict Resolution, University of Cape Town, South Africa; senior trainer for the Center for Empowering Reconciliation and Peace, Jakarta, Indonesia; and an adjunct faculty member at Hartford Seminary, Hartford, Connecticut. She was educated at Agnes Scott College, Edinburgh University, and the University of Wisconsin. She is co-author of numerous books, including *Casebook for Christian Living, Pastoral Theology from a Global Context, Peace Skills for Community Mediators,* and *Transforming Urban Ministry.*

Robert A. Evans is executive director of Plowshares Institute, Simsbury, Connecticut; senior fellow at the Centre for Conflict Resolution, University of Cape Town, South Africa; senior trainer for the Center for Empowering Reconciliation and Peace, Jakarta, Indonesia; and an adjunct faculty member at Hartford Seminary, Hartford, Connecticut. He studied at Yale University; Yale Divinity School; universities in Berlin, Basel, and Edinburgh; and received his doctorate from Union Theological Seminary, New York. He is the author, editor, and co-author of numerous books, including *The Future of Philosophical Theology; Globalization of Theological Education; Human Rights: A Dialogue between the First and Third Worlds;* and *Pedagogies for the Non-Poor.*

Christine E. Gudorf is professor and chair of the Department of Religious Studies at Florida International University. Her doctorate is from Columbia University in joint program with Union Theological Seminary. She has published a number of books, journal articles, and book chapters in feminist ethics, Christian ethics, and ethics and social policy. Her books include *Catholic Social Teachings on Liberation Themes; Victimization: Examining Christian Complicity; Body, Sex, and Pleasure: Reconstructing Christian Sexual Ethics; Ethics in World Religions,* co-authored with Regina W. Wolfe; and *Boundaries: Case Studies in Environmental Ethics,* co-authored with James Huchingson.

Robert L. Stivers is professor of Christian ethics, Pacific Lutheran University, Tacoma, Washington. He did his undergraduate work at Yale University; his M.Div. at Union Theological Seminary, New York; and his M.Phil. and Ph.D. at Columbia University in joint program with Union Theological Seminary. He has authored, co-authored, edited and co-edited numerous books, including *The Sustainable Society; Hunger, Technology, and Limits to Growth; The Public Vocation of Christian Ethics,* co-edited with Beverly W. Harrison and Ronald H. Stone; *Reformed Faith and Economics; Christian Environmental Ethics: A Case Method Approach,* co-authored with James Martin Schramm; and *Resistance and Theological Ethics,* co-edited with Ronald H. Stone. He has worked extensively in the Presbyterian Church (USA) on social issues.

CONTRIBUTORS

William P. Bristol, now deceased, was a physician in private practice and former dean of Mercer University Medical School, Macon, Georgia.

Frank Gudorf is executive director and president of Jubilee, a community-development organization in Miami, Florida. Jubilee was jointly founded by the regional offices of the Catholic, Methodist, Lutheran, and Presbyterian churches and builds affordable housing, both condominium and rental developments. A graduate of New York University School of Law, he worked as a corporate lawyer in New York and Cincinnati for almost twenty years before coming to Jubilee.

John F. Kilner is the president and CEO of The Center for Bioethics and Human Dignity in Bannockburn, Illinois. He received his B.A. degree from Yale University, his M.Div. from Gordon-Conwell Theological Seminary, and his A.M. and Ph.D. from Harvard University. Author of numerous articles in journals, he has also written or edited fourteen books: *Does God Need Our Help?; Life on the Line; Who Lives? Who Dies?; Cutting-Edge Bioethics; The Reproduction Revolution; Dignity and Dying; Genetic Ethics; The Changing Face of Healthcare; Genetics, Stem Cell Research, and Cloning; Basic Questions on Healthcare; Sexuality and Reproductive Technology; Alternative Medicine; End of Life Decisions;* and *Suicide and Euthanasia.*

The Rev. Dr. Tom Tuma is an ordained Anglican priest in the Church of Uganda and director of the Planning, Development, and Rehabilitation Department, Church of Uganda, Kampala, Uganda. He resides in Jinja with his wife, Ruth, who is a member of Parliament.

J. Shannon Webster is an ordained member of the Presbyterian clergy; executive presbyter of the presbytery of Sierra Blanca, Roswell, New Mexico; and past president of the Association of Executive Presbyters.